THE BASIC ENCYCLOPEDIA FOR YOUTH MINISTRY

THE BASIC ENCYCLOPEDIA FOR YOUTH MINISTRY

Copyright © 1981 by Dennis C. Benson and Bill Wolfe

Library of Congress Catalog No. 81-81967

ISBN 0-936664-04-5

Third printing

THE BASIC ENCYCLOPEDIA FOR YOUTH MINISTRY

BY
DENNIS C. BENSON
&
BILL WOLFE

BOOKS

P.O. Box 481
Loveland, Colorado 80539

DEDICATION

We dedicate this publication to those special persons with whose support and insights we have grown immeasurably in what youth ministry can be:

Marilyn, Amy and Jill Benson

Martha, Janita, Maria and Christina Wolfe

ABOUT THE AUTHORS

Dennis C. Benson

•A free-lance theological media consultant. Author of 14 books (from Abingdon, Word, Friendship and John Knox). United Presbyterian minister, member of the Pittsburgh Presbytery.

•Award-winning radio host and producer for youth programming on WDVE-FM (the Gabriel, AFTRA and Golden Mike Awards).

•Co-editor of **RECYCLE** and **SCAN** newsletters.

•Has served in the past as seminary lecturer in New Testament Greek and Exegesis (McCormick Theological Seminary), suburban pastor, hospital chaplain, college chaplain, radio and TV producer for interdenominational agencies and youth director for many churches.

•200,000 of his audio cassettes are being used around the world.

•He is a jogger and student of karate.

Bill Wolfe

•Director of Senior High Educational Ministries for the Board of Discipleship of the United Methodist Church (approximately one million youth in 39,000 local churches). He is responsible for programs related to youth and young culture, worship, human sexuality, recreation and mission. Consultant to all youth curriculum produced by the United Methodist Publishing House.

•Covers the nation in workshops for conference and district events, interdenominational youth events and large group presentations. He has led events in every part of the nation, plus Mexico and Canada, and has conducted a media survey with 4,000 participants. (The results were published in 1980.)

•Edited the music tip sheet "Music and the Young" for 10 years.

•Produced the award-winning cassette series "Young Culture Lifetime Cassettes" for six years and the award-winning syndicated radio series "Lifetime" for 13 years.

•Co-edited the **UMYF Handbook**, the first such handbook for the Methodist Church in 22 years.

•Wrote **Music You Wear** (Tidings).

•Served for ten years as director of Christian education in two local churches, working daily with those who work with youth in fellowship groups.

CREDITS

Art

Bettman Archive—41
Rand Kruback—37, 50, 55, 172, 177, 178, 258, 348
Laurel Watson—29, 40, 68, 82, 105, 106, 116, 132, 133, 162, 251, 303

Photography

American Broadcasting Corp.—100
Bob Combs—184
Paul Conklin—39, 44, 51, 102, 204, 269
Rohn Engh—34
Lucasfilm Ltd.—199
Robert Maust—90
Paramount—324
Charles Quinlan—223
Rising Hope—48, 95, 109, 296
Schwinn—47
Thom Schultz—15, 16, 17, 18, 20, 33, 36, 42, 43, 53, 54, 69, 70, 96, 114, 128, 131, 137, 142, 145, 151, 169, 171, 180, 181, 185, 188, 189, 193, 195, 200, 202, 211, 220, 228, 232, 233, 235, 241, 253, 257, 280, 283, 294, 299, 304, 308, 312, 314, 319, 323, 329, 331, 332, 343
Ben Smith—81, 207, 226, 317
Lee Sparks—146, 176, 260, 262
David Strickler—30, 31, 45, 56, 59, 61, 63, 65, 71, 104, 110, 124, 127, 143, 147, 152, 170, 181, 187, 238, 242, 245, 265, 273, 300, 301, 304, 309, 310, 321, 325, 326, 332, 337
Leo Symmank—335
Bob Taylor—197, 275, 341
Jim Whitmer—19, 52, 57, 66, 73, 78, 85, 87, 91, 99, 113, 120, 134, 141, 158, 214, 219, 224, 247, 271, 289, 291, 345
World Vision—160

CONTENTS

TOPICAL GUIDE FOR THE BASIC ENCYCLOPEDIA FOR YOUTH MINISTRY

As you circle through the pages of this ministry-helping tool, you'll find that certain topics hook together to provide a wealth of information on a broader youth ministry topic. For instance, individual topics such as **Balance, Consultation, Evaluation, Finances** and **Job Description** form a common thread that becomes the broader topic of "Youth Group Management."

If you have a specific youth ministry pinch point, or a special area of interest, take a look at the following topics. Be prepared to sift through a treasure chest of ideas.

ADULTS AND YOUTH MINISTRY

Access
Adults
Advising
Advocate
Burn-out
Commitment
Conflict
Criticism
Counselor
Devotional Life
Diversity
Encouragement
Friends
Goodbye
Love
Mentor
Newcomer
Rebellion
Relating
Respect
Risking
Support System
Touch
Training

INTERPERSONAL

MEDIA

**WHEN THE GOING
GETS TOUGH**

Aaugh
Blues
Burn-out
Despair
Doubts
Encouragement
Failure
Panic
Hostility
Risking
Support System

YOUTH CULTURE

Age Level Characteristics
Body
Cars
Cliques
Clothing
Commitment
Dating
Dieting
Drinking
Drugs
Emotions
Heroes
Identity
Keeping Current
Language
Lifestyles
Loners
Malls
Movies
Peer Pressure
Parties
Public Schools
Rebellion
Records
Rowdies
Rumor
Runaways
Self-image
Sex
Sexuality
Smoking
Suicide
Youth

CREATIVE MINISTRY

Adventure Camping
Bell Choirs
Bikes
Bubble
Bus
Camping
Choirs
Clowning
Creativity
Drama
Earthball
Exchange Programs
Fall Celebrations
Festivals
Fund Raising
Group Media
Ice Breakers
Intergenerational
Interviewing
Journals
Lock-in
Malls
Mime
Module

Movies
Multi-media
New Games
No-loser Recreation
Parachute
Parties
Portable Ministry
Publicity
Puppets
Records
Recreation
Retreats
Role Playing
Serendipity
Singing
Simulation Games
Slides
Speakers
Stories
Taming
Team Teaching
Trips
Washington-U.N. Seminar
Weather Balloons
Worship
Youth News

YOUTH GROUP MANAGEMENT

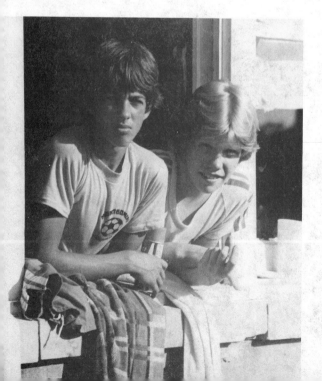

YOUTH GROUP PROBLEMS

PREFACE

We poised over our typewriter keys for some time before striking in the imposing title to this book. Thirty fat volumes of fine print are often pictured when the word encyclopedia forms in our minds. These reference tomes seem to contain much more than a person wants to know about everything. Yet, it isn't the dusty and all-inclusive attributes of the encyclopedia genre which drew us to this format.

We have probably been most influenced into going this quaint route because of many of the books we have read concerning youth ministry. It seems to us that the past few years have spawned texts which assume that the average youth worker is seminary-trained and has years of experience. However, most churches have a membership size under 150. These congregations do not have a full-time youth minister. The youth work is usually done by a couple recruited one Sunday after church. They have been away from youth for the past 10 years. Yet, they are finally convinced that it is their duty to take on this important task.

These youth advisors or sponsors have not studied the latest youth ministry literature. Yet, most of the books freely season each page with spicy alphabet recipes (P.E.T., T.A., T.A.T., etc.). The part-time advisors also discover a number of code words, and phrases (gaming, serendipity, faith development, etc.) which have layers of meaning for those in the know, but very little significance to them. These good folks aren't stupid or uninformed. Yet it is easy for them to get that impression of themselves.

It is always difficult to make the jump from the clever skills of most youth ministry resources to the practical "pinch point" or problem facing you in tonight's youth program. Clowning may be a neat project for the group, but what do you do about the complaining parent who challenges your program because her daughter didn't get home until midnight?

As we probed the historical soil in which the concept of encyclopedia developed, we found that it suggested a circular or general learning. It took only a minute for us to realize that our real growth in youth ministry took place as we circled around and around our work. Insight and hope came only as these arcs of experience intersected again and again. The simplest strand of solving a problem became woven into our tapestry of experience next to a conceptual thread. It was then we understood a piece of the pattern which was a mystery a minute earlier!

Hopefully, **The Basic Encyclopedia for Youth Ministry** will help you to circle and circle around your ministry. We hope you will follow the journey through these pages guided by the moments of need in your work. Each item will stand by itself. Yet, you will soon find that one entry will suggest an exploration of others. This book is a circling collection of moments from experience which can enrich your youth ministry. You are in control of what you learn and how you learn it.

You will soon discover some basic hinge points upon which our philosophy/theology hang. This is not an idea book with fast answers to every program need. We also don't offer the answer to every question. Each entry defines the narrow focus of one moment from your life together as youth and adult. We then share a story or illustration of how this kind of experience was faced or utilized by someone who has crossed our path.

We work from an understanding of ministry as that of shared community. This book is drawn directly from the kindred spirits who have taught us and dreamed with us across the world. These folks come from every part of the theological spectrum. The one thing we all share is that we so love our youth and are so committed to our faith that we will do just about anything to bring the two together.

We invite you to circle through these pages. Meet a cast of thousands. Your authority to do youth ministry is not based on your education or your mystical vision. If these were the sole qualifications to your work, you would have to retain your authority by seeing to it that the youth were always behind you

as far as insight or spiritual power. We believe that
learning and preparation are important for every
facet of the ministry. We also are convinced that
youth need adults who are on a serious spiritual
journey. However, your only authority for this vital
ministry is the illogical fact that God has called you
to this moment of service. You and your companions
are the only ones who are called at this time to ministry with these folks. No one can take that authority
of vocation. This is a very freeing gift. It means that
you can permit your youth to be more learned or
more spiritual than yourself at a given moment
without being threatened. God only calls you to be
faithful to this calling.

We invite you to enjoy this portable feast. May
God continue to bless you with the courage to risk
for others.

Dennis C. Benson
P.O. Box 12811
Pittsburgh, PA 15241
(412) 833-7524

Bill Wolfe
Board of Discipleship
P.O. Box 840
Nashville, TN 37202

We are most grateful to our super typists, Jean
Morales, Renee Beard and Joanna Leatherman.

DIRECTIONS

In your hands is a collection of possibility, hope and common sense. This tome is filled with the best gifts from hundreds of friends, neighbors and those whom we have passed in the night. The mini-case studies included in most separate articles have been whispered in our ears, written on the tops of pizza boxes, sent by cassette tape and imposed upon us as students and participants across the world.

We don't intend you to use this encyclopedia like a fill-in-the-blank workbook or read it as you would the latest novel. There is no starting or ending place. It circles around. As you read the articles which are closest to your needs, you will find a reference to another item. We hope that your curiosity will force you to read that suggestion.

This book is designed for a creative and exciting hopscotch approach. Just flip it open and read an entry aloud. Then discuss your reactions with members of your planning committee.

You might even want the whole youth group to use this book! Pass it around your circle and ask each person to pick out one article from a certain letter of the alphabet. Invite him or her to read it aloud. Ask the simple questions, "So what? What does that article say about or to our group?" Let the discussion roll. You might tape some newsprint to a wall and write down the ideas which flow from the book or are developed by the discussion.

You might also want to use this book to encourage adults in their understanding of youth ministry. Let them borrow your book. Ask them to mark the entries which excited them the most. Once they grasp the spiritual power and love in such a ministry they will be your strongest supporters.

Most of all, we hope you will use this book as a beginning point. Help us expand and change it for future editions. We will enjoy hearing from you.

May God prepare you for the excitement and possibilities of his Spirit as you are led to risk for your young people!

Aaugh

"Aaugh," Charlie Brown's cry of anguish, is known by every youth leader.

Okay, let's say you've really blown it! You've said the wrong thing at the wrong time, did the wrong thing at the wrong time, zigged when you should have zagged. And now you think you are a total zero in youth ministry.

Wrong.

The fact that you admit a mistake is the first indicator that you are not a total failure. Admitting your queasy feelings is also the first step toward starting to straighten out the problem.

Working with youth is seldom a well-lighted route between right and wrong, and all of us who risk the journey will be able to look back and see countless wrong moves, some of them seemingly serious. Admitting our mistakes does not encourage blundering and unconcern at all, but it does confirm the person who gets up from a mistake, cleans up as much of the mess as possible and starts over by looking for a better way.

The same thing is true concerning our work with other people. Again, mistakes by those we work with are plentiful. As observers we can become experts at goof tabulation. It is so easy for us to judge the same person with radical differences: "If she wouldn't take over so much, the youth could more easily assert themselves," or "The kids are floundering, they need her to give more direction." (This may reflect more about our perception than the other person's faults.) And it is easy for us to blow out of proportion the possible long-lasting consequences of obvious mistakes.

The Christian message should be: Your mistakes are forgiven, proceed with God's help. God is not a failure and can supply your needed help on any occasion, even from the bottom of the deepest self-imposed exile. It is very true that God can work through apparent goofs, mistakes, even serious failure— which may turn out not to be so disastrous after all.

Always keep in mind that each of us makes mistakes regularly, sometimes serious and often intentional. But what is really important is that God accepts us, blunders included.

See also BLUES, CONFLICT, DOUBTS, PANIC, SUCCESS

Access

"I can't understand it. There has been a drastic change in our volunteer youth leaders in the past three years. Our program requires youth advisors to move through the four years of high school with the teenagers. But lately, the adults seem to realize they can't handle the emotional intimacy youth ministry requires."

The speaker of these words captures aptly the problem facing most youth sponsors. Before you become too involved in youth ministry, you must

Youth need to share your everyday life.

answer the question, "Do I really want to carry the emotional burden demanded by this work?"

No one can answer this question for you. Youth need actual and emotional access to you. You will become a very significant person in their lives. Once they pass into your life in this way, real teaching and sharing can happen. They are going to be touched by your faith no matter what methods you use. When looking closely at those popular para-church religious youth movements, you quickly realize that their youth leaders are accessible to their youth.

Access also means spending quality time with youth. Your phone may ring at odd hours. Three or four youth may drop by after a date just to talk. These idle moments are the times in which growth takes place.

Access as a youth leader also means that you permit teens to share their personhood with you. Can you listen to a story without stepping on it with a sermon? As you become involved in participatory listening, you will be amazed how a teen will conclude with the insight that something he or she did was a dumb thing to do.

It is easy for the youth advisor to give too much. There are many stories of burn-out. An adult gets overburdened and ends up neglecting self and his or her family. The tension between total accessibility and nurture of selfhood is always a Christian challenge.

It is hard to be accessible or present with youth every time they want or need you. It becomes difficult if you are married and have family interests as part of your priorities. When do you

withdraw into your own legitimate personal concerns and when do you remain
available?

It is sometimes embarrassing to see
what happens when you are accessible
to youth. "You're so friendly, you are
not like other adults." You have only
done what any person should do for
another person. Your real gift to youth is
the gift of yourself. It is painful and
frightening to give yourself and receive
the personhood of another. However,
this is what the faith is all about.

Resources
1. **Fully Human, Fully Alive**, by John
Powell, Argus.

*See also BURN-OUT, RELATING,
SUCCESS*

Adults

**One of the biggest problems adult advisors face is their
opinion of themselves.**

One of the biggest stumbling blocks
for adult advisors is their own opinion of
themselves. A new youth sponsor feels
scared as he or she faces 18 high school
students for the first time. Even after
years of experience in meeting new
youth groups it is frightening to poise for
that leap of faith across the chasm of the
unknown.

This knot of uncertainty can twist off
into all kinds of unwise options. For
instance, it is easy to become defensive
as a means of dealing with fear. This
self-protective stance gives off an odor
which makes for an unpleasant relationship. It breeds the same response in
the youth.

It is also a temptation to interpret the
fright of uncertainty as an inability to
build a successful ministry. "What am I
doing here? The kids will never accept
me. I am just too square." This reaction
is natural—and unfair. For starters, you
have very special qualities of maturation which are vital to these young folks.
Your perspective can provide a new
context for the journey of these teens.

The youth group members are
worried too. They are uncertain about
how you and the other members in the
room will accept them. Your faith will
enable you to push
through this unknown
zone. It takes great
amounts of emotional
energy to force yourself to
create a climate of love
and acceptance.

Another chancy option
for many when faced with
the natural gap between
teen and adult is to forget
that they are adults. You
can't be that which you
are not. This doesn't
mean that you can't be in
touch with the childlike
qualities of the spirit. Yet
you are not competing
with the college football star. Young
people do relate in a significant way to
secure adults. They want you to be who
you are.

Dan was not your model youth
worker. At least, he didn't look like most
of the folks produced by those campus
religious groups. He wasn't tall or mus-
cular. Instead, he was 35 years old, had

four children and looked more like Santa Claus than a football player. No one ever remembered his wise sayings or sermons about our failings.

One of Dan's major qualities was his availability. A teen would feel free to stop by after taking a date home. Dan knew how to listen. He nodded, sighed and laughed at just the right times. He would also raise a one-sentence thought which would open all kinds of new insights from the teen.

In Dan's years of work with youth, many young people found a path of faith. Several went on to become clergy. In fact, many youth advisors look back on the model Dan provided for their current work. He gave the best he had—himself.

Resources

1. **Creative Youth Ministry**, by Jan Corbett, Judson Press.
2. **Youth Ministry: Sunday, Monday, Every Day**, by John Carroll and Keith Ignatius, Judson Press.

See also BIBLE KNOWLEDGE, COMMITMENT, DOUBTS, KEEPING CURRENT, MENTOR, TALENTS

Adventure Camping

Stretching, challenging, terrifying situations such as these stress the importance of depending on God, self and each other.

There has been a strong interest in a new kind of camping. This model is designed for a small group of teens and usually runs for one week. With a strong staff of experienced adult leaders, the group spends a week conquering their fears as they face physical challenges.

The wilderness or survival camping style was first developed in Germany for special school situations. It was later introduced in the United States and used with troubled youth. These programs have found that creative crises forced participants to become interdependent with others in the group. This style of camping is now used extensively around the world. Many business executives and other adult leaders have gone through these programs.

Smokey is the dean of a fine adventure camp program. He leads teens in mountain climbing, white water rapids, boating and other outdoor experiences. The importance of depending on self and the interdependence between people becomes very clear in this physical challenge. There is a focus on facing and pushing through fear. Many stu-

dents find a huge emotional and personal release as they press through and beyond fear. The power of God is very much a part of this program. The interviews before and the reflections after the week reveal an amazing sense of personal and spiritual growth.

Earl has created a program which combines the physical challenge with the study of the person from the perspective of the impact which comes from all the influences of life. He has found that many teens can reflect on many aspects of their lives as they face and overcome physical challenges. Earl has built a course for this kind of experience. For instance, there is a twenty-foot wall and a group of five have to find some way to get everyone over it.

It is important that you realize that you don't have to be the one who has all the skills in youth ministry projects. There are other people who will help you if you should want to try adventure-type camping. Seek and you will find.

Resources

1. Institute of Creative Living, 3630 Fairmount Blvd., Cleveland, OH 44118.
2. American Wilderness Institute, P.O. Box 11485, Highland Station, Denver, CO 80211.
3. Sierra Treks, Mount Hermon, CA 95041.
4. Wilderness Learning Center, Wheaton College, Wheaton, IL 60187.

See also BIKING, CAMPING, MOUNTAINTOP EXPERIENCES, PORTABLE MINISTRY

Advising

Advising is an inherent youth ministry responsibility.

According to comments from various youth leaders, one of the least sought after responsibilities included in their position is advising youth about their problems and questions. It is one thing to be with a group, to attend their meetings, to be up front in leadership when it is called for and even to share personal faith concepts. But it is something else to be asked to be a contributor to significant choices that a young person is making.

Whether you seek such responsibilities or not, it is very likely that as a trusted "significant other" (respected and much admired non-parent), you will often be turned to as one who can offer loving concern and valued wisdom at this particular moment in the youth's life. The reasons are obvious: You have often been involved in what seemed to be momentous decisions in the life of the group; you have experienced both the youth and the adult worlds; you care about youth or you would not be in youth

ministry and in all probability, you value youth very highly as persons. If you were a youth, what better person would you turn to?

You may think that we are describing the functions of a professional counselor. This is not the case. It is true that the advisor does function from the same baseline of trust and sensitivity. However, you are not called to be a therapist. You are not treating a patient. In fact, one of the vital roles of your special relationship with teens is that you spot serious problems which need professional counseling rather than advising.

The problems young people bring to you are basically coping concerns and not life and death matters. However, each problem is important to the concerned young person. Therefore, the problems, no matter how small, are worth your time and concern.

In coping with the natural stress of adolescence, young people are designing the foundation for their lives.

You will want to find some backup help for the occasional serious problems. A professional counselor in your community should be happy to develop this kind of arrangement. You may want to have regular appointments to talk over your advising role. Many professional therapists offer this kind of support.

A recent study showed that most of the emotional help given to people in trouble is done by volunteers, youth workers and neighbors.

So it's up to you.

Go ahead, muster the courage and be an advisor. Listen with every bit of sensitivity you can gather to what the person is saying (not just the words but the emotions, fears and hopes); explore the alternatives as this person understands them; check out the advice he or she has received from others and probe the relative value that the individual has placed on alternatives. Then share some of your feelings, explaining that these are just initial reactions and that additional time and exploration will probably be needed by both of you, perhaps together, perhaps not.

If time does not warrant, a projected schedule for working on the problem may be outlined at the first meeting. Allow yourself some contemplative and consultative time with persons who can advise you. When possible answers appear, check them carefully with the individual, because they may apply only to what you first understood the problem or question to be and not to the real dilemma.

Pray with and for the individual. You should be open not only to God's strength and direction but also that the problem or question can be visualized within God's framework of time and concern for the world.

The terms *advising* and *counseling* might be used interchangeably, except for one matter: The youth is usually asking for your opinion, not merely an impersonal problem-solving process. You are being turned to as a friend who might have a helpful opinion, some useful advice.

Quite often, you will need to realize that the problem is far beyond your abilities and that the young person needs to be referred to someone more qualified. The referral should be done as quickly as possible after you have located the person or agency that can provide exactly the help that you perceive is needed. Realize though, that the person came to you, and you can aid the youth in making the transition to the more specialized help.

There are some times when your caring and listening may help the individual begin to discover answers without much help from anyone. The answers may have been there all along, but the panic and uneasiness of what seemed to have been an overwhelming problem might have clouded their presence.

Where does the time for advising come from in your busy schedule? Amazingly enough, other matters may lose some of their priority. You alone will have to determine when you are spending too much time with certain individuals (for their good and yours), and when it would be better for them to look to their own resources.

You will also have to decide when too much of your daily schedule is spent in this advisory role. You may decide, as many persons have, that this is such a significant responsibility that it should be a regular contribution, maybe even a vocation.

Resources
1. **On Caring**, by Milton Mayeroff, Harper and Row.

See also ADVOCATE, COUNSELING, PEER COUNSELING

Advocate

Have you ever needed an advocate, someone who would speak a good word for you? Most of us have. An example: The teacher came back to the classroom and found us in a very suspicious place. Even though we were innocent, we hoped some of our friends would help defend us. Another example: A bill before Congress proposed major changes in our community. Everyone hoped that our representative could convince his congressional friends to vote the way he wanted them to. The best example: Jesus promised his disciples that he would send the advocate or comforter in order that we might be advocates (John 16:5-15).

It didn't take long for you to realize that you inherited a role no one told you about and with which you felt unfamiliar and unprepared. That is, your role as a youth advocate probably came as a surprise. No getting around it, since you work with youth, it is obvious that you have a spiritual interest in them. And because you care, people will come to you for your advocacy role. . .

"Hey, did you see those kids get into the women's pies last night?"

"Now, are you sure that if we let them use the cabin, they won't wreck it?"

"What will it hurt if we knock $100 off next year's youth budget?"

There will be many other times when you have to initiate and sustain your advocacy function. . .

"Would it be possible to let a youth help with the worship service from time to time?"

"Moving the youth class to that other building will cut them off from contact with the other members—and both groups need each other."

"Is there any way that we could put a regular youth column in the church newsletter?"

As a youth advocate you can function

Your actions should tell youth that you are 100 percent for them.

best if you know the needs of the people in your group. This is not simply a process of asking the group what they want and then pleading their case with the proper authorities or bombarding kids with questionnaires and discussions regarding their needs. You'll need to carefully and prayerfully analyze the group's underlying needs before working toward solutions. Maybe the group needs a service project more than a new ping pong table. Your advocacy role will be to open up opportunities for the group to give themselves away in service rather than be given a less-needed piece of equipment.

Often your advocacy role will be most needed in church committees and councils that make decisions about general programs. For instance, the group may be talking about an attempt in intergenerational Sunday school classes with children, youth and adult classes meeting together. All at once you realize that this would be an excellent opportunity for some of your youth group to contribute their musical and leadership talents. You are an advocate on behalf of potential growth both for those who will contribute and those who will receive the contribution.

Advocacy is wanting the best for those you represent. It is giving your life resources for theirs.

See also ACCESS

Age Level Characteristics

No two youth are alike. The obvious similarities often lead us to compare and contrast, but every such conclusion is demeaning and inhuman to the persons being so appraised.

No youth is at the same stage of development (physical, mental, spirit-

ual, moral, etc.) as another. Lisa is 14 years old and an 8th grader in school (which means in her case: 7th grade in grammar, 5th grade in spelling, 6th grade socially, level 3 on a moral development scale, advanced physically, an infant in athletics, and she doesn't realize it, but her heart is weak and the symptoms are affecting her in ways she cannot explain).

Margaret is Lisa's best friend and they do look somewhat similar, but it would be so unfair to each of them to be grouped as "just alike," since Margaret is quite the opposite from Lisa in many important ways.

Even though this uniqueness should not be forgotten for a moment, it can be extremely useful to those in youth ministry to be aware of insights that have been gathered from many fields of study into general characteristics of persons who are progressing through adolescence.

Differences in males and females are never more pronounced than in the early teen years.

Volumes of helpful studies concerning these general characteristics are available in most libraries, and they are also provided by many doctors' offices. Many public school teachers have found the characteristics most helpful in realizing the various stages of development of students prior to the grade they are teaching, what might be occuring during this year and what would be following.

It is important to know that these are general trends. No youth ever follows the pattern exactly. The temptation must be avoided to conclude, "Don't worry about Tom. It's just a stage he's going through. He will pull out of it like they all do."

While profiting from the contributions of these generalized youth profiles, it is important to remember that no two groups are alike. Everything that makes individuals unique compounds to make each group unique. Methods that worked so well or so poorly with one group cannot be predicted to have that response again. Expectations must be seen only as subjective projections, perhaps necessary but highly fallible.

You are not in any way similar to any other leader. You have different attributes, and it is a waste of time trying to decide if those are better or worse than those of another leader. Realize that you are the best leader who has ever been with this particular group at this particular moment.

Resources

1. **Twelve to Sixteen: Early Adolescence**, by Kagan, Coles, W. W. Norton.
2. **Normal Adolescence:** Group for the Advancement of Psychiatry, Scribner.
3. **Growing Through Life**, by Rhona Rapuport and Robert Rapuport, Harper and Row.

See also BODY, CLOTHING, PASSAGE RITES

Attendance

Too often we get caught up in the flurry of activities and the concerns of the persons who attend regularly to remember those who are not presently attending.

Rolls of the active, inactive and potential membership should be diligently kept up-to-date so that adequate notice can be registered when members do not show up for a couple of events. Then a note or a phone call could let them know they are missed. All kids like to know that they are valued by the group, even though outwardly they may seem to discredit that desire.

Regularly looking over the potential attendance list and the known interests of non-attenders can help in remembering them while designing future programs. This concern is especially true for those who were once a part of the group, but for some reason have not been seen lately. When you send out news concerning upcoming events, remember the non-attenders too. Even though they may never attend, it could easily be that your contact with them, even through general notices, is very helpful. Jesus talked a lot about going after the lost sheep even at the neglect of the many who were present.

Some groups have become very aggressive about reaching the non-attenders. Everything from personal cards to phone calls on a regular basis to kidnap breakfasts (literally coming to their house, kidnapping—with a little help from their parents—and bringing them to a breakfast with other non-attenders, plus the entire group).

Everyone is worth the effort.

However, it is possible for us to get so caught up in numbers that we forget persons. The numbers game is encouraged by many elements of the church, everyone from the pastor to the

All young people like to know they are valued by the group.

parents. And acknowledgement of leadership capabilities can get tied up with numerical references. ("Joe is better than John as a youth leader because more people come when Joe is in charge.")

Of course, you cannot spend inordinate amounts of energy and time with those who never attend. (It may be that other groups are meeting their needs better.) Constant focus on the ones who do not respond can dissipate your concern for those who attend regularly. Even Jesus shook the dust from his sandals where persons did not respond, and he advised his disciples to move on to where the response was better.

Groups tend to be much stronger when they bring together a diverse group of individuals. Each individual difference provides a way for the group and the other persons to realize something of the splendor of God's creation. It is easiest for persons to recruit persons like themselves to join the group, but the long range effect is exclusiveness and a deficiency of perspective. For instance, persons with handicaps contribute as much to the group as they receive; persons from other races offer insights that could not be gained apart from their presence.

See also DIVERSITY, HOSPITALITY, INTEREST, LARGE GROUP VS. SMALL GROUP, LONER, NEWCOMER, VARIETY, YOUTH NEWS

Balance

One of the most luring pitfalls that can occur in youth ministry is to continue doing some activity or direction that has worked well in the past. Whether it be outreach-type of involvement, recreation, spiritual development, dramatics, or a myriad of other emphases, it can become so easy (and often so rewarding at the time) to continue doing exactly as before at the expense of other equally valid directions which are necessary to meet the needs of additional youth.

Some youth are attracted to a group because of its involvement in athletics and fellowship activities, for example. But if athletics and fellowship are all that ever happen, there will be very little depth to the overall ministry. Likewise, totally serious programming without any fellowship consideration is a mistake. Concentration on just those in attendance, forgetting about an enormous potential of other youth who might like to be invited in various ways to attend is nearsighted. Likewise, spending all the time trying to attract newcomers and forgetting about the personal needs of those faithful regulars is farsighted.

How can a proper balance be maintained? There are several reliable ways, two of which are long-range planning and continual evaluation. Week-by-week and month-by-month planning can be done with more ease and wisdom if some overall planning has been done for the year, keeping in mind short-term and long-term goals. This way, steady progress can take place for areas of concern that might not be emphasized each week. Checkpoints for assessing achievement can keep the group aware of its varied work.

Evaluation can take place at regular intervals to test not only the attainment of goals but whether additional goals should be included. Evaluation need not be a heavy or threatening process, but simply a way to see if anything is missing. For instance, it can be a significant discovery when a group member realizes that, even though the group has been very active for the past few months, added several new members and learned much about numerous subjects, service to others was totally overlooked.

An extremely valuable gift that can come to a member of a group seeking balance for its life is that same sensitivity for themselves.

Jesus' teachings are filled with double emphasis: concern for the needs of others while not forgetting one's own worth or spiritual well being; giving one's self away in order to find it; keeping one's attention on eternal matters but not worrying about the next day. Our tension should be to seek to do well in each activity but always be aware of other needed activity in which we help our young people to grow spiritually, mentally, physically and socially.

See also EVALUATION, FEEDBACK, GOAL SETTING

Bell Choirs

The melodious sound of handbells fills the sanctuary with a stirring accompaniment to worship, and persons of all ages are inspired by the echo-like effect achieved by the variety and combinations of tones.

What happens to the worshippers in the congregation is important, but often something of much more significance occurs in the lives of those in the choir.

Handbells can be the voice for the persons who would prefer not to sing in a vocal choir. In fact, handbells can be a godsend to junior high boys whose voices are changing.

Of course, handbells are an excellent way to learn music. By waiting to ring a particular bell or bells, the choir member must learn to understand tempo, volume intensity, tonality, rhythm changes and other necessary concepts. When several bells are rung at the same time, the choir learns about harmony, dissonance, composition of chords and other information concerning combinations of sounds.

Teamwork is a must. Everyone depends upon everyone else. The notes that each person is responsible for are as important as those of anyone else, since the melody is complete only with the inclusion of each component part. The group thrives on mutual respect.

Bell choirs do not need great throngs of participants like many other youth programs do, and this makes it a natural for the youth group with few members. As few as three persons can handle many musical selections, though if eight or ten persons are available, the possibilities are almost limitless.

Often bell choirs are composed of youth and adults so that an intergenerational mix encourages communication across age and background categories. Since the contributions of each member are equally valuable, many of the former walls that separate persons are erased.

Handbells might seem to be expensive, but if a small budget is your only worry, don't give up the idea just yet. Many larger churches have usable sets of handbells to sell because they have progressed to a more advanced set. Newsletters for choir directors often list used sets for sale. Some churches will loan a set to help your choir get started.

Some bell choirs have acquired bells through memorial gifts. Since the bells are lasting gifts, each concert may constitute a living memorial.

National handbell organizations with regular festivals and a wealth of exciting music have given handbell choirs tremendous growth in the last decade. Bell choirs are effective outreach channels into the community: shopping malls, schools, airports, nursing homes, etc.

Attendance at festivals is also an interdenominational outreach and rewarding personal experience.

The American Guild of English Handbell Ringers, Inc. (100 West 10th St., Wilmington, DE 19899), is a major organization providing programming, magazine and resources for bell choirs.

Resources
1. **Joyfully Ring**, by Donald E. Allured, Broadman Press.
2. **A Manual of Handbell Ringing in the Church**, by Ellen Jane Lorenz, Lorenz Publishing Co.
3. **Let the Children Ring**, by Jerald P. Armstrong, Broadman Press.
4. **Tintinnabulen [The Liturgical Use of Handbells]**, by Richard Proulx.
5. Director of Publications, American Guild of English Handbell Ringers, 72 Lake Morton Drive, Lakeland, FL 33801.

See also CHOIRS, MUSIC

Belonging

Youth advisors have always asked, "How can I get more youth to come?" This query will be around as long as we care about young people. It is clear that teens will attend groups where they think something is happening and where

A creative mailing approach is one way to help group members feel needed.

they feel wanted and accepted.

This book is filled with many ways these two goals can be fulfilled. Yet, you as youth advisor are the only person who can make an exciting place a reality.

Fred goes to great lengths to see that young people experience authentic excitement and welcome. For instance, one week he created fake telegrams. Using the electric typewriter in the church office and envelopes with plastic windows, he simply stated, "I need you." Fred listed a time and place. He had a college student unknown to the teens deliver the telegrams to each of the church young people. There was no one at the church and the youth could not call in an excuse. The meeting time was unusual. Every young person except one appeared! The group spent this special time talking about the needs and future directions of the youth program.

Another time, he created S-shaped links. He asked each member of the group to decorate one link in some special way. There were paints and other items available for the task. He had screwed a hook into the ceiling of the meeting room. Individual links formed a chain group. The group had discussed the idea of *covenant* as it applied to this study class. "If someone is missing, the chain isn't complete." Each young person was given someone else's link. They were told that the chain would be reassembled when the group met to add their links to the chain. It was surprising how many teens began coming to the Sunday morning class.

There are so many little strategies that can help your youth experience the importance of belonging to a gathered community. Teens who stay away from church programming are saying something to us.

See also ENCOURAGEMENT, HOSPITALITY, LOVE, NEWCOMER

Bible

The scriptures are a youth ministry's best resource!

The Bible is not only the rule of faith and life, but also the source of endless creative ministry ideas. We know that folks don't often link the word of God with innovation. Since there is something forbidding about the study of the Holy Book, people often stumble when it comes to teaching the scriptures. A teacher usually visualizes a narrow range of possibilities when approaching this task. The study of scripture has traditionally fallen into certain patterns:

- Expository method (verse by verse)
- Cross-reference method (comparing passages and words)
- Unit method (studying a block of Bible material)
- Conversation method (each member expresses his or her understanding after study and reflection)
- Historical context method (searching for meaning from the text alone)
- European SCM method (creating paraphrase, prayer and meditation)
- Reading versions (comparing readings in various versions)
- First-century method (reading large sections and sharing insights from the text alone)
- Scientific method (detailed observation, selection-interpretation, and conclusions)

A close, creative study of scripture often opens up new understanding.

material. It also supposes that the student can be drawn into the passage rather than having the passage made relevant to the student. The points of contact are the natural senses, the emotional and intellectual experiences of the youth. It is absolutely incredible how the close study of scripture opens up new ways of studying the Word!

Many youth leaders are tempted to be popular with youth by focusing all Bible study on the concerns of youth problems. While there must be a connection between daily life and the historical Word, the flow must begin with scripture. It is saddening to see a group randomly leafing through the Bible and sharing ignorance. The experiential mode of study demands sound research and study while introducing the group to new areas of creative study.

For instance, a group was studying the Book of Acts. The leaders struggled with the text of Acts 9:1-19. The passage describes Paul's conversion as a complete physical and spiritual experience. This must be an important clue to the teaching of the passage. As the youth gathered, they were stopped at the door to the room, blindfolded, led to a table and seated. For the next hour and a half, the group experienced human situations quite beyond the usual suburban setting. A tape recording was played of a young girl's attempt to express the desperation and confusion she felt upon being released from prison after the death of her lover. "How would you respond if this were your daughter speaking?" The members of the group responded with academic and textbookish advice on the counseling she should receive.

The tape recording was played again and each person was asked to place his or her hands on the table. A woman, who had been in the room without the knowledge of those present, stopped at each person's place. She took the stu-

However, one of the most promising starting points for the developing youth group is to focus on experiential Bible study. This approach assumes that the Word has come to us in its present form for a reason. Many "biblical" preachers and teachers interpret every passage by the same means. It seems that a Psalm, a historical narrative, a parable or a teaching passage becomes a three-point message with a concluding story.

The experiential technique searches deeply within the passage to find how the passage suggests that the text be taught or communicated. This internal method draws upon the study of the language, images and context of biblical

dent's hands in hers and said, "Help me." The earlier round of intellectual responses was suddenly replaced by deep Christian encounters with another person. One young man stammered with great feeling, "I would put my arms around you and tell you that I love you." The physical touch of a person in need enabled a new level of involvement with the power which also touched Paul's life.

After sharing the burden of a refugee family (or migrant workers and other oppressed persons) and wrestling with the point that we need the love of the poor to recover our humanity (as Ananias needed Paul to fulfill his ministry), the leader removed each person's blindfold with the words: "Brother (or sister), the Lord Jesus has sent me that you may regain your sight and be filled with the Holy Spirit" (Acts 9:17). They parted with the question, "What do you see now as Christians about your lives?"

Resources

1. **Switched On Scriptures** series (Six cassette tapes and guides). Each tape contains instructions and materials for a six-week course. Write P.O. Box 12811, Pittsburgh, PA 15241 for more information.

2. **Translating the Good News Through Teaching Activities**, by Donald Griggs, Abingdon.

3. **A Theological Word Book of the Bible**, edited by Alan Richardson, Macmillan & Co.

4. **These Stones Will Shout** (Old Testament Study), by Mark Link, Argus Communications.

5. **The Seventh Trumpet** (New Testament Study), by Mark Link, Argus Communications.

See also BIBLE KNOWLEDGE, MIME, PUPPETS, RESOURCES, STORIES, SUNDAY SCHOOL

Bible Knowledge

Youth leaders aren't asked to be biblical scholars, but rather biblical students.

"What is the shortest verse in the Bible?" If you are stumped by such a question, don't turn in your youth advisor uniform. It is important for adults working with youth to frequent the pages and the spirit of scripture. We don't worship the Bible, but the major source of our Christian commitment is found in this rule of faith and life.

How do we "know" something? We can repeat every word of the Bible from memory and still not experience the gospel. On the other hand, we can know Christ personally and not be able to repeat the books of the Bible. Yet, the Christian must become comfortable in this landscape of salvation. It is the struggle with the Bible's "hard" sayings and teachings which brings the gift of insight and truth.

Playing within the familiar context of biblical parables and stories will bring hope and peace.

Youth ministry advisors are not asked to be biblical scholars, but rather we are called to be biblical students. There is an old story about a simple, illiterate Christian who was new in the faith. He was able, however, to recite the complete Sermon on the Mount. His teacher was amazed. "How did you accomplish this?"

"Each day I tried to live one of the teachings," was the man's reply.

It is this kind of biblical "knowledge" that young people need to experience in their advisors.

We encourage youth and youth advisors to study the biblical languages (Greek and Hebrew). This is not as extreme a suggestion as you might think. There are pastors in your church or town who have been trained to read the scriptures in the original languages. Ask them to set up a course for yourself and some committed young people. It will be one of the turning points in your faith experience! There is hard work built into this suggestion, but I think that we often expect the faith to come too easily. Maturity costs. It is also an amazing experience for you and your teens to learn together. What a super model you will provide as a growing Christian!

You need a growing and developing relationship with the Word of God!

By the way, the shortest Bible verse is I Thessalonians 5:17.

See also BIBLE

Bikes

While many junior highs may be anxious to dump the transportation they used during their childhood for the chance to drive a car, don't miss the value of the bike. The two-wheel wonder has great possibilities for youth groups. Many churches have organized bicycle outings which take the teens for hundreds of miles over several days.

These biking trips can have all kinds of teaching opportunities. Imagine a Beatitude bike journey. Each day the group has to find an encounter or situation which illustrates one of the teachings in this passage. Perhaps the group even makes the trip without money! They must work or beg for food and lodging. They can repay the hospitality of others by serving them in some way.

This model brings together solid physical activity with a good learning situation. You might want to combine such a trip with a special fund raising drive. If your youth are interested in the hunger situation, they might get people to pledge so much a mile for the cause.

Some groups have enjoyed using tricycles! They have races at their regional youth conferences. This is a fun activity.

Bike Organizations
1. Out-Spokin', Box 370, Elkhart, IN 46515.
2. Wandering Wheels, Taylor University, Upland, IN 46989.
3. Bikecentennial, Box 8308, Missoula, MT 59807.

Resources
1. **Camping on the Move**, by Charles Kishpaugh.

See also ADVENTURE CAMPING, CAMPING

Put your group on wheels for ministry, spiritual growth and just plain fun.

The best way to deal with the blues is to bring them out in the open and evaluate them carefully.

Blues

Phyllis gets a headache every Sunday night at nine o'clock. She has finally concluded that the headache comes from being a youth leader and feeling that things are not going as they should. The headache goes away before long, but the discouraged feeling remains— she is not being an effective leader. She had great expectations when she was recruited as youth advisor, but now things are different.

Most of us could probably fill in a long list of personal reasons we have found for falling into the blues.

The best way to deal with the blues is to bring them out into the open (to defuse their mystical quality) and evaluate them carefully.

Try listing on paper all those parts of your youth ministry that do not seem to be going well. Note the word *seem*, since it will be imperative to check later to see if the items you list are subjective assumptions open to rebuttal. Be specific in your listing to the point of describing situations in which the negative conditions are at their worst.

For contrast, make a list of all the positive conditions, again being very specific about what makes the good times begin and continue. Which ministry is the most active? Why?

The point is not to see which list is the longest but what factors are at work to cause such divergent reactions. What individuals, systems and assumptions are making the differences?

Peter confessed that he was ready to give up working with youth after having to call off two well-planned retreats just because registrations were too low. He was further upset when he discovered that in both instances, there was a scheduling conflict with the youth choir director. After taking some time for reflection, he realized the problem was not the retreats (they were well-received by those who wanted to participate), the date (it was obviously a good one for the choir), the choir director (it turned out he did not know about the retreat since both choir programs had been planned prior to the retreats), or himself (an important consideration since at first he felt he was incapable of helping to arrange something for the youth).

Peter's follow-up was positive action to call together all those involved in the church's youth ministry to do some cooperative scheduling so that the youth were not forced to choose between competing programs.

You may come to some of the same kind of conclusions as you examine your list very carefully. That deadlock you may have mentioned concerning a particular person or circumstance might be resolved by getting together with the ones you may be convinced are immovable.

Invite other persons who care about you and your ministry to evaluate the items on your list. Ask their help in suggesting alternative ways of reaching youth ministry goals. Some programs may have to be dropped or altered drastically, while others may require more help for you.

There's little doubt why our friend Phyllis in the opening anecdote gets headaches. Her expectations of what the group could quickly become are too high and probably are not at all the expectations of the group members. It would have been fairer to the group and to herself if she had told the group at the beginning about her expectations instead of trying to work on a secret agenda. Then there could have been some negotiation and a time for combining goal expectations. The larger reason for her frustration was her mistaken belief that it was all up to her to pull off the successes. She is involved in a group ministry that could be aided greatly by her sharing this responsibility with the group.

She is also involved in a team ministry with God, and his abilities are certainly sufficient to make a youth group function (in his own time and way). When we share our ministry with God and depend upon his strength, we have no gauge capable of measuring the fantastic results.

See also AAUGH, CRITICISM, DESPAIR, DOUBTS, FAILURE

Body

The button was clear in its message: "I want your body!" Even coming from a health spa, it says much more than one might suspect. The human body is more than we might assume. A wise woman once said, "You are not in a body, you are a body!"

Teens know and feel the implications of the human body. At times, they feel imprisoned by it. Their bodies are in the process of changing daily. They see zits pop out on their faces overnight. Joints stretch as the young person grows. The chemistry of the teen body is amazing and frightening to the youth in your midst. Sexual awakening is more of a burden to youth than a license for abuse.

The social pressures on the body are overwhelming. Insecurity about self is threatened and affirmed by the need for acceptance. "Do I look right?" "I hate those shoes." "My shirt is horrible!"

Of course, advertisers appeal strongly to the bodily fears and needs of youth. They know how to promise physical acceptance by treating the body

Many teenagers view themselves as less attractive than they really are.

with the right odor, shape and appearance. The body is important because it is important to the teenagers.

The body is also a matter for concern because God chose to become flesh and dwell among us in the human body. Jesus permitted others to attend to his body. He knew that they realized that he was a person/body. The one could not be separated from the other.

This means that your program must be aware of the shifting, and sometimes confusing, needs of your folks. For instance, some teens at points in their development cannot sit still. Jim was a bright junior high student. However, he was always giggling and punching others in the Sunday morning class. When the advisor talked to him alone, he was always apologetic for

Helping youth accept rapid bodily changes is an integral part of youth ministry.

what he had done. The youth sponsor who taught the class responded to Jim's physical needs and asked him to fold the bulletins during class. There was a radical change. Jim could now do something with his hands and still participate in the discussion. It was as if his body wanted activity while his mind was at work.

Some youth advisors have turned to strong physical activities as a way of dealing with this concern. This may be a partial answer. However, such an approach can lead to continuous sports without any other option.

See also IDENTITY, SELF-IMAGE

Boredom

A teenage girl in California stayed home from school on Monday. She was bored. She took a gun and started shooting at the children in the schoolyard. When the police finally subdued her, she had shot several people. She said the only reason behind her act was that she didn't like Mondays.

Boredom is one of the most dangerous human states. The human being is not designed to endure the state of boredom without falling into deep trouble.

"Man, I do some pills before school. I hit on some more at the free period. A lot of us do this kind of thing."

"Why?"

"I don't know. It just seems . . . like I need something."

"Is it hard at school?"

"Not hard. It just means nothing. It is so boring. The teachers don't care."

What is boredom? In western culture, the kinetic activity of life (fast transportation, fast sports, fast moving enter-tainment, fast cures, etc.) seems to view any lull in the movement as boring. Many a church teacher has cried, "How do we keep the young down on the Sunday school farm after they've been stimulated by TV's rapid fire programming?"

There are many teens in your world who do not feel challenged. When signs of boredom among youth become obvious, adults usually try to think up activities to keep the kids off the streets. The local church also has that kind of mentality at times. "We must do something for the young people."

Young people will judge your work according to this kind of thinking.

The antidote to boredom is not activity imposed upon the bored by others. Our theological commitment places responsibility for ourselves on ourselves. Too many youth programs do too much of the wrong things for youth. We must draw upon the faith to guide us in challenging youth to work out of boredom by ministering to others. The cults have won many because they demand a great deal from converts. Their ideology may be foolish or worse. Yet, they do challenge their followers.

The roof had fallen on the poor woman. At least, this is the way it seemed if anyone looked into her life. Her husband died early in their marriage and left her with three children. She fought to keep the family going. Mary worked hard while battling her own bad health. She had two cancer operations during the last ten years.

One day she shared her story with a group of teens who dropped by to offer some Christmas cheer. "Some terrible things happened to you. How did you keep going?"

The old woman smiled, "I don't know. It was hard sometimes. I remember what my husband said to me before he died. He told me to fight any self-pity, loneliness or boredom by helping somebody else. It works."

Indeed, Mary was one of the most active folks in the local church.

It is clear to those who work with the sick and dying that there is a trade-off between helper and helped. You come to serve but you are served in the process. This is a major Christian insight which young Christians must experience. Utilizing concerns like peer ministry, young people have a special opportunity to touch the lives of others. Boredom is the misdirection of vital energy. When the life turns outside of self to care for others, new sources of talent and strength appear.

Maggie Kuhn, the Gray Panther person, claims that many old people die of boredom. She urges the old and young to engage more fully in the lives of others. "I don't want to dry up on a park bench in the sun. You know, those of us who throw ourselves into helping cure the suffering of the world live longer!"

There are times of the year when the sources of energy release are turned down in the youth world. Ironically, the church usually closes down at these times. You can play a significant role in getting young people to discover the faith understanding of full stewardship in life.

The Christian faith demands a view of life which turns things inside out. We are called to act upon life, and the flow of our enthusiasm for life is our responsibility. This kind of ministry equips youth to replace boredom with zeal.

See also ADVENTURE CAMPING, GROUP BUILDING, MOTIVATING YOUTH, WORK PROJECTS

Ministry to others is the best boredom breaker.

Brainstorming

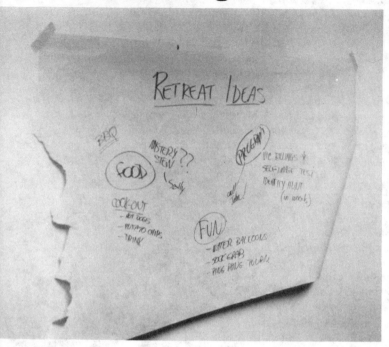

This is a method of shaking ideas loose from a group that might be a bit slow in starting a discussion or realizing how they are personally related to the topic at hand.

The procedure is to announce the topic and briefly introduce the topic's significance for the group. Designate someone to write down what is said. Use a chalkboard, newsprint, posterboard or overhead projector to list the thoughts and ideas. Newsprint can be hung in different places around the room to remind people visually of their progress in dealing with the subject.

To begin the brainstorming session announce a general request, perhaps stating that it would be helpful to see how everyone feels about a particular subject. For instance, "Give us the first words that come into your mind to describe your feelings when you hear this subject mentioned." The secretary lists the words or phrases contributed. Once completed, this listing could be placed in another position in the room where it can be easily seen for future reference.

Next, the leader may wish to ask a more advanced question, such as, "Where have you found help in dealing with this subject?" Again, every response is noted.

Brainstorming can take place with each person urged to give a response or it can enlist general responses from the group at large. (This process is sometimes called popcorning, since ideas seem to burst forth from around the room.)

Brainstorming helps group members realize that they have plenty of feelings about this subject and it does affect their lives. Not only are all members of the group affirmed by the leader's anticipation that each person has something to contribute, but each opinion is given a prominent position.

Brainstorming has one simple rule, which must be enforced constantly. No one is allowed to judge or comment on anyone else's contributions. There are no stupid or dumb contributions. When the listing has been completed the group can look at the list as something it owns. Without going back to the original contributor, the entire group can expand some details about the words and phrases. For instance, if the subject were "War," and a word listed was *scary*, the group might wish to embellish that concept by offering reasons why war is scary. By then, your discussion is well underway!

See also DISCUSSION, CIRCULAR RESPONSE

Bubble

A window fan and masking tape can transform a large piece of plastic into a bubble large enough to hold your entire group.

One of the most delightful environments which you can create easily and cheaply is right at hand. The "Bubble" or "Whale" is built out of 4 mil plastic, masking tape and a large window fan. The plastic can be purchased at any lumber yard. We like to use the roll which is 18 feet wide and 100 feet long. Greenhouse suppliers sell plastic of this size which is sealed like a tunnel.

If you can't find the tunnel-type material, roll out plastic until it can be doubled into a 50-foot length, Have the youth fold about two inches of the outside edges along the long sides. Use masking tape to seal these edges. Also seal the open end up to the corner. Using spare plastic, form a short tunnel and connect the window fan. You now have a giant Baggie! Cut a long doorway by slitting a six-foot opening in the closed end. Turn on the fan and a giant bubble or whale will be ready for entry. You can get 100 or more youth in this structure. Use it again and again.

For example, in a recent event the bubble became a whale when a leader was conducting the concluding worship. Drawing upon the story of Jonah, he led a prayer asking God to bring forth a creature wherein they might find refuge. The bubble was flat and the fan was turned on as he prayed. They then entered it and had Communion. The benediction picked up the reference to Jonah being sent to minister.

Warren used the whale as a survival shelter when he led his youth group through the simulation game "Ralph" (from **Gaming**, Benson). They spent several hours working on a way to live "now that the world has been destroyed." Other groups have used bubbles as the site for the youth group meeting each week. They simply turn the fan on and the environment appears. Pillows and bean bags can be scattered around the floor. Filmstrips and slides can be projected on the side of the bubble.

Let your young people build the structure. It will take about 20 minutes. The environment will change the whole tone of the meeting or worship service.

See also EARTHBALL, PARACHUTE, WEATHER BALLOON

Burn-out

If you are a typical youth worker, you are a prime candidate for burn-out.

Joe and Betty had worked with the youth group for four years. They were the best! The kids loved them. Their home was always open. Even after midnight young people could be found in their house. The entire church was surprised when Joe and Betty resigned.

Peter was the finest. He was right out of seminary. His wife and young child were the joy of everyone in the congregation. The youth group exploded in size. It seemed that he was gone every night and weekend. "I have to give myself to the kids." Peter has left the church. There was a scandal about him and a girl in the group. His wife took the child and moved away.

These folks were dropped by different problems. Yet, it is the danger of burn-out which usually leads to other factors that overcome the youth advisor. Most serving professions face this risk. For instance, while the medical field utilizes rest periods, support systems and other safeguards to protect their people, the church has been the slowest to build preventive factors for its workers. Protect yourself! Be sure that you have a board of people (adults and youth) who supervise and guide your ministry. These folks should be connection links to the power structure in the local church. They can fight the fights for you.

It is also important that you have a support system which helps you reflect on your ministry. You cannot develop a proper perspective alone. If you do a lot of counseling, find a professional counselor for support. Share your cases or encounters with youth and allow the counselor to give you an overview of your involvement. This resource person can also help you work on your relationship with your family. You may be advised to turn out the porch light earlier as a signal that youth cannot drop by. You are important to your young people, but you are indispensable to your family!

It is also vital to monitor yourself. An 80-year-old friend reminds us, "Listen to your body! If it says to you, 'Out of the pool!' Get out!" If you are overly tired, confused and tense, you are getting too close to the youth group action. It is not selfishness to care for yourself. You will be no help to youth if you are burned out.

Many churches are now using youth advisor teams made up of several couples or individual adults. This means that the team can absorb the emotional impact of close youth ministry. We are not suggesting a rotation scheme which brings a fresh face every week. The whole team should be known by the group. The "up front" aspects of the program can be shared by one couple with other adults being present in a less visible role. In fact, the love and care between the members of the adult team can teach a great deal to the youth.

Burn-out comes to those who are doing too much of the work which should be done by the youth. The role of the youth advisor is that of enabler. You should be thrusting young people into positions of growing, stretching and working.

The great miracle of youth ministry is that we are called to balance deep involvement and commitment with a sense of self-preservation.

See also DESPAIR, SUCCESS, WORKSHOPS, YOUTH COUNCIL

Bus

Ed and his youth were floundering. They had no focus to their program. It seemed that there was a different mix of kids every week. They got into a meandering discussion one night. One of the boys started a conversation about music. He was a real "Who" freak. This early rock band was the center point for his pop music appreciation. He produced his audio cassette and after a bit of fiddling, asked everyone to be quiet. The strong introductory strains of "Magic Bus" filled the room with distorted sound. "Man, I wish I had a magic bus—I'd visit the world."

Out of this passing comment came a dream which changed the direction of the youth group. Ed picked up the remark at face value. "Why don't we get our own bus?" The teens suddenly realized that he wasn't kidding. They got a bus!

Well, it didn't happen that easily. They spent the next six months working on this project. Of course, as the idea gathered steam, so did the kids involved in the program. Once the teens made it their idea, Ed backed off and raised the problems. How are we going to get the money? Where do we find a good bus? Who will pay for the upkeep? What will we do with it? Why should we have it? What can we do as Christians if we have a bus? The youth came at those questions from every perspective and with a widening group of people. They got adults into the discussion. The young people were amazed when the senior citizens got most excited about it! "Could we share the use of it with the young people?" The group also found a mechanic in the congregation who

would help them find a good used bus.

The congregation agreed to appeal to its members for this project. One announcement from the pulpit by a young person resulted in $5,000! They finally found the right used school bus. The man who dealt with used buses offered them special seats which would give them more space for long distance travel. Yet, it would cost them another $500. They decided to sell seats to members of the congregation. All the seats were sold after one announcement.

The group had much work to do on the vehicle before it was ready to roll. In their state, it was necessary to paint it a color other than yellow. They also had to obtain insurance and find someone equipped with a special driver's license. Since the church was near a recreation area, they decided to build a stage area which could be attached to the side of the bus. This would give them a performance area for a new beach ministry.

There are many questions to be answered before you consider such a move. Ed and his folks were ready to move. This bus project just became the occasion on which they could focus their restless energy. A bus does not promise success. Yet, in this time of critical energy resources it might be important to look into ways by which to transport folks.

For a more complete treatment of this subject, see **The Youth Group How-To-Book**, GROUP Books, Box 481, Loveland, CO 80537.

See also CARS, PORTABLE MINISTRY, TAMING

Cable TV

America has been wired with special antennae which enable each home to receive a variety of television stations.

Agreements to set up community antennae can be made between a company and a local community. Most contracts contain provisions for locally produced shows. This "narrowcasting" means that a group of folks can produce a show about highly focused interests. In some communities local churches have their own channel. Theoretically, every church can reach out through localized cable. However, in many locations there has been very little interest either by the cable operator or the community in producing local programs.

How can you get started in this opportunity? Youth can provide an exciting ministry through cable. Many have learned about television and media production at school. All have spent hours consuming media and are experts at determining what's good.

Stations that encourage cable involvement will help you produce the shows. Perhaps you and the teens could do a show about the shut-ins in the community. Instead of funding programs for your young people to watch, make them the stars! The video tapes could also be used for an in-church interpretation of community needs.

The most important step in creating a cable production is to cast off the mythology of mass media. The slickly-produced video material we see on commercial TV is intimidating. The quality of shows produced by most cable studios will seem raw and flawed. You and your youth must realize that this is narrowcasting and not network television. It is proper to produce homespun shows which communicate the honest interests and concerns of your community. There is a challenge of how much you can create from very little. You will be amazed by the possibilities.

John and his youth are interested in cable. He worked for months to give himself and his group the basic experience of producing cable. They now plan to put together a summer youth program

After the mystique of TV production wears off, you may be amazed at the endless possibilities for creative ministry.

based on cable production! They hope to have 25 to 50 young people involved in a nightly magazine format show! The production will take all day. Using a van and portable video equipment borrowed from the high school, the group will range through the community, gathering the life stories of the people in the region.

The full utilization of cable depends on local pressure and creativity. Most franchise operators can truthfully claim that the community doesn't take much interest in cable opportunities. However, does this disinterest reflect little interest or encouragement in media production? The youth group can open a vital realm of self-expression and communication through this ministry.

There is a special quality to the communication attitudes of the faithful person. He or she has been raised on a special sensitivity to the process of translating stories into life. The whole biblical experience is lived again and again in the Christian's life. This means that symbols and images important to cable production naturally work within his or her imagination. An enabler only needs to awaken this connection and our folk will spring into action with exciting media creations.

We also do not approach media production from the usual pattern of the world. Some professionals in the secular environment are elitist and guarded about their skills. They assume that what they know about production is unique and almost magical. This is untrue. Media creation is simply hard work. While the professional expert may protect his or her skills, the church community gives away everything possible. We are natural enablers. We are eager to bring others into our circle of knowledge and experience.

Christians also approach the production of other persons' messages from a strong viewpoint. As directors of video, we work to enable a guest to be fully and honestly presented. We want him or her to affirm that special personhood via the media presentation. Many secular directors will produce people to fit their convenience or outlook. But the person of faith uses media to release the special way God is working through the life of the person. How can he or she be most natural and comfortable? What setting will best reveal this guest's authenticity? What questions will open doors to the guest's world of thinking, believing and suffering?

Cable also assumes that you will create an audience. Folks do not usually keep their set tuned to the access or church channel. Gene was very sensitive to this problem. He spent from his church budget to promote a Lenten discussion series. They dealt with the addictions of the times. Young people and adults gathered in the studio and discussed the community's problems. Viewers called with questions and comments. The production group produced bulletin inserts, posters and even a couple of newpaper ads. On the Saturday before the program, young people called cable subscribers in the community and invited them to watch the program. The cable outlet was delighted by this kind of work. It meant that more people used and appreciated the offerings of the service.

The future promises more complex cable possibilities. There are two-way systems in operation, where the sub-scriber can talk back to the station! You and your youth can be the vanguard of this new media ministry. Do not be frightened by what you do not know. You are invited by this person-centered medium to explore and learn.

Cable may also provide a key resource for the energy-scarce future. What will happen when gasoline prices make it hard for every person to drive his or her own car to church? How can meetings be conducted when folks cannot afford to gather? This may sound like a fantasty scenario. However, there will be major changes in our movement patterns in the latter part of this century. Cable certainly could provide an alternative to physical gatherings. Nothing can take the place of a gathered community in worship. However, there is a stratum of church work which can be transacted without expenditure of energy for mobility. As you work with youth in the process of combining media, Christian values and the needs of the society, you are undertaking the major thrust of the ministry. There are few institutions which have such a vast sweep of concerns as the community of faith.

Here are a few steps which can carry you into this world of communication if you have a cable operation in your community:

1. Make personal contact with the persons at the cable station.

2. If you know nothing, admit it and ask for training.

3. Pass around your new knowledge by training youth and others from the faith community.

4. Map out a format for a weekly show (magazine—segments; discussion panel on community issues, worship—a communion service at a table with several people, etc.).

5. Take your group and your plans to the cable manager.

6. Develop a strong community

support campaign for the show.

7. Urge the cable operation to add portable equipment in order to produce the new idea you and your youth have just developed.

See also MULTI-MEDIA, RADIO, SLIDES, TELEVISION

Camping

The best equipped classroom in the world is the out-of-doors. It provides groups with varied experiences and helps them relate to this complex business of being a responsible earth inhabitant.

Whatever youth program you relate to (choirs, fellowship, church school, confirmation class, whatever), consider having some of your activities in a camping environment. Camping will take nothing away from your overall objectives, and it will add a dynamic dimension unavailable elsewhere.

Structuring camping experiences to meet your group's unique needs adds a dynamic dimension to your programming.

There is almost any kind of camping experience available to meet your group's tastes. The more rugged persons can choose trail hikes, survival training, cross country skiing, adventure camping, cave exploration, mountain climbing, rappelling and long bike camps. Less strenuous people will like the tent and covered wagon camps, canoe trips, rafting, horseback trips and overnighters in the woods. And for the motel crowd, most church groups have access to state and church camps that provide bedding, meeting rooms and perhaps even a dining room with a dietitian.

Many church groups make the mistake of planning their camping outings while they are sitting in someone's basement and forget to schedule plenty of time to be outside. Nature has so much to teach, but unfortunately, many groups plan a full schedule and keep all the participants locked up inside.

Concentrate on what is not available in the city—let people experience the massive and the miniscule. Have plenty of telescopes and binoculars around so that they can notice the grandeur of the mountains, clouds and lakes. Make available plenty of magnifying glasses so that they can notice the smallest crawling creatures that spend their lives under leaf mulch.

Be quiet. Give your people time to walk by themselves through the forests and by the marshes. Let them hear the wind whipping against the hills and trees. Let your singing and scripture reading mix with the night sounds.

If possible, have your closing worship near the most scenic spot you have found during your time in this setting.

Make sure to promote the summer camping programs, winter retreats, fall cookouts and all those other occasions when the church allows itself to be taught by all those magnificent creations that our Creator has provided.

There are many sources for locating just the right camp or camping spots. The Rand McNally camping guides are thorough and objective. You can find copies at most libraries or bookstores.

Auto clubs usually offer their services in locating and recommending various types of campgrounds, as do recreational vehicle clubs. Also, check the

state tourism bureau in the state you wish to camp. Most tourism bureaus will flood you with information.

If you're looking for Christian camps and conference centers, contact either the regional offices of your denomination for camps your church supports, the American Camping Association (Bradford Woods, Martinsville, IN 46151) or Christian Camping International (P.O. Box 646, Wheaton, IL 60187). The latter organization is comprised of over 700 Christian camps and conference centers.

Resources

1. **Responsible With Creation**, by Ted Witt, John Knox Press.
2. **Camping Together as Christians**, by John and Ruth Ensign, John Knox Press.
3. **Singing the Lord's Song in a Strange Land**, Bethany Press.
4. **Environmental Handbook**, edited by Farrett DeBell.
5. **Acclimitization: A Sensory Approach to Environmental Awareness**, by Steven Van Matre.

See also ADVENTURE CAMPING, MOUNTAINTOP EXPERIENCES, RE-TREATS, TRIPS

Cars

American youth have a romance with the automobile. From the low riders of Los Angeles to the pickup trucks of rural areas, youth are wild about wheels. In many high school circles, the boundary line between being accepted and being a loser is drawn by ownership or regular access to a car.

Some experts link the sexual revolution to the availability of the car. Others have written how the car has been marketed as a sex symbol e.g. television ads showing girls on automobile hoods. The automobile accident record of young people is frightening. For all these reasons and others, youth advisors are nervous about the use of cars in relationship with the youth group.

How do we channel a natural desire into opportunities for creative growth as a community of faith? Jack developed a special Saturday program called "Rally." The teens were invited to bring cars and be prepared to take a journey. It was important for them to see their car trip as a journey of faith. Each team within the car was given a list of things which had to be completed.

Along the way there was a stalled car with a man and woman standing by the road. This was an opportunity to help. But everyone passed by without stopping! There were other moments when the "race" took on aspects of the Christian's trek through life. At the end of the event, they debriefed who really "won." The teams were judged on the quality of driving as caring people and not the speed of their travel.

However, some youth groups have found that cars tend to solidify cliques and divisions within the church youth community. Who rides in whose car becomes a matter of status. Those who are left out of the car pecking order are left out of the community. There is also con-

Many churches design programs to take advantage of their youths' love affair with the car.

cern for safety in the use of cars in relationship to youth programming.

It has been suggested elsewhere (see also *Passage Rites*) that it might be meaningful to mark the passage rite of receiving a driver's license in worship. A service of dedication in the Sunday morning worship might help the young person see the responsibility of the automobile as part of his or her faith commitment.

Some folks have developed interesting ways to loosen up the tight cliques. For instance, during a caravan journey one group has a "fire drill" every so many miles in order to change the mixture of each car's occupants.

Another group adds an exciting element during a long trip by picking up a hitchhiker. (Some folks do not recommend this practice.) However, Wes knew that the seven kids in the van could handle themselves. The stranger was welcomed and encouraged to tell his story. They happened upon an unusual character who had run away two years before. His journey had been filled with pain and danger. "I don't like it . . . but I can't go back to my dad. He drinks and would beat me up all the time. I hate his guts."

When the vans gathered for the evening meal, there was an energy which carried the group long into the night. The stranger had opened whole new areas of concern and feeling. Someone mentioned the time Jesus met his disciples on the road and they did not recognize him until they ate together. Should they have invited the stranger to stay with them? Was he a messenger of Christ for them?

We do not suggest that you pick up strangers. However, the car can provide an opportunity of unexpected possibilities. How do you keep it from being misused?

See also CLIQUES, CULTURE

Certification

This is to certify that

....
has completed all requirements in the
**Splice and Plug School
of Movie Projector Theology.**
Gratefully bestowed on

....
this day, the .... day of ...., 19 ......
This certificate allows bearer to attend
all SPSMPT annual conferences
in Split Screen, OR.

Specialization in various ministry areas allows leaders to become certified to train other leaders.

Many denominations and other agencies (i.e., Television Awareness Training, Parent Effectiveness Training, New Games, etc.) sponsor training enterprises to prepare leaders for delivering a particular program. Often, the persons who have completed a basic preparation unit are certified to conduct training on their own, following specified guidelines set up by the agency.

Many such programs exist to help youth leaders in doing their work. For example, leaders in vocational guidance, human sexuality, laboratory training and many other programs have been trained and certified to offer services either directly to the youth in your group or to persons like yourself who will use the training. The availability of these persons can be known by contacting leaders in your church or in the program for which you have interest.

As you become interested in a part of youth ministry that has special meaning in your work, you may wish to become certified to provide leadership for others.

See also TELEVISION AWARENESS TRAINING

Children

Occasionally, a younger brother or sister of a group member may attend youth group meetings or be in a car as the group is being transported. And your own younger children might be included from time to time in various activities.

These occasions can be beneficial for the children and the group, provided they do not happen too often and are properly acknowledged when they do occur. Talk with the group about how the younger persons were treated and should be treated. You can help your group prepare for future occasions with persons who are quite different from them.

Many of us are like Nancy and Herb who admired a number of youth in the group they led. Every time the group met, Nancy and Herb wished that their own children, ages 8 and 10, could be with the teenagers and experience some

of the fun times. Inwardly, they hoped that the positive attitudes of the youth could serve as models for their children. Further, they felt that the youth would learn how they affect younger persons.

All of these desires can be fulfilled. The child ministers to the youth in many ways. Young people need experiences with children so they can practice caring skills. It is an invaluable occasion when a youth can hold a child and show attention and support.

In many ways the youth will get to know you and your values better by being acquainted with the members of your family. But never forget that your primary attention should be given to the group, which is often difficult when your responsibilities are torn between your group and your children.

Invite the group to your home occasionally and let the relationship with your family develop naturally.

What if one of your children (a teenager) is a member of the group? Sometimes this can be helpful while other times it is disastrous. Your success will depend upon the amount and quality of communication between you, your son or daughter, the other youth, and the rest of your family. If the youth member of your family is embarrassed and upset by your presence, take a closer look to see if the reason is real or imagined. Perhaps the idea of having a parent in the group seems restrictive. However, many youth have concluded that their parents are glad for this willingness to support something they enjoy.

Whenever you and your child are in the same group, be careful not to listen only to your child (a temptingly accessible member) for group consensus. Not only are other opinions necessary and other youth need to be encouraged to give feedback, but you may unconsciously encourage your child to use you as a power figure.

See also INTERGENERATIONAL

in church music programs as midget adults. The youth end up dressing and sounding just like the big choir.

Walter, an incredible enabler of persons, has struggled with the youth choir concept. "People like to see the kids looking just like the adults. However, the real question we must face is, *What are the unique gifts youth and children can offer to the worshipping people?* That is a hard one to answer."

You are in the unique position to strengthen the musical dimension in your life together each week, even though the pastor and music person may not give you much of a chance to help out.

Sociologists note that the strength of the early grassroots labor organizations paralleled their use of music. In the early days when working people had to practice solidarity, they sang hymns and reworked church music at each meeting. In recent days when there has been a much smaller degree of grassroots activism, music is almost nonexistent. It would be interesting to run that

Choirs

Youth music has always been troublesome in many churches. In some settings, the youth advisor and youth music advisor are different people. In most cases the youth advisor has little input into that part of the youth program. This can be difficult because many music directors tend to be a cautious lot. Perhaps they have been caught once too often in the crossfire between critics of worship changes and the pastor. Many music advisors look upon youth

Your job is to enable your youth to find ways of expressing their faith. Perhaps a choir is the key for your group.

measurement scale next to the life of the local church and the youth group.

The youth ministry program should take music-as-shared-experience very seriously. Don't be frightened if you are not a musical person. It is true that Martin Luther said that no one should enter ministry if he or she can't sing. But perhaps we are chosen because of our weaknesses! This enables us to permit others to give their ministry by supplementing our weak spots. You will be amazed how often an honest call for help in an area of skill at a group meeting will result in expert help. Almost every crowd has musicians skilled in vocal and instrumental talent.

Perhaps you could develop your own musical group for Sunday evenings. A congregation in Adelaide, Australia, and another in Riverside, California, have their own Christian rock bands. They play for the early service every Sunday morning! The funny thing you will discover is that once you value music, your group will start growing. When the youth group's musical direction is solidified you can offer these finely honed contributions to the choir director and church.

Encourage the use of original material. The process of deciding what the content will be and the development of lyrics and music is religious education at its finest. When word gets out that your youth group is exploring new music forms for the expression of faith, you will discover many new people with talent.

Your job is to enable all of this to come together. It is the scope of your vision and the bottomless hope in the gifts of others which will carry this kind of musical interest.

See also MUSIC, BELL CHOIRS, CHRISTMAS

Christmas

This is one of the biggest seasons in the life of the Christian, when even the most traditional congregation longs for something different to celebrate this special time. Christmas is also a time when we are asked to give in response to what God has given us. This means that we have a perfect opportunity to strengthen the ministry of youth during the Advent celebration.

How can young people minister to others in the community and church? Music is one of the favorite means of touching others at Christmas. Caroling can be an ideal program. It is based on community and sharing while it reaches out to shut-ins and others.

A terrible storm hit the night of one youth group's outing. They decided to use the phone for caroling! They dialed the people they had planned to visit, gathered around the phone and sang their carols.

One of the most exciting examples of the ministry of youth during a Christmas season is reported by Pauline, a creative youth worker in Australia. On the Sunday before Christmas Sunday, the young people polished apples, wrapped them in foil and placed them on the communion table. At the end of the service they passed them out to each worshipper. A teenager asked that during the week the congregation give the apple to someone they did not know. If they felt comfortable, they were to tell the person that this gift was given as a response to the gift given in Jesus Christ. If this was too intimidating, they could just say the apple was a gift of love. The youth group president then asked the people to return the following Sunday prepared to share what had happened to them when they gave the apple to a stranger.

The following week the message time was filled with the stories of the experiences encountered through the giving of the apples. Everybody seemed to have something to say. The youngest child and the oldest person had something to contribute. Many stories revealed encounters which went on for several minutes to over an hour. One young woman visited a neighboring house. An old man answered her knock. His gruff expression melted as she explained why she wanted to speak with him. "An apple for me?" He pondered a moment. "Would you please come in and give it to my wife. She is very sick and would love a visitor."

The woman visitor spent over an hour with these folks. She was able to bring them comfort by her friendship and their prayer together. It was a joyous Advent celebration with the whole congregation sharing. The youth group made this worship possible through their ministry.

Resources
1. **Preparing for the Messiah**, Donald and Patricia Griggs, Abingdon.
2. **Alternatives Celebrations Catalogue**, Alternatives, 1124 Main Street, P.O. Box 1707, Forest Park, GA 30050.

See also FESTIVALS

Circular Response

This excellent discussion stimulator is particularly helpful when a youth group needs to be coaxed a little to talk about various subject matters. This exercise gets its name from everyone sitting in a circle so that each person can be seen as the contributions are made.

If your group is larger than 25 persons, subgroups could be formed of 15 to 20 in each.

The leader states the topic and gives whatever preliminary information is available and appropriate. Then the person on the right is allowed to state his or her opinion without any comment or debate from anyone else in the group. (A time limit can be imposed if necessary.) Then the person on the right is allowed to speak. The talking proceeds around the circle with comments allowed on other persons' statements during the next time around.

This procedure allows the shyer or less assertive person to gain the podium and be encouraged to share. It also promotes listening and heightens the anticipation of debate.

See also DEBATES, DISCUSSION

Citizenship

Youth group meetings are excellent places for youth to debate and investigate what it means to be a responsible citizen of the city, county, state and nation. Certainly, there will be intense disagreements, which can occasionally turn into heated exchanges, but such processes can help the youth to compare the various sides of an issue and the implications of a certain stand.

It is important for youth to begin to understand that they are global citizens with responsibilities for persons on the other side of the planet. Soon they will realize that most decisions of one country affect the well-being of the citizens of other countries.

Political and social leaders could be invited to speak to the group on crucial concerns that affect the life of the young. The group might prefer to travel to the leader's office and tape interviews that can be added to those of leaders with different opinions. In this way the youth can search for the motives that cause the differences and perhaps discover ways that they can influence the changes they prefer.

Many youth groups keep a bulletin board in the youth room filled with newspaper clippings, announcements and other information regarding issues related to prior studies on citizenship or upcoming matters of interest (changes in voter registration, legal rights of youth, the draft). Some groups appoint a person or small group to be on the alert for issues that should be brought to the attention of the group, either through an announcement or a more extensive program.

It can be a very valuable experience for the group to visit their state legislature in session, travel to Washington to see Congress in session or see the United Nations in operation.

Resources
1. **Casebook on Church and Society**, by Keith Bridstone.
2. **God and Caesar: Case Studies in the Relationship Between Christianity and the State**, by Robert Linder
3. **The Politics of Jesus**, by John Howard Voder.

See also WASHINGTON-U.N. SEMI-NARS

Cliques

It is a rare group that is not blocked from time to time in its work by small groups of persons who link themselves together so tightly that no one else can gain access to them. Such cliques become doubly threatening to the life of the group when they attach themselves to positions of leadership responsibility.

When such tightly constructed cliques exist, it is quite common for other members to eventually give up and leave. When asked about such departure, those leaving may utter something like, "Well, I just didn't fit in anywhere" or "I found some better things to do" (often meaning, "I do not want to remain where I am made to feel less than accepted and appreciated").

Cliques exist for numerous reasons, probably chief among them is the promise of protection and security. A clique is a homemade social insurance policy. The clique contract assures the loyal devotee that he or she will never appear to be lonely or unappreciated. If anything in the larger group does not go as desired, the clique alternative is always present.

Cliques become their own popularity rating system, since most participants are close friends and admirers of each other. This grants the clique plenty of political clout over elections and group decisions.

Keeping such adverse conditions from occurring or continuing may require a variety of approaches and patience. Talking about the situation may reinforce existing cliques since they have now been acknowledged, and that may encourage other cliques to form in retaliation.

A better approach for many groups has been to dissipate the cliques by helping clique members become interested in activities in which the clique cannot always remain together, and in which persons get to know and appreciate others in the larger group. For instance, drama or musical productions can scatter clique members into meaningful configurations with other persons, and these new involvements offer the same social security that once seemed available only in the tight-knit small group.

The key is to offer a variety of involvements so that persons are continually changing configurations. Some possibilities include: clowning (perhaps grouping participants by twos for many assignments); travel (one person from the group and a clique member journey to an out-of-town meeting where they meet new friends and upon return relate better to persons they have not known well in the group); media production (where skills of a wide variety of persons are needed); visitation (again, two-person involvement); serving as a group representative on an important responsibility, where it will be necessary to hear what various group members feel about an issue.

Often cliques have evolved from long-developed friendships and were never meant by any of the participants to be vicious or threatening to others. Therefore, it is unwise to approach them as if they understand the danger their clique poses, even though you may feel that it is very threatening.

Actually, a clique is not all bad. Its concern for its participants can be a crucial ministry. The breakdown comes when this situation becomes exclusive, full of pride and limiting.

It is preferable to help the group to broaden its circle to include everyone. If you can discover ways of offering rewards in the form of affirmation and support, they will receive so much more from the group than when they limited their world to mirrors of themselves.

One thing is obvious about God. God loves variety. The more we learn to appreciate this unlimited variety, the more we learn to appreciate ourselves.

Resources
1. **Interpersonal Communication**, by Bobby Patton and Kim Griffin.

See also COMMUNITY, CONDUCT, CULTURE, GROUP BUILDING

Clothing

To the casual observer, the clothing worn by youth at any occasion might not seem to be very noteworthy. Just jeans and T-shirt in the summer, jeans and sweater in the winter. Right? Not exactly! Those jeans represent endless decisions between designer styles versus regular, flares versus straight leg, tight versus loose, prewashed versus new, fancy pockets versus plain, and on and on. The same is true for the shoes, shirt, belt, jewelry.

The casual observer might also conclude that youth clothing is all alike. Again, not exactly. A young person's wardrobe is often uniform-like and the overall objective of dressing is to be totally in line with everyone else. But there are subtle attempts at individuality and upmanship. A hat, necklace, the wording on the T-shirt are all carefully chosen to fit the profile that a person has adopted.

If you think all of this is chosen haphazardly, try hanging around when the clothing is purchased or planned for a special occasion. The "perfect" three pairs of jeans have to be ready for the upcoming trip.

The point is that the clothing selection speaks loudly regarding the way the person wants to be seen—not challenging the crowd but screaming out in subtle ways to be noticed as an individual. Young people see clothing as an extension of the individual, and to belittle it in any way is to presume to think less of its owner. Therefore, compliments and criticisms of the clothing are direct appraisals of the youth.

Activities that might in any way harm this clothing should be avoided unless the group has been warned in sufficient time to dress accordingly. Many a youth leader has been surprised at the rebellion that resulted from a suggestion that a group sit on a floor, little realizing that the jeans they had on might appear old and worn, but were aged to the exact preferred style. Floor dust and mud were intolerable.

Hair styles have for a long time been symbolic of the individual's feeling for society, and adults have wasted their time by trying to get these changes. It is difficult to understand the significance of such styles unless a person lives daily within that same culture. Only then is it possible to feel the peer pressure to conform and to understand the individual's compulsion to add a personalized statement that says in effect: "*I live here*, in the midst of *this* culture."

Members of a youth group may often encourage the adult leaders to dress as the youth do. This is a compliment and signifies an invitation to join the culture. At the same time, even though the adult may want to keep in touch with the fads and trends in youth culture (to love a person is to at least remain in contact with their "trivia"), these need not be selected as one's own. Adults need to remain authentically adult so that their own life has meaning.

The youth culture can be shared rather than be an adult's futile attempt at mimicking youth. Youth desperately need friends who can help them to see life in broader perspective than the next exam or dance.

We are needed to love the individual within his or her culture and not try to judge or change him or her based on external appearances. We can share with them who we are (without dumping our own culture, traditions and social trappings) by the way we find meaning in the way we live.

See also BODY, CULTURE, SEXUALITY

Clowning

"Send in the Clowns" might be the theme song for one of the most interesting youth ministry outreaches. Clowning is particularly important because the youth become the instruments of ministry. They are transformed through makeup, costume and art forms to impact others with love and care.

Some folks stumble when they first think of clowning as part of the faith. They just can't fit the two arenas of life together. Actually, there are many compelling reasons why this universal servanthood figure easily takes on Christlike implications. The old person in us dies through white face (universal symbol of death) and becomes resurrected through the attributes highlighted in the colors, persona and character.

It is important for Christian clowns to reflect on who they are and whose they are. They are not going into the world to scare, entertain or force themselves on others. Good leaders spend time with youth and adults to develop a capacity by which the clown creates a space and relationship. The person on the street, in

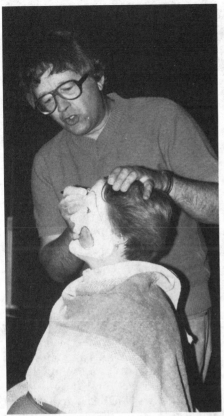

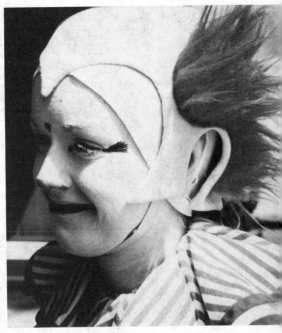

People become more than themselves once they add a costume and makeup. Christian clowns have a life-changing message to share.

the hospital bed or in the retirement home is invited to enter this special world of hope. It is a spiritual realm of play, joy, drama and love. The clown gives selfhood for the pleasure of others.

There are several different approaches to clowning. They are all strong and helpful. You will probably want to create your own breed of clowning philosophy. It will be the mix of clown philosophies from others (history), your folks (present) and yourself (future) which makes this your ministry.

There are three interesting models for us to appreciate. Charlie Sweitzer has been probing the possibilities of clowning in workshops which focus on the total impact of many influences from a person's life. How do all these experiences work to make up the person? By using individual mirrors for self-reflection and meditation, Charlie has the students transform themselves into clowns. They bring this clown focus of self into relationship with others on the street or in the shopping center. They then return and debrief, long and hard, on the impact of this experience with others in their lives. He has had amazing results.

Floyd Shaffer is a Lutheran pastor who has built his clowning ministry experience around strong, traditional theological themes. Using the liturgy, he has created a deeply moving worship experience which is done without spoken word. He transforms each part of the service through the vision and character of the clown. For instance, he takes the loaf and wraps a towel around it as he cradles it. The bread has become the Christ Child! If you watch information about national and regional youth events, you will have a chance to be with Floyd. He has trained thousands of clowns. You will want to experience him at some point.

Bill Peckham, who has also traveled widely and trained thousands of clowns, provides another variety of clowning ministry. He draws junior and senior high youth into this exciting ministry by encouraging them to do what feels comfortable for them. They are permitted to talk and communicate in any way possible with the people receiving their ministry. He has found that the clown figure enables shy and uncertain youth to give more of themselves since they can try out caring skills as a different character. Bill has enabled a network of faith clowns called "Fools for Christ." There may be a group in your area. This would be excellent contact if you want to get this program going in your church.

Clowning is a wonderful way to equip your folks for a ministry of youth. It might be worthwhile to send several youth to a workshop experience. They can then return and train others in your group! You will be amazed how popular this kind of outreach is. Your troupe of clowns can be kept busy all the time by going out to other church and community groups. In one city, the clown troupe includes 35 young people. They have more invitations than they can handle.

One of the beautiful aspects of this model is that you have to start at the same place as the young people. Together you can grow and risk. It is a wonderful example of solid youth ministry. Significant adults and young people can probe God's will in a situation of growth and risk.

Resources

1. Funny Farm Clowns, Inc., Route 2, Butler, GA 31006.
2. Clowns of America, 1633 Dyre Street, Philadelphia, PA 19124.
3. **Be a Clown** filmstrip, Contemporary Drama Service, Box 457, Downers Grove, IL 60515.
4. **Getting Started in Clown Ministry**, by Tim Kehl, Office of Communication Education, 1525 McGavock St., Nashville, TN 37203.
5. Floyd Shaffer films: **The Mark of the Clown, A Clown is Born** and **That's Life**, from Mass Media Ministries, 2116 N. Charles Street, Baltimore, MD 21218.
6. **The Complete Youth Ministries Handbook**, by J. David Stone, Abingdon.
7. **The Complete Floyd Shaffer Clown Ministry Workshop Kit**, produced by Dennis Benson, P.O. Box 12811, Pittsburgh, PA 15241.
8. Holy Fools, P.O. Box 1828, Springfield, IL 62705.

See also DRAMA, HUMOR, MIME, PUPPETS

Commitment

"Why can't those kids stay with a project long enough to see it through?"

"I think the youth just come to the youth group for the fun of it and couldn't care less about the serious side of it."

"How can you teach people to care anymore?"

We have all heard those feelings expressed, and we have certainly had those feelings ourselves. There are so many times in youth ministry when we feel that everything depends upon us, since the interest span of the youth appears to be so short, their commitment so short-lived. At least, that is how it seems to us more often than we want to admit.

It does not help to tell ourselves that youth are extremely busy; that someone else has to do the detail work because we know that youth are able to do ultimate detail work for projects in which they believe. We also know that our doing the work for them is setting a horrible example.

We may also wonder about our own commitment. Is there some immature motive that prods us into what appears to observers as an ultimate commitment? Are we masochistic to walk into such demanding responsibilities? Every adult who works with youth must deal with this nagging question: Am I trying to remain the eternal youth, to somehow relive a teenage existence, either a memorable one I would like to relive or a miserable one that I would like to make better through this group of youth?

No one knows another's motives. Neither can we know the future and whether the youth or our adult team members or even ourselves will be able to completely follow through when we choose a future project or direction. All we can do is to assess as wisely as possible the strength of the commitment at the moment, allow a bit of time to recheck the strength again after some discussion and testing with each other, and plunge into the future with the highest expectations that our shared commitment encourages.

Not every project will be completed, and often they do not need to be. At times it might be unwise to proceed when we learn that the need was not as great as we first surmised or when another priority or urgent need legitimately demands our attention.

Often we are able to look back on a project several years later and realize that the planning for the project or program was far more meaningful to the group than its completion. This is not to encourage schizophrenic, haphazard planning that never leads to fruition, because the completion of plans is extremely important to youths' needs of closure and shared reward. However, sometimes the best group experience is to locate a need, do the ground work to discover if the need is real and how it might be met with the efforts of other persons.

Planning meetings should include a time for progress reporting, such as, "It's been a couple of months since we got so excited about helping to get playground equipment for the day-care center. Tom, you and Joan were going to follow through. Based on what you found, should we try to get an adult Sunday school class to work on it and make it more of a church-wide concern?" "Mike, I noticed that your task does not sound like it will take very long. Would you like to spend some more time with the small group to see if anyone has any further ideas?"

Strengthening the commitment of youth for seeing that the details and follow through get taken care of takes persistence. So much of the world of youth is based upon short attention spans, and television fosters a belief that any problem can be solved in an

hour with plenty of time left over for commercials. It may be that your group will need to approach a project in parts and divide out the responsibilities so that few persons will need to be involved over the entire range of the activity. This may also be necessary for the adults working with youth.

Each of us comes to this ministry offering the best motives we have and the most dedicated commitment. The weaknesses are not important, because with God's presence in our work, miracles do happen and our efforts can be transformed. Therefore, we should offer whatever time and insight we have. Sometimes we may realize we are doing more of the work than others. So be it. Sometimes there will be those golden breakthroughs when every group member pitches in and is pleased with their contribution. Sometimes other adults and the youth will have to hold the responsibility alone. So be it. Sometimes time and energy will vanish and the progress will stop at its current level. Be pleased with this, feeling that it may be picked up someday. If it is not, perhaps this was as far as it needed to go.

See also BURN-OUT, MOTIVATING YOUTH, PRIORITIES, RISKING

Communication

Since we are inundated with the communications explosion in every part of our lives, we assume that communications skills are easy to acquire. Yet the opposite situation seems more probable. The more we observe communications, the harder it seems to become a skilled participant. And the more those with whom we seek to communicate are themselves involved as observers, the more difficult it is for meaningful dialogue to occur.

An additional frustration occurs

when we fail to recognize that the problem is not with any of the human participants in the exchange but with the attempts at transmitting understandable thought symbols between the persons.

Your group may find it beneficial from time to time to define words to see how various persons attach different meanings to the same word. Phrases, expressions, hand movements, body language and other forms of communication occasionally need to be defined.

Youth culture constantly picks up different meanings for words. When adults use the term intending another earlier meaning, young people may misunderstand them. Sharing the new meanings shows a form of concern and respect.

The group will find it exciting to develop some communication skills for telling the rest of the congregation and community some of their most important concerns. Try interpreting, perhaps through slides and tape, the various experiences that took place during a recent trip, outing or project. Try interpreting, perhaps again through slides and narrative, what the Christian faith offers youth or how the community can help in a meaningful project in which you are engaged. Try communicating, perhaps through slides and narrative, what the Christian faith offers youth or how the community can help in a meaningful project in which you are engaged. Try communicating, perhaps through posters or banners, reasons for celebrating our faith in these days.

Resources
1. **Something to Believe In**, by Robert Short, Harper and Row.

See also LISTENING

Community

Community is electric, life-giving, renewing. The means of building group together-ness are unlimited.

This term is used quite often in youth ministry circles. It refers to the delicate but valuable process of blending an individual group member's caring qualities into a group unity that is much stronger than the separate parts. *Community* happens when all of the group members realize their own unique gifts, the composite strength of the union, and the dedication to each other that survives any threat or weakness.

Community is electric, life giving, renewing.

It is worth striving for.

There is no magical formula to develop community, though concern for it is the first step toward its realization. When two or more persons become aware of their need for each other, it is already within reach.

Rarely will a cohesive feeling of community exist for an entire function. Some people may say, "All this togetherness and group building makes me nervous; that's not the way the world is." Though others may not be that candid, their

actions may betray some uneasiness. That is to be expected because such times of community are seldom known today, and most of us do not know how to act in community.

Still, community evokes the highest sense of what it means to be human and deposits within our mind unforgettable, treasured moments.

That sense of community can be obtained through a common experience, such as a trip, work project, drama—something that the group members live through together and feel a sense of mutual investment in the outcome.

Some tight-knit groups look back on their roots and realize that their unit really began during a miserable experience in the rain one cold winter morning or during a meal that was less than delicious.

The safest place to reach for this important quality is the theological foundation. This may be hard for many churches because there has been great neglect of this dimension of the congregation. Community is linked to the communion forged by the life, ministry, death and resurrection of Jesus Christ. The gift of the spirit provided connective tissue in which all authentic Christian fellowship lives. This is a given. It has been nurtured, fleshed out, and preserved through the fathers and mothers in the faith who have preceded us.

Community occurs when people reach out to each other. Sometimes all we as leaders can do is to prepare the environment where that can possibly happen. No-loser recreation can sometimes help one group; mountaintop experiences work for others, or insights gained during a Washington seminar do it for others. Yet, nothing can replace the experience of worship as the source and the experience of community building.

One of the most moving examples of this kind of celebration is the widely used water ceremony designed by John Washburn. He utilizes John 4:7-15. Drawing upon the biblical use of water and thirst, he groups teens into units of 12 to 16. He tells them the symbolic use of water sharing in the novel, **Stranger in a Strange Land**. The rite of drinking precious water makes the participants kin. In the partaking of water there is the wish that no other will thirst. Each circle now passes a bowl of water. After a teen drinks he or she shares a blessing or wish for the rest. (For a full account of this moving experience of community see the **Recycle Catalogue**, page 72.)

Community has been given. It can be claimed, celebrated and shared. The means of experiencing such a reality are unlimited.

Resources

1. **Relationships in Adolescense**, by John Coleman, Routledge and Kegan.

See also CLIQUES, GROUP BUILDING, SERENDIPITY

Conduct

Some groups develop their own code of conduct which lists the consequences of broken promises.

It is never easy for one individual or group to tell another how to act. It may not be possible. And yet, every time a group of individuals does anything together, there must be an understanding among them of the responsibilities each person is expected to accept.

What a group will or will not tolerate is not the easiest thing to determine. Less easy is to determine what a group wants its members to do.

When planning for an upcoming event, especially one that involves travel and housing, discover what this particular group expects of its members and also what it will not tolerate.

Should group members attend every part of the function? Help with the event's duties and responsibilities? Pay certain fees? Be willing to do something upon return? (For instance, give a report.) What else?

What should they not do? Any special hours for being in the building or in rooms? Any places that everyone can not go? What about alcohol, sexual conduct, non-prescription drugs? What else?

Will the adults abide by the rules set for the youth?

It is imperative that your group discuss what should happen if someone breaks the rules. Not everyone must agree on the discipline or punishment, unless the entire group administers the consequences (a questionable procedure). More preferable is a small group of youth and adults which deals with each situation and which is willing to discern the details of the infringement. It is important for this group to know the various options: being sent home, extra chores, whatever.

The code may need to be changed or modified as the event progresses. Rather than someone adding a new rule, the group should agree to it. Otherwise enforcement will be extremely difficult.

The code is a servant of the group, not the reverse. It is merely a plan for living and growing together in harmony. The two important considerations of the code are respect for each person and each person's respect for the whole group.

Some groups have used covenants with great success. In this process the group develops the rules at the beginning of the event. Drawing upon the biblical understanding of *covenant*, the group is reminded that broken promises are followed by consequences. When someone violates the code, he or she must suffer the punishment. The danger of this approach is the temptation to be overly legalistic.

Covenants shift the responsibility for behavior from the leaders to the entire group. The group members first draft a list of agreements, then sign it as a symbol of mutual trust. Such a covenant signifies the submission of personal freedom to the good of the group and the good of its individuals.

A covenant is different from a set of arbitrary rules. It is a living instrument that binds persons together in love and wills that the best happens to everyone.

Regardless of the approach you use to guide the conduct of your group, remember that law and gospel work best together when balanced.

See also DISCIPLINE, RETREATS, RULES

Conferences

The large youth gathering has both advantages and negative aspects. It is great to get a lot of kids crowded into a college gym. They are able to see that they belong to a faith which has many other followers. It is also a great way to get youth excited about God. By careful planning, most events can get the young people as emotionally high as desired. These brief experiences can build an intense sense of caring and community.

Large group gatherings have some drawbacks too. There are some things you can't do with such large numbers. It is easier to equip youth with new skills when there are fewer people.

Some of the less experienced youth can get lost in the vastness of a large conference. This happened to some young people when they participated in the huge gatherings (25,000-35,000) organized by several denominations a few years ago. It was hard for a small youth group from a small community to deal with making a choice of a workshop when there were 150 offerings! Several groups almost withdrew from the seemingly infinite number of choices.

Some denominations have alternated the large and small conference each year. Some 3,500 young people would attend one year and only 450 would be permitted for the next. The first event utilized the attributes which such a gathering could give: lots of input from speakers, rich texture of people from different places, an exciting trip. The smaller event was designed for study and action. There are lots of small groups dealing with the issues of faith in the world.

Bernie was responsible for coordinating a large denominational youth conference. He concluded that the hardest part of such planning was to trust the young people who are leaders. While it

Small and large churches alike find conferences an effective means of building an intense sense of community.

is vital to have them plan with the adults, it is also so easy to step in and take over the areas for which they have chosen to be responsible. *They will always come through. You have to trust them. Your job is to encourage and surround them with possibilities.*

When you are asked to help plan a regional youth conference, insist that teenagers be included as part of the process. You will also want to move carefully about asking a speaker to come in and do everything. It is tempting to invite someone else to carry the whole load. Yet, it is not fair to the guest or the kids to solve the planning challenge by just buying a superstar package. What is the purpose of the event? Whom are we trying to reach? What can be accomplished with the size of group in mind? What will be the benefits after the experience is over?

See also FESTIVALS, SPEAKERS

Confirmation

The moment of initiation is always special—those historical points when we realize that our lives are beginning to change. The first time a young person is an acknowledged part of the adult community of faith has enormous power. Different traditions handle this passage rite differently. However, do not underestimate the impact being accepted as an adult in the faith community has upon the young person.

Many traditional churches precede the initiation rite by a period of study and discussion. There is a wide variety of preparation times. Some churches utilize several weeks; others have programs which take up to two years. The clergy are usually in charge of these special classes. Many of these confirmation teachers are uncomfortable with the available materials and have a hard time finding the right approach. Every local church community has a unique sense of what its life together means. This context of faith is what must be passed on. The task is made harder because the clergy is often unfamiliar with the youth who are recipients of this experience.

You can be a great help in the process. Find a way by which you can aid in the confirmation, membership or communicants' class. What you can add is a sense of the youth's faith development. You know the questions which must be faced in such an enterprise. What is the nature of this new state of full membership? How does one prepare for a faith affirmation at this point in life? What new responsibilities and privileges are being offered by the faith community to the young person? Is the church prepared for this moment of initiation? What are the intellectual, physical and emotional acts which will make this passage point effective?

There have been many creative responses to this challenge. A cluster of churches in Missouri use an interesting learning center approach for the formal learning part of the course. They organize a number of Sunday afternoons for family groups to undertake the steps of learning about the faith. The parents must go through the confirmation course with their children. Even if they have several young people, they take the journey with the young person each time.

Symbols are often used to mark this important event: Crosses or Bibles are usually given. Doug has an exciting proposal for the symbol to be used in confirmation. He suggests that a confirmation ring be developed. This is a symbol which is valued by young people and it can be retained as a lasting sign marking a special event in the life of a believer.

Pastor John stopped by the home of a student in his confirmation class. He talked with the teenager's father. "I am sorry that I have done a bad job with the confirmation class. I simply underestimated the young people."

John did have trouble getting alignment on his students. However, he was wrong about the kind of job he did with the class. John was accessible. He invited them to share the faith and the ministry. The class also experienced that their lives made a difference. The service which celebrated their public confession of faith was a special worship experience. That Maundy evening these young people declared their faith and celebrated the Lord's Supper. These teens knew that they were different after that moment. John did the job he was called to do.

In many cases, the church is not ready for teens who have become adults in the faith. It is the adult who cannot make the adjustment in his or her view of the youth. The older members of the church don't seem to grasp how the Spirit of God can move into and change the lives of the young. Belonging to the family of faith is the content and context of confirmation. This moment of passage confirms the nature of this people for all members. The course which prepares for this event must be given the importance suggested by it. You can be a catalyst for this exciting and meaningful passage rite.

See also ACCESS, PASSAGE RITES, SYMBOLS

Conflict

Dear Reverend James Nelson:

I feel that it is imperative that I hereby resign as Advisor to the Senior High Youth Fellowship. During last week's winter retreat to Lake Glisten, I realized that I could not continue.

Our group had agreed to a 12:30 lights out time for everyone. I had already gotten the group in my cabin in bed by then. The girls had been very cooperative, and I certainly appreciated it since I had worked all that day until 5. No sooner had most of us started to sleep when we heard the boys up making noises. Apparently, your friend Bob Johnson decided to go against the covenant of conduct that all had agreed to.

I do not feel that I can continue working in this situation. Please find a replacement for me by the end of the month.

Yours truly,

Mrs. Warren

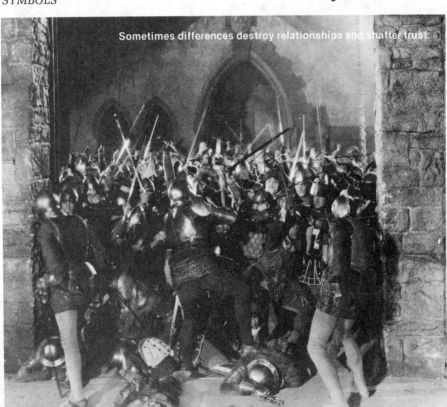

Sometimes differences destroy relationships and shatter trust.

Dear Jim:

I thought I would let you know that things with the Seniors are not working out very well. Maybe you'd better get someone to take my place.

You see, last weekend the whole group went up to Glisten for an overnighter, and Jane Warren blew her top. You know how we had been trying to get those three boys from the project area to begin to feel a part of the group? Well, we just about did it Friday night. Everybody had gotten in their bunks and Tim, that's the tall one of the three, asked a question about the church that opened up an unbelievable discussion. We really didn't make much noise, except once when Tim and Joe came across the room to shake hands and the rest of us let out a whoop. Wow! Then Jane about knocked the door down and that ended it.

Maybe I'm just not cut out for all this. We apologized the next morning, but it didn't do much good. Anyway, we tried. I'll stick around a couple of weeks, but maybe you better get someone else by next month.

Bob

Dear Reverend James Nelson:

This is just a short note to thank you for not letting me resign a couple of months ago. Your idea of forcing us to write what was bothering us really worked. I guess Bob had told me the next morning about the breakthrough that he had experienced with Timothy, Joe, and Michael but I was too upset to hear.

Your suggestion about not working all day before a retreat made all the difference in the world during the spring retreat.

Thanks again. I've got to run. Bob and his family are coming over tonight.

Sincerely,

Jane Warren

Each of us has a variety of opinions in youth ministry. And sometimes those differences threaten to undo relationships and destroy trust. It is during those vulnerable times that we often draw up our forces around us and fight back, slinging words and actions against those who come near.

Mediators can help to hear both sides. Time and prayer can also bring their magical transformation. It is a time for quiet and listening. And usually, somewhere between us is a lost cord of cooperation that can be retrieved and shaped into a new bond of support.

Resources
1. **Why People Fight**, by James Boller, United Church Press.
2. **Church Fights: Managing Conflict in the Local Church**, by Speed Leas and Paul Kittlaus, Westminster.

See also CRITICISM, DIVERSITY, HOSTILITY, RUMOR

Consultation

This term has several meanings, two of which could have special value for the youth leader.

Consultation can be the title of a gathering of persons who have unique experiences or special insights into a particular subject of interest. Church agencies will call together persons who have a background in missions or early teen ministry or specific ethnic minority ministry, for instance, and enable these "experts" to share their understandings with each other and with large groups of persons through publications or changes in program direction. You may be asked to participate in a consultation on youth ministry and share from your experience. If you discover that your church has sponsored consultation, it will be extremely helpful for you to read through the findings and conclusions for insights that will help in your work.

A less formal consultation can occur when one or two persons are invited to share their expertise. In fact, you might prefer to request a specific consultation. For instance, the group may want to tackle a project for which there are no leadership skills available. A logical approach is to request consultation. Arrange a meeting for yourself and other leaders in the group (both youth and adult) with those who have the needed skills and insights. You may wish to go where the consultants can use their skills as examples. Or maybe they could visit your church and evaluate your unique situation. A number of persons are usually available through the various agencies of your church to assist you through consultative services.

See also WORKSHOPS

Counselor

We are not talking about the person who decides what college your young people can attend, nor are we discussing the person who has perfect answers to every youth problem. Nor the person who will immediately tell others about a silly case of "puppy love" to the entire group. Nor the person who sermonizes after someone has shared a problem.

There are obviously many different kinds of counselors, some like the ones described above. In our understanding of youth work, we are really looking at two kinds of counselors: the trained professional and the lay person who is a professional at caring. There is a place for the professional person who spends his or her time in this one crucial activity. Every community needs at least one

Counseling young people is one of the youth leader's most important roles.

of these folks. They usually are specially trained and are in some sort of supervised arrangement. The best professional counselor is being counseled or supervised by another trained person. Some counselors simply don't understand or care about youth. But they will let you know about these feelings. Don't be afraid to ask.

Where do you look if you need a professional counselor for one of your young people?

1. Check with your senior pastor first. Find out to whom he refers adults when they need more help than he can give. Perhaps your senior pastor is a trained, certified counselor. If so, use him. In many instances, senior pastors think they are effective counselors when they really aren't. If your pastor is untrained and incapable of counseling young people, you'll need to handle this situation carefully—to find expert counseling for the young person without alienating your senior pastor.

2. Contact the state or county mental health agency in your area. These trained folks are experienced, willing to help, and are probably the least expensive source of professional counseling.

3. Look in the yellow pages under American Association of Marriage and Family Counseling. The association is made up of ministers and pastors who are specially trained for various counseling situations. If there's no listing in your phone book, write to American Association for Marriage and Family Therapy, 924 W. Ninth St., Upland, CA 91786, and request a list of members in your area.

In most of your work, you won't utilize such folk. But when you feel you're in over your head, take your youth to such a referral. Be sure that there isn't a break in the transfer from you to another person. Most of the problems facing your young people can be called "coping" problems. These emotional stumbling points in the lives of young people are very important. While they may not need professional counseling, they do need what we call "a significant other," people whom they value highly. This is your most important role! You have earned the right to be such a person because you have lived through your own process of becoming. You know how it hurts when that girl or guy dropped you before the big dance. You remember the emotional pain of having those zits filling your face just before your first date.

The unique characteristic of being a significant other is that you are in touch with your youth. While you know that the extreme despair of losing your boyfriend or girlfriend will pass, you don't treat painful experiences from that perspective. You can feel and empathize with the suffering person. You know that the manner of dealing with this level of pain can help him or her grow to face the escalating trials of adulthood.

Resources

1. **How to Start Counseling**, by William Hulme, Abingdon.
2. **Growth Counseling**, by Howard Clinebell, Abingdon.
3. **My Brother Dennis**, by Dennis Benson, P.O. Box 12811, Pittsburgh, PA 15281.

See also ADVISING, ADVOCATE, LISTENING, MENTOR, PEER COUNSELING, PREMARITAL COUNSELING

Creative Models, Inc.

J. David Stone, professor of youth ministry at Centenary College and president of Youth Ministry Consultation Service and formerly a co-leader with Lyman Coleman in Serendipity workshops, has teamed up with a number of experienced youth leaders who lead various workshops around the country and have contributed chapters to the **Complete Youth Ministries Handbook**, volumes I and II (Abingdon). Contact David at 500 Common St., Shreveport, LA 71101.

Creativity

Some terms have a bad reputation. The term *creative* has become an elitist label. Creativity really has nothing to do with particular skills. While it is true that this sensitivity does include finely honed abilities, creativity is something deeper. It is the capacity to make something new, something meaningful from life's different fragments. In other words, the new is not really new. The great artist or musician does not invent the colors or the notes. He or she is able to weave the existing pieces into a new pattern. The person with this kind of vision is a creative person.

People of faith should have a special sensitivity for this kind of creativity. We are a people of the Spirit. There is a wholeness to our perspective of creation. It all comes together because God put it together. The sad reality is that most Christians don't think they are creative. Many youth advisors don't consider themselves creative persons.

If we are a new creation in Christ, then the old, broken way has passed. The new has come. It is our responsibility to live out this wholeness.

One of the important things we learn from living this life of reconciliation is that we do not work alone. All creativity comes out of community in order to go back into community. All the great artists sought the community of ideas and stimulation in order to have more pieces of existence. The moment of writing, composing or organizing that youth program may be a singular task. However, we bring to that moment all

Creativity is putting the familiar into new and exciting combinations.

the collective contributions of the community.

Unfortunately, many folk in local leadership undertake their church task in the Lone Ranger model. They wonder why they soon break down. No one can be creative without the community of others. This means that the youth advisor must draw upon the resources of the community. If you are a single youth advisor or a lone couple doing the job, find some kindred spirits to put you into the creative stream once again. Develop a creative covenant with someone else in the area. Meet a couple times a month and share ideas. Debrief your failures and successes.

The church is the most creative gathering on earth! Where else could you join one week and be leading a youth group the next? If you do a decent job, they don't care what you do! If people don't support your creative ideas, it is either a dumb idea or they don't understand you.

YES, BUT . . .

YOU ARE A CREATIVE ENABLER.
Yes, but . . . I don't have time.
YOU ARE A CREATIVE ENABLER.
Yes, but . . . I don't have the experience.
YOU ARE A CREATIVE ENABLER.
Yes, but . . . I don't have the equipment.
YOU ARE A CREATIVE ENABLER.
Yes, but . . . I don't have the resources.
YOU ARE A CREATIVE ENABLER.
Yes, but . . . I am more interested in "content."
YOU ARE A CREATIVE ENABLER.
Yes, but . . . I need clear directions and guidance to teach.
YOU ARE A CREATIVE ENABLER.
Yes, but . . . my kids are too unruly in class to do anything different.

YOU ARE A CREATIVE ENABLER.
Yes, but . . . I will try something different later on in the year.
YOU ARE A CREATIVE ENABLER.
Yes, but . . . I don't have any special skills like music or art.
YOU ARE A CREATIVE ENABLER.
Yes, but . . . my people don't go for tricky approaches to learning.
YOU ARE A CREATIVE ENABLER.
Yes, but . . . I need help to do these kinds of things.
YOU ARE A CREATIVE ENABLER.
Yes, but . . . our classroom facilities are not right for such things.
YOU ARE A CREATIVE ENABLER.
Yes, but . . . it is too hard to prepare for such things.
YOU ARE A CREATIVE ENABLER.
Yes, but . . . I was satisfied as a child with the linear forms of teaching.
YOU ARE A CREATIVE ENABLER.
Yes, but . . . I might fail if I try different means to do my teaching.
YOU ARE A CREATIVE ENABLER.
Yes, but . . . other teachers might make fun of me.
YOU ARE A CREATIVE ENABLER.
Yes, but . . . I am too old for changing my ways.
YOU ARE A CREATIVE ENABLER.
Yes, but . . . I might offend Mrs. Jones.
YOU ARE A CREATIVE ENABLER.
Yes, but . . . I am afraid.
YOU ARE A CREATIVE ENABLER.
Yes, but . . . I am only one person.
YOU ARE A CREATIVE ENABLER.
Yes, but . . . I am lazy and comfortable with my old approaches.
YES.

Resources
1. **Creative Youth Leadership**, by Jan Corbett, Judson Press.
2. **Recycle Catalogues I and II**, by Dennis Benson, Abingdon Press.

See also HUMOR, MENTOR, RECYCLE THEOLOGY, VARIETY

Criticism

You will encounter criticism as you engage in youth ministry. Even though this is normal and certainly to be expected, it usually comes as an abrupt surprise and disappointment. And almost always the criticism triggers a defense mechanism deep within us that recounts every ounce of effort that we have put into whatever activity we feel is under attack. The ensuing battle can be devastating—and it is all unneccessary.

Often what we identify as "criticism" is not that at all. The person making the comment may have shared what he or she felt was a useful perception. A person telling you, "Did you know that two of the junior highers were still in the church parking lot at 10 last night?" may not mean "You are such a negligent leader that two lonely young people were left stranded until I came along." Instead, the real meaning could be, "In my support of you as a youth leader, I would like to pass along a fact that may be useful."

Let's face it, we often wear our feelings where they can get hurt easily. Maybe it's because youth ministry involves us with a group that is often powerless and ignored. It also invites the investment of considerable time and effort, which we often tabulate just in case someone challenges the work. This much fuel will ignite with anything that resembles a spark!

Some reasons for criticism:

• The comment may be one of envy for your involvement with youth.

• There is no perfect youth ministry program, and almost anyone in your church has a suggestion to improve yours.

• One age group is often suspicious of another (yes, envious as well).

• No two people agree on the right amount of money to invest in such a ministry as one with youth.

• Current news focus and entertainment content encourage distrust in any group of which an individual is not a part.

When the comments are made to you, acknowledge them, even write them down. Thank the person for his or her interest and support. Try to discover what is being said below the surface. If any part of the comment is helpful, let the person know and encourage more support.

If, after analysis, the criticism is apparently meant only to be disruptive, you may wish to go no further than to your prayer concern list. However, if the intent is obviously to be harmful to the program, yourself or any of the group, go to your pastor or to one of the church leaders whom you respect and begin to deal with the issue before it can be allowed to fester any further.

See also CONFLICT, RISKING

Cults

What is a cult to one person may be a grassroots religious group to another. It is quite easy to label the newest religious organization in town as being unorthodox. Orthodoxy ("right praise" —that which is accepted) is always defined by those who are the successful or dominant group.

Yet, there are some basic factors which we must use to evaluate the new religious group. The following questions can help:

1. Does the group depend solely on one strong authority figure?

2. Does the philosophy or doctrine include bits and pieces from many different places which appear to have been added just to gain followers?

3. Does it demand an allegiance which tends to exclude family and other in-

volvements?

4. Is there a strong appeal to fear?

5. Is hostility expressed for those who disagree with the group's views?

6. Does the group focus on special rites and practices which appeal to the strange or theatrical needs of followers?

7. What is the line of accountability for the local group in terms of regional, national or international organization?

8. What is the opinion of others whom you trust in the community or nation about this movement?

As you can see, most traditional organizations would have a hard time with some of these queries. Yet, every adult working with youth must monitor

Asking certain basic questions will help youth uncover extremist cults.

the many youth organizations seeking teen participation.

On the other hand, these questions will quickly reveal the kinds of groups which cut youth off from the mainstream of life. A cult is usually an extension of one person's ego. He or she appeals to those youth who want the answer to every question. In this setting, everything is good or bad. The cult leader often demands absolute control over the follower's life. Again, many youth who have been battered by an unclear set of religious values will find such a context very comforting.

The best way to face this kind of challenge to young people is to develop a preventive program. Dan and his folk provide an excellent example of a session for junior highs. The advisors researched cults and isolated several basic characteristics. They asked the teens to decide which group they wanted to join. One group had had Fritos and Seven Up for refreshments while the other had Pepsi and potato chips. This was the enticement.

When the young people had chosen a group, they were asked to sign a paper. The leaders said that they needn't read it. When they had done this, the leaders announced that they were now members of the Loonies and Marahpetties. After refreshments, the tone changed to a much stronger and directive approach. "In this group, we believe these things and we must do these things." The leaders then gave the rules: 1) Everyone is important; 2) You must wear these costumes (the kids put them on); 3) We believe in the sanctity of life; 4) The leader is the boss over all things; and, 5) We only sin when we go against the wishes of the leader.

The leader placed one of the previous rules at each point of a five-point star. To show their allegiance to the creed, the members were given a star and ordered to place it on their foreheads. This was the mark of the cult. They then developed their own chants and code of ethics, which had to be followed because the leader said so.

The experience went on for about 30 minutes. The students were really getting excited about it when Dan and his folks stopped the process and gathered the two groups into one room.

Then the deprogramming began. Every point the leaders wanted to make about the cults was pointed out by the students in the discussion! The junior highs shared how easy it was to get sucked into this kind of group and how reasonable everything sounded at the beginning. The teens also noted some good things in the beliefs, which were only a little different from their faith. Everyone experienced how such an allegiance could easily lead to terrible things.

While many community-oriented youth groups are fine, you will want to help teens and adults understand how to make choices that are consistent with their faith commitment.

Resources

1. **Know the Marks of Cults**, by Dave Breese, Victor Books.

2. **Cults, World Religions, and You**, by Kenneth Boa, Victor Books.

3. **Youth, Brainwashing, and the Extremist Cults**, by Ronald Enroth, Zondervan.

4. **The Kingdom of the Cults**, by Walter Martin, Bethany Fellowship,

5. Spiritual Counterfeits Project, P.O. Box 2418, Berkeley, CA 94702. Ask for their catalog, the SCP Journal and the Spiritual Counterfeits newsletter.

6. **The Occult Revolution**, by Richard Woods, Seabury Press.

7. **New Gods in America**, by Peter Rowley, David McKay Publishers.

8. **Cults, Charisma and Mind Control**, a filmstrip by Human Relations Media.

Culture

Culture is whatever is created and sustained by a person's society. A person's culture includes music, clothing, housing, attitudes, standards —whatever is valued by those we value.

While the culture in which a person lives begins as external and valueless to the individual, it always becomes internalized. We begin to enjoy a particular kind of music or book or film and before we know it, some of the attitudes in the song or story begin to rub off on us, whether we notice it consciously or not (usually not).

Of course, no two human beings react to the same culture in identical ways. The same song may strike good friends in totally opposite ways because no two persons have the same background or tastes.

Since 12 or 14 years is a rather short living span, youth are particularly susceptible to cultural influences. They have had little time to put together their own sensing devices. And culture, with its implicit social approval, tests whatever sensing mechanisms a youth can employ.

Adults who work with young people often have difficulty in dealing with the youth culture. Some adults feel they can relate to youth only if they match the current youth culture standards of dress, speech, music and lifestyle. Other adults go the opposite extreme and assume that youth need adult models, so they avoid all youth culture images. Both types of leaders are open to admiration and criticism: admiration because they are seeking to identify with those they would serve, and criticism because they are treating culture as something you can deliberately put on or take off.

The adult must recognize that youth live in a culture all their own. Some of that culture is universal (songs that speak of a search for meaning in life, clothing styles that reflect times of affluence or scarcity, etc.) but most of it relates directly to students who walk high school halls every day.

At the same time, there are similarities between the present adult and youth cultures (alcohol and drug abuse and concern over energy are currently components of both). Nevertheless, it is true that only a person enmeshed in life at that particular time and place can feel the impact of that specific culture.

What young people need from the adult is not an imitation of youth culture (though adult values and a lifestyle consistent with present youth culture is valid and authentic), but help in discovering workable standards which they can use to evaluate their culture for themselves. It takes special skills, time and insight for a person to scrutinize his own culture. Regularly, it takes stepping away from the daily grind and looking back at it.

An adult can help this discovery process by encouraging youth to search for the positive models in the culture. For example, one youth group in the midwest uses meaningful contemporary music when they are in charge of the worship service. From the group's musical selection process to individual presentations, the effect is to highlight cultural ingredients that are uplifting and help the church's members to grow.

The negative aspect of the youth culture must also be explored. And often this means listing alternatives and making choices. Struggling with the issues as a group can be extremely supportive to individual youth.

The church has often backed away from its responsibility as a social critic with a prophetic word for culture. But we live in a day when group voices, even minorities, are heard better than individuals. We need to make our constructive voices and concerns heard. Youth desperately need to develop their skills in speaking to a culture that so loudly speaks to them.

Resources
1. **Christ and Culture**, by H. Richard Niebuhr, Harper and Brothers Publishers.

See also AGE LEVEL CHARACTERISTICS, CLIQUES, DIETING, DRINKING, DRUGS, KEEPING CURRENT, PEER PRESSURE, SEX

Curriculum

Sounds dull and routine, doesn't it? Even the term sounds like school. That's why some youth leaders take one look at their lively, seemingly carefree students, then at those flat wordy booklets and decide, "Aw, my kids deserve a break. Let's talk about last night's game." And on the way home, the leaders might add, "You know, those kids don't want to learn about all that stuff in those books. Maybe I could bring some of my projects from work. We would talk about the way decisions are made. Now, they would like that."

It is true that no curriculum writer or

publisher has yet figured out a way for the material to leap off the pages and dramatically pull together a raving audience. Heaven knows, curriculum publishers have tried. They've included pictures of every size and color, wall charts, foldouts, maps, even cards that spill all over your lap when you open the package. They've added cassettes, filmstrips and a mind boggling assortment of balloons, banners, sound makers and anything else that was shippable. And some of it worked. The cassettes and the wall charts did make teaching and learning much more exciting.

Some people might ask, "Why all the effort? Why not just let teachers bring an interesting book or magazine to class and discuss that?"

Actually, there are a number of crucial reasons why the extra effort is worth it, and why youth leaders need to check out the material that is being offered very thoroughly before deciding to develop their own curriculum.

Reason #1: Denominational curriculum is based on the denomination's beliefs, and leaders do not have to screen each page for detrimental concepts. That is not to say that there will not be a wide span of viewpoints expressed in the curriculum. Most denominations find it helpful to utilize the talents and insights of varied writers to give more latitude to each understanding. Obviously, it is a tedious task to stay within the guidelines of belief held by most persons in the denomination while presenting a broad spectrum of viewpoints. (But this struggle adds life to the curriculum.)

Reason #2: Each piece of curriculum material has been carefully developed in light of the most extensive research possible into the needs of persons at each age level. The words and concepts have been painstakenly chosen to be understandable and useful to those in the age level for whom it was created.

Reason #3: Those who want to design their own curriculum often forget the continuity factor that's built into a comprehensive curriculum. Somewhere in the design of each of the curricular pieces is a connection to the overall plan for what needs to be taught at what age. In order for a youth to come into contact with every segment of the Bible, different passages are included in the various age-level lessons. Some denominations plan for the youth to spend time studying a special passage of the Bible in-depth. This special study is suggested to come the year prior to a study of Christian beliefs or ethics or church history. Just as the plan includes a study of the Lord's Prayer for children, so a certain topic, never before mentioned in previous materials, appears in youth materials and may be prerequisite for subjects young people will encounter in adult materials.

Reason #4: The curriculum development folks are responsive to your suggestions. When you get insights of ways to make studies come alive, let those who plan the youth curriculum know about it. Such suggestions are extremely valued and sought after. That "flat, wordy booklet" is not dead; it is infused with the hopes and concerns of youth leaders just like yourself. The youth curriculum can have even more life as you add your own intensity and unique touches to it.

Every group gathering should use a curriculum. Both stream of conscience debriefing of a rumble at the drive-in and the latest design from a Sunday school publishing house are learning contexts. The question is whether you are intentional or not about what happens in the learning event.

See also AGE LEVEL CHARACTERISTICS, BIBLE, MATERIALS, MODULE, RESOURCES, VALUES CLARIFICATION, VARIETY

Dancing

The final Psalm in the Bible urges believers to "praise Him with timbrel and dance"(150:04). Second Samuel (6:14) tells of David who "danced before the Lord with all his might." Ecclesiastes (3:04) speaks of "a time to mourn, and a time to dance." In fact, there are over thirty references in the Bible to dancing, none of them with any negative connotation.

However, over the years dancing has not had an easy time in the life of the church. It is often counted high on the list of activities that are characteristic of non-believers and is therefore to be shunned.

Many Christians feel that to engage in dancing is to give into sensual desires that would return them to a state they left before their conversion. Social dancing, they feel, is inappropriate for the Christian, especially within the church building.

On the other end of the spectrum is another large group of Christians who view dancing as a way of expressing their faith with their bodies. Social dancing, in the church or elsewhere, they feel demonstrates their affirmation of life and other persons.

Somewhere between these two groups are endless varieties. The spectrum might be represented this way:
- Dancing permitted in any location
- Social dancing in church building
- Folk dances allowed in church building
- Some folk dances in programs at camp
- Dancing allowed only outside church building and program
- Dancing allowed outside church building in a place where alcoholic beverages not served
- Members can join square dance groups in town
- No dancing allowed anywhere

The reasons for this wide diversity come from tradition, culture of the past and present, family position, theology, biblical understanding, as well as those experiences that took place in a person's childhood. These positions must be honored because they usually involve complex emotions. Youth leaders should not go against the positions of the parents, and it might be wise to call a brief meeting of the parents to discuss their stance on this issue.

The use of liturgical dance (dance expression of a faith concept) within the worship setting is also an activity that needs some feedback. Many youth who are in various types of dance training would like to offer this talent as an expression of worship, though many congregations need to be prepared to accept the gift.

For many youth groups, folk and novelty dancing has consistently proven to be of immense value. The descriptive term "folk" underscores the fact that this is a creation for the ordinary (not just the skillful) folk. The steps are contributions from the past and are open to improvements for the future.

It is possible to understand the culture of another civilization by participating in some of their dances. The "World of Fun" phonograph record-set offers a wide diversity of dances that express cultures of an international flavor.

In the secular environment dancing is often used competitively to make advanced dancers look better than other persons, thereby encouraging feelings of insecurity among many persons.

Resources
1. **Guide for Recreation Leaders**, by Glenn Bannerman and Robert Fakkema, John Knox Press.

2. **A Time to Dance**, by Margaret Fisk Taylor, United Church Press.
3. **Dance for the Lord**, by Lucien Deiss and Gloria Weyman, World Press.
4. **Social Recreation with Music**, John Knox Press.

See also PARTIES

Dating

Work to develop a youth group climate where non-daters feel accepted and comfortable.

"A good youth group is a great place to find a date," is a thought that's in the minds of most teens. Yet, the youth group can provide a context where young people can experience acceptance and freedom from the tight dating patterns of some youth circles. The fellowship aspect of the Christian youth group should be broad enough to include both those who date and those who do not.

The climate of acceptance and belonging to a group is vital to the theology you represent. Christian kinship provides a security of belonging which permits males and females to be brothers and sisters without the world's sexual games. Yes, couples do form and people do fall in love as part of a youth group. But the real test of whether you are drawing upon the spiritual essence of your faith as a group comes when a couple breaks up. Do both people continue to come to the group? Does the change in status as a couple alter their kinship as members of God's family?

The youth group can become a place where teens feel acceptance when they experience real or imagined problems of fat, zits and immaturity. You don't have to date to have others as friends. The youth group is also an excellent place to explore those other commitments of love youth face elsewhere. The youth group should be talking about the Christian's faithfulness in the face of sexual and social demands. If we don't confront these areas of concern, we are inviting those who exploit the need for love and acceptance to use our youth.

You might want to explore ways to find a counseling mode for dating couples. Our participation in the growth of love between men and women often comes only after there is a problem. Why can't we enter into the relationship when it is new and growing? Teens actually love to talk about their relationships if the significant adult really cares.

One campus pastor came up with a brilliant way of creating such a mode. He called a number of people at different stages of love commitment (dating, married, divorced). Charlie asked them if he could interview them on tape and use sections of their story to help those who are just beginning the journey. He found that people were eager to share. In fact, they often noted after the conversation that this was the first time they had ever told anyone about these aspects of their love. Charlie created an edited tape of short comments from these folks.

When he talked with a dating couple, he would give them the tape and ask them to listen to it together. "When you come back next time, we can talk about those points which are most interesting to you." They would, of course, pick out the sections which related to the problems they were having.

Resources
1. **Equal Dating**, by Jean Stapleton and Richard Bright, Abingdon Press.

See also ROMANCE, SEXUALITY

Death

The shadow of our demise encroaches on youth in our culture. The veneer of activity and distractions do not fool many people. The American lust for eternal youth is crumbling. Yet, the young are caught between the mythology about youth and the harsh reality.

It is always natural for the young to be closer to the vigor of living, but the cosmetic sheen of the media images continues to have a great impact on them. Many young people do not want to grow older. With this kind of emotional twisting it is not suprising that teens are extremely interested in the exploration of death. At large youth conferences, seminars on death always seem to outdraw other offerings.

Tim Morrison has developed a course on death for junior highs. This three-week experience begins by sending the parents a letter describing the study Using several different ways to get the young people to consider their own death, he invites them to develop a life map and write their own obituary. After

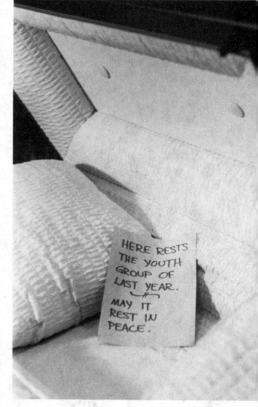

HERE RESTS
THE YOUTH
GROUP OF
LAST YEAR.
MAY IT
REST IN
PEACE.

this exercise, they discuss how they died, what they have accomplished, etc.

Session two is a visit to the funeral director who is open and honest. Together, they follow the process of dealing with a person after death. Session three focuses on the questions and concerns of the young people.

Other folks have related the whole process of grief and loss to the concept of death. There is loss in many different ways. In fact, one youth advisor was confronted by a group which did not want to welcome the new freshmen into the high school group. They had had such a fine time during the past year, and they didn't want to give it up.

Wes asked the youth group to meet the first week without the new members. He borrowed a casket from a funeral director and had several teens carry it into the church. There was funeral music. The youth advisor asked the group members to gather around the casket. He opened it. On a piece of paper were written the words: "Here rests the youth group of last year. May it rest in peace." Using the funeral service from the liturgy book, the leader read the passages and prayers. When he came to the sermon section, he asked the members to share the good moments of the group which had passed away. After a long period of sharing, the leader noted that the service is really a witness to the resurrection. They then heard the promise of scripture and shared their hopes for the new group. Wes found that this session was an excellent way of helping his group to face the grief of the nonreturnable past while embracing the present and future.

There are also moments when classmates, parents or other significant folk die. This is a prime time to link the theological truth which supports our faith to the deep emotional impact of this loss. Divorces, loss of job, moving away and loss of an arm or leg may even fall within this area of concern. The Christian youth group can approach the question of grief and death like no other organization in the community. We have something special to share and a supernatural ability to care.

Resources
1. **On Death and Dying**, by Elisabeth Kubler-Ross, Macmillan.
2. **To Die Is Gain: The Experience of One's Own Death**, by Johann Christoph Hampe, John Knox Press.
3. **A Matter of Life and Death**, by D. P. McGeachy, John Knox Press.
4. "Say Goodbye," five film case studies, Mass Media Ministries, 2116 N. Charles St., Baltimore, MD 21218.

See also BIBLE, DIVORCE, MEDIA

Debates

One of the most important resources for youth groups is that of controversial issues. The church often tries to shirk the points where its members may disagree. Yet, the community of faith should be the one place where folks can disagree and still be brothers and sisters. It is the centrality of Christ which should draw us into community, not common political or social views. It is important to encourage young people to develop a mind which questions everything and yet respects the views of others. Such a vigorous style of searching and caring will also overcome those moments of silence when you are leading a discussion.

For instance, Peg helped a group of junior highs develop the duality of debating and the respect of opponents. She asked them to bring their favorite toy of the moment to their discussion: the water gun. Peg collected them at the door. She then selected a number of hot issues from the morning paper. Styling the debate in a charade presentation format, the topics were given out to the students. They had to take one side or the other. After each debate, the whole group voted for the side with the most impelling defense. The people on the losing side were then lined up against the wall. Peg passed out the water guns and the students were permitted to "execute" the losers. After doing this several times, they shared their feelings about being "killed" for having an unpopular view. This discussion moved in many different directions. They explored human rights and the idea of toleration for minority views.

Another youth group has an annual "great debate." After sponsoring a dinner for adults and young people, the leader gives everyone a topic and a position he or she must take. Mini-debates are held as pairs of people sit in chairs placed in the middle of the circle of people and debate their issue. A general discussion follows each encounter. The most popular topics are those dealing with ethics, youth freedom and behavior.

It is also helpful to put teens in positions where they have to defend positions unfamiliar to their experience. This strengthens their minds and ultimately makes their faith positions even stronger.

See also CIRCULAR RESPONSES, DIS-CUSSION

Despair

"Youth ministry stinks!"

There are days when this thought will overwhelm you. There were only six at the meeting last night. The superstar speaker for next week has cancelled. The neighbors complained because of noisy cars in the parking lot last night. You don't see any growth or change among the teens in the group. None of your young people go to Sunday school or church. One parent has called already this morning about her son not joining the confirmation class.

After a second cup of coffee, you still don't feel much better. "Maybe it is my fault. I really don't know what I am doing or what to do. I am getting too old for this kind of work."

Periods of despair come with the territory. It would be nice to know that all your efforts will result in vast spiritual growth, renewed faith and a change in behavior. However, those moments of encouragement as a youth advisor only come occasionally. Life in the trenches of youth ministry is tough.

The way to counteract this malaise is to get rid of your individualism. It is true that American religion seems to draw upon a Lone Ranger mentality—all you need is a horse and a Bible. Such mythology goes well in the film scenario. However, this isn't the way to sustain creative ministry.

If you can't find kindred spirits in the congregation, look around the community. There will be another youth advisor who has also been through the jungle. Even though you may not be able to have the two youth groups meet together, you can still form a youth advisor covenant.

As a cadre, you can form an alliance against despair and other traps that threaten the solo role. Meet once a week and debrief last week's experience. As trust grows, you will be able to celebrate both success and failure without despair. Your kindred spirit can rejoice in the good things and mourn with you during the misses.

It helps to share some of your youth ministry burdens with youth. This does not mean that you have license to dump all of your problems on them. You will be surprised to see how well they push themselves out of the doldrums. Just ask,

"What are we going to do about the state we are in?" This is not a challenge for them to decide what should be done. It is rather an invitation to share the burden of their group. Just sharing the concerns that led to despair will free you to see many new options.

Despair often arises out of self-centered concerns. You want to have a great victory or you want the youth to be where you think they should be. Pride can only bring more disappointment.

See also AAUGH, BLUES, FAILURE, SUCCESS

Devotional Life

Many adults are misled because they often think of devotional models from their past. It is important in your preparation to look into the long history of meditation. There is a strong witness of faithful sisters and brothers who have had deep communion with God. Some of these folks have also been very committed to serving the needs of people in the world. The most impressive conclusion one draws from such a historical survey is that there is quite a wide variety of meditation styles in the devotional spec-

Many groups develop a spiritual closeness through experiencing a common devotional life.

trum. We should also encourage and acknowledge the possibilities for different styles of meditation among youth.

Marc is a resourceful New Zealand youth worker. He calls eight or nine teens and tells them that he is going on a jogging devotional journey. He will jog by and "pick them up." The group grows as each person is picked up. They do a variety of devotional exercises as they move. They might jog in silence and reflect about the people they pass. Then they talk about their thoughts. They have even found that scripture takes on new meaning in this active devotional context.

Covenant groups of youth have also been helpful. They gather for sharing. Then they agree to meditate at the same time during their time apart. One group of youth used the symbol of a bolt as a way of mutual responsibility. They carried the bolt and reflected on it at an agreed time each day. When they gathered together, they held the bolt and shared around the circle in what way the symbol represented something about their lives.

Resources

1. **Alive** Magazine, Box 179, St. Louis, MO 63166.
2. **Alive Now** Magazine, Box 840, Nashville, TN 37202.
3. **Power** Magazine: Personal Reflections for Youth by Youth, Box 803L, Pierre-Laclede Station, St. Louis, MO 63156.
4. **Making Tracks**, by Dennis Benson, Abingdon.

Dieting

Pencil-thin models, pre-teens staring for years at inhumanly proportioned Barbie dolls, diet plans on every page we pick up, even the slim-line design on many products can have their effect. When an affluent society decides that slim is "in," it has a brutally devastating affect on young teens who are caught two ways: at a stage in which their body needs extra nourishment and also at a stage in which every fad is taken literally.

Dieting has become a major compulsion of many youth. This compulsion will

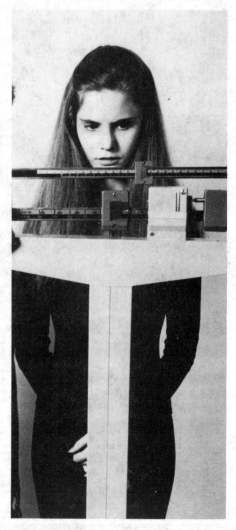

A body-conscious society puts brutal stress on vulnerable young people.

Photo courtesy of American Broadcasting Company

affect your youth group because some of the dieting youth actually know very little about nutrition and may cause themselves to encounter physical abuse, sometimes major.

One of the extremes of dieting is Anorexia Nervosa, commonly called "Skinny Sickness." This very serious illness is brought on by persons, usually female youth, who become so fixated on their figure that they want to become thinner and thinner, just like what they perceive to be the "perfect" size of all the persons they admire. The lure of dieting becomes obsessive until their perception is distorted so that other people are seen as thinner than they really are, and the individual sees herself as fatter than she really is. This compulsion is aggravated by feelings of unworthiness and inability to cope with society.

You are in a unique position to observe the young person in a different context than a parent or teacher, and it may be your task to gather the support team (parents, physician, psychiatrist) to provide the needed help.

Thankfully, most youth stop dieting before they get to this stage. Many youth will appreciate learning as much as they can about nutrition, and this can be brought when the group is planning meals for an upcoming trip, snacks for a hike or refreshments for a party. Not only is this concern related to valuable resources that should be wisely used (as opposed to refined sugar, overprocessed flour, etc), but it includes the sustenance of the body as God's temple. In the Christian faith, the mind, spirit and body are closely connected, and therefore, as participants in youth ministry, it is our responsibility to encourage youth to take proper care of their bodies.

See also BODY, HUNGER, REFRESH-MENTS

Discipline

Several weeks ago Jack's youth group worked out some rules for their once-a-year trip to the beach. During the first afternoon, Jack had a visitor who announced that she was a representative of some of the youth. The group wanted to know if the rules really would be enforced. They would plan their behavior accordingly. Would that all groups were that honest! But almost every group will test the rules to see if and how they will be enforced.

The word *discipline* comes from the same root as *disciple*. To be a disciple of tennis or running, a person has to alter behavior, watch his or her diet and change his daily schedule in noticeable ways. To be a responsible member of a group, especially on a trip, requires extra personal considerations.

The group will have to think through what is best for its welfare. If possible, a group should come to a consensus on a few needed agreements that are fair and can be consistently upheld.

Tricia had been invited to go with her best friend's youth group on a skiing trip. It was her first skiing trip—she had been saving money for months. As soon as she received the registration materials, she quickly returned them all signed, paid and unread. She didn't realize that registering implied consent to the rules.

The second night on the trip Tricia stayed out almost an hour beyond the curfew. She did not think much about it until she realized the entire group had been all over the slopes looking for her, risking their own safety and health. She was even more upset when she realized the punishment for breaking curfew: spending the next day at the lodge.

Tricia complained that she had not seen the rules and this was her only chance to ski. A small group set up to handle such matters met and retained the punishment. It was not until the next evening before she spoke to anyone in the group. During the last night's devotional period, Tricia stood up and explained how she had disliked everyone the night before but had come to realize that the rules were really for her welfare as much as anyone else. She thanked the group for enforcing the rules because it showed they cared about her. If the group would let her, she said she would like to return with them the next year.

See also CITIZENSHIP, CONDUCT, DRINKING, DRUGS, MOTIVATING YOUTH, REBELLION, RULES, SEX

Discrimination

Klan Terrorizes West Virginia Minister. Many church folks might be surprised to read a headline like this today. Yet, groups dedicated to spreading racism will be with us for some time. It is hard to eradicate the virus of hatred, which flares up on every level of society.

There is often a great deal of prejudice among young people. Most youth groups are built around tight ethnic, racial and economic patterns. The old saying about the church on Sunday morning being the most segregated hour of the week is still very true today. In the late '60s and early '70s it seemed that

Imagine that you belong to a different race [or economic background or culture]. How would your group react to you?

blacks and whites would gather around the Word. But the unity didn't happen, because each race had to get its own house in order first. Each race searched for a sense of identity as it sought its roots. When will we again seek the promise of being one family of God?

Perhaps you live in a community in which housing patterns have loaded your church with homogeneous membership. The young people have never worked, talked or worshiped with teens of a different racial, economic or theological background. Teens are placed in great jeopardy by this exclusive pattern. They are prone to be swept away by prejudice. Yet, whenever the composition of the Christian community becomes exclusive, the gift of the Spirit is not present in its fullness, the diversity of texture in the community of faith is the heart of its faithfulness to the Word.

Each person has the potential to be a unique instrument of God's Word. The Good News is known only as others share their faith with us. We are fragments of life joined into a meaningful wholeness through God's love.

How do you open up the experience of your youth? Conferences and youth congresses are a good way of breaking out of your local church ghetto. Use this time to set up some exchange programs with different ethnic or racial groups.

The refugee may be the true bearer of this gift of inclusive community. Many churches have discovered a whole new surge of spiritual power when they have offered hospitality to refugees. One church of 150 members has taken in 75 refugees! Imagine the sense of community this challenge has given them.

Why couldn't your youth group take on the responsibility of relocating a refugee family to your community? This would demand a great deal from youth. However, such an exchange of care between your youth and folks from another culture would change your teens' lives. As our friend Lenore reminds us, "Jesus was a refugee."

It will be hard to defuse the jokes about Poles or the lack of concern for "lazy poor people." You will be running against much of the nation's racial mythology. Yet, in Christ there is neither "Greek" nor "Jew."

A racial experience

The two groups of teens were evenly divided racially. They had agreed to meet for a day of communication. After a few simple communication exercises, the teens were teamed and told to walk around town. They were to find lunch and to note how people reacted to them. We then tied brightly decorated ribbons on their arms.

After two hours the teens returned with amazing stories about the hostility and anger they evoked in strangers. People were upset, not because of the racial mix, but because of the suspicious-looking arm bands. As the group examined the shape of this prejudice, they started telling other stories from their worlds.

The session ended several hours later in a moving communion service. There was a rich sense of community as Christian brothers and sisters.

The view of the church as the family of God means that we should encourage a variety of Christian experiences. In fact, if we do not seek out those in the faith with whom we differ radically, ethnically, socially and theologically, we are not being true to the gospel.

Resources
1. **A Christian Declaration on Human Rights**, edited by Allen Miller, Eerdmans.

See also CLIQUES, DIVERSITY

Discussion

Someone has said that lecturers are discussion leaders who cannot stand the suspense of hearing someone else answer their questions.

A discussion leader must summon a certain amount of bravery as well as trust in the group. Discussions have a way of traveling into totally unsuggested places and taking unexpected turns. Of course, there's also the possibility that a discussion group will just sit there and stagnate.

Over the years discussion leaders have discovered a number of methods that can greatly aid the prospects of having a lively and rewarding discussion. Here are some of the time honored ones:

Method #1: Divide into smaller groups. Form dyads (groups of two persons), triads (groups of three) or larger subgroups to deal with specific assignments. For instance, a dyad might be asked to tell five significant facts about themselves and then to join another dyad with one person introducing his partner to the two new persons. A triad might be asked to engage in observation/dialogue in which two of the persons would discuss a topic with the third person observing what is said and reporting the observations at a set time. Then the roles would be rotated. The small groups could be asked to report back to the large group. (Perhaps the person whose last name was closer to the beginning of the alphabet could be moderator and the person whose last name was closer to the end of the alphabet could be reporter.) Setting a time limit for discussion increases the involvement.

the topic. Roles can be reversed after evaluating what took place during the discussion period.

Method #3: Modified Fish Bowl. People in the outer observation circle can enter the inner discussion circle as they feel inclined by changing places with someone in the inner circle.

Method #2: Fish Bowl. Divide the group into two equal subgroups with one group in a circle for a discussion and the other group in the larger circle around the first group. The outside group observes how the first group reacts to

Method #4: Observers. Plant observers in the discussion group who will look for specific activities. (Did the group really deal with the subject? When was the group the most involved?) The observer can help the group in becoming more aggressively involved.

Method #5: Case Histories. There is nothing like a real situation to get the group involved. Explain how a person coped with a particular situation up until a crucial decision had to be made. Then ask the group what they would do. You may wish to tell how the real person handled the situation following the discussion.

Method #6: Film, Tapes and Other Audio-visuals. Audio-visuals can be most invigorating to the discussion but should not take the place of it. Too often, a film is shown and the group is dismissed without sharing insights. Various group members can recall certain scenes and reap benefits from other persons.

Method #7: Interviews. By recording or writing out the comments of other persons, you can add any number of stimulating opinions to your discussion. With a cassette recorder you can interview persons on the street, in the church, on TV or radio, and any number of others who would be difficult to bring to your group for such contributions.

Basic Guidelines for Leading Youth Discussions:
● Scan the group's emotional environment for clues to the entry point of your discussion (behavior, small talk, clothing, seating patterns and so on).
● Probe for contact points between the chosen subject (film, reading, play) and the group's feelings (laughter, sadness, expressions of boredom).
● Freely utilize means by which students can make comparisons between the topic and an immediate experience. For example, read 1 Corinthians 13 and hand each person a spoon. "As you look into the reflection in the spoon, what do you see about God which is only seen darkly?"
● Always draw upon the resources of the whole group. Even the giggles in the corner are a contribution.
● Let unresolved points remain in the minds of the group.
●Don't be afraid to pursue aspects of the topic you don't know.
● Be patient when silence reigns after your invitation to share.
● Affirm those who contribute their opinions.

Resources
1. **Youth Worker's Success Manual**, by Shirley Pollock, Abingdon.
2. **Learning Together in the Christian Fellowship**, by Sara Little, John Knox Press.
3. **Discussion Starters for Youth Groups**, Ann Billups, Judson Press.
4. **Developing the Art of Discussion**, by John H. Bushman and Sandy Jones, Judson Press.

See also BRAINSTORMING, CIRCULAR RESPONSE, DEBATES, LISTENING, QUESTIONS, ROLE PLAY

Diversity

Ever hear these comments?:

"I don't feel a part of this youth group. Most of the members go to a different high school than I do."

"I hate it that I'm the only (person in a wheelchair/blind/retarded/deaf/black/Asian/Hispanic/Native American/only child/left-handed/heavy-set/poor)."

The first comment is the one heard most often. The others are usually thought and expressed in other ways.

Each of us has something that makes us different from the rest of the group, and we often find ourselves believing that this difference gives everyone else an advantage over us. We survey the rest of the group and conclude that everyone else is alike and we are the only odd one.

A young person tends to play upon differences as if they were of ultimate importance. ("Everyone is always staring at my big nose/toes/knees/ear lobes. Why do I have to go through life like this?") Youth of all generations try to dress and act alike so they will not be considered different.

While it is difficult, adult leaders need to help each youth to begin to feel good about whatever unique qualities he or she possesses. Certainly, we should emphasize the value of the group and the unity we all feel when we are together, but we also need to accept our individuality. Unity can never be achieved at the expense of diversity.

Help your group members to develop an attitude like this: "It is *because* I go to a different high school, am a member of a race other than the majority of the group or am handicapped that I can offer unique and significant insights that the rest of the group needs."

Some of those who study infants believe that newborn children perceive themselves to be everything they see. As they get older they learn where their body ends and the rest of the world begins. In many ways the youth years are similar. The youth are beginning to recognize where the life they have known in elementary school, the nearby neighborhood and the family tapers off and the rest of the world begins. The task for the youth is to discover what capabilities are contained within his or her body for entering into the world and coping with it.

The church youth group can help in that discovery. By affirming and expanding the horizons of the youth, the youth group can help the young person begin to notice special talents, skills, insights, perceptive abilities and other unique gifts God has given him or her to discover and develop. A wide variety of programs is needed to enhance this discovery process. If your group has only three or four members, you may want to join other groups occasionally to widen the discovery possibilities.

Leadership responsibilities of the group should be passed around to various members of the group in order to bring out other interests and talents. Many youth never felt that they had any leadership interests or skills until they were given responsibility, opening up a whole new world of talent investment for them.

Vocational interests and skills can also be cultivated within the group. Obviously, the youth group is not a job training center but it can introduce its members to a wide variety of talent applications as it maintains a wide sweep of program diversity.

See also AGE GROUP CHARACTERISTICS

Divorce

The two 14-year-old boys shifted in their seats nervously. They wanted to talk about their feelings. "My parents are divorced. There are five kids in the family. We gave my folks a hard time. Perhaps if I had not gotten into so much trouble at school, they would still be together."

As he finishes his comment, the other teen nods, "My parents split too. I guess I pulled it down. I would stay out late. My parents would fight over me. I am sorry Dad left. I just disappointed him too much."

Two young teens caught blaming themselves for their parents' divorces may seem unbelievable to you. However, these are just two examples of how the young often misunderstand the dynamics of families in collapse.

If the home cannot always help youth walk through this pain of separation, the church must deal with this sensitive area of concern. You just don't know how close your youth members are to a divorced situation. At one youth meeting, the leader played a short interview on the cassette tape recorder. The voice was of an agonized father describing the day of his divorce. "I said goodbye to my son. I told him that Mother and Dad couldn't live together without fighting. I told him that it was not his fault in any way. We hugged and he got out of the car. As I drove down the street, I could see him running after the car. He was yelling, 'Daddy, Daddy!' "

The sobs of the father echoed through the room. At the end of the session a high school junior came to the guest. There were tears in his eyes. "My dad is leaving this week."

Joe has found that group sessions with teens from broken homes are very helpful. There is a sense of common wisdom to be shared. It is also acceptable to express some of the heavy feelings which would be uncomfortable to share in most general meetings. Teens caught in the transition of the family need special ministry.

Resources
1. **I'm Divorced, Are You Listening Lord?,** by Peggy Buck, Judson Press.
2. **Parents Book About Divorce,** by Richard Gardner, Doubleday.
3. **Creative Divorce,** by Mel Krantzler, New American Library.
4. **Divorce: Prevention or Survival,** by William Arnold, Westminster Press.
5. **"My Parents Are Getting a Divorce"** a filmstrip by Human Relations Media.

See also DEATH, FAMILY

Doubts

Feelings of doubt can signal the beginning of significant personal and spiritual growth.

Here you are—a person your church has named to lead its youth. But in spite of the church's confidence in you, you are filled with doubts, little ones and big ones.

For instance, you may have serious reservations about your motives for working with youth. You may not feel capable of answering their questions or meeting their demands. You may not

adequate for the unexpected. And in the midst of daily schedules and personal involvements, God can seem very far away.

Doubts can signal the beginnings of new personal and spiritual growth. Sometimes former conclusions have to be pruned away for newer, more constructive and reliable conclusions to grow in their place. For sure, anyone who regularly communicates with youth gets his or her personal convictions challenged constantly. But seldom does the pruning and repotting of convictions fail to result in a greater harvest for you and the youth.

even be sure if you really like youth. Even though your family members say they are glad for you to be working with the group, you often feel guilty about not spending your extra time at home with your own children. And yes, there are times when you have doubts about God's presence.

Before dumping the youth program too hastily, let's look at what you are saying. You're thinking responsibly about who you are in relationship with others. You're aware that your concept of ministry is evolving. Our beliefs grow by testing, questioning, even arguing about them, and only the less alert minds among us are still thinking as they did months ago.

You're also expressing honest growth, a realistic process of appraisal—no one likes any age group all the time. Families do get jealous occasionally when a member is involved in meeting demanding obligations. None of us feels

Have you ever met a highly respected church leader whom you were sure had all the answers, then discovered (usually to your astonishment and disillusionment at the shattered image you had built) that this person had some of the same doubts, questions and misgivings you did? Even though the bubble you had for the person may have burst, it is helpful to realize that each person has to daily put meanings together in order to keep growing in understanding.

Youth are riddled with doubts, and they will look to you as one who totally has it together. Sharing your doubts with them may also burst some of their bubbles, but together you can journey in search of clues to the truth.

Each person's life that intersects with ours can help us to have better views of truth. When working with youth, the journey is a matter of pilgrim helping pilgrim to realize the magnificence of the search God is letting us share.

Don't hide your doubts. Share them openly with your church, your family, your youth, yourself and God. Actively follow them with a search for answers, and invite other persons to join you. None of us is perfect. We don't have to be (though many persons feel that they have to be before leading youth).

Thankfully, God is not finished with us yet, and our doubts could be the very next step of growth that is before us.

See also AAUGH, BURN-OUT, COM-MITMENT, PANIC, SELF-IMAGE

The Draft

A key point of ministry for the youth advisor is dealing with this decision for youth. You may be fully supportive of the draft (or you may be totally anti-draft). However, how do you respond to the young man who has a question about his response with *his* life?

A young man came to the youth leader after a large group meeting. "I am concerned about registering for the draft. I don't believe in war. I have terminal cancer. I know that they won't take me. However, my faith demands that I not cooperate with a system of killing." The adult and youth talked for some time. The leader urged the teen to talk with a

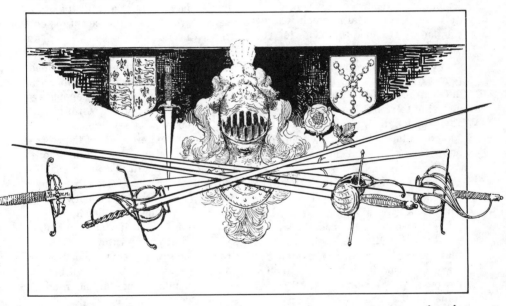

One of the most uncomfortable struggles for the local church is the question of military involvement. While the topic might be a spicy debate for adult discussion groups, it becomes a very personal matter for youth. It is the young who go into the service. The New Testament presentation of the Christian life leaves no doubts that we are called to be peacemakers. The crunch comes when we must determine just how to fulfill this injunction for our own lives.

trained counselor in his home church.

The role of the adult youth leader is to walk with a youth through the steps of becoming a faithful person. This may be a hard role for an adult who has very strong opinions about the military, nuclear energy or other issues. It is the advisor's task to provide the context of faith in which the young person can make the decisions which God calls him or her to make. No one can answer another person's questions about discipleship.

It is very risky for you when the youth of your group deal with issues which touch their lives. Other adults may be fearful about the quest of the young to find God's will in the world of confusion and challenge. Yet, youth ministry is the thrust which encourages you in their quest for full participation in the society as a mature person of faith. This means that the rough texture of real, ethical questions must be experienced as personal concerns.

As soon as you announce a discussion of nuclear power or military policy, don't be surprised by criticism from someone in the church. It is your maturity as a person of faith which will give you courage to open the doors for your youth to explore these issues. This means that you may be called to accompany a young person as he registers for the draft and stand with another as the decision to resist is taken. The adult advisor must draw upon a deep theological commitment to the growth of young people in order to stand before these conflicting issues.

A youth advisor went to the draft board with a high school youth member during the war in Vietnam. The young man was seeking a conscientious objector status (C.O.). The two people had spent many hours in discussion and prayer. The youth advisor was called as a witness for the young man. "I served in the service during the Korean War. I believe in the draft and our effort in Vietnam. Tom and I disagree on this issue. However, I know him as a Christian of depth and I support the decision he has made."

Tom was given the C.O. classification.

Resources
1. **Christian Attitudes Toward War and Peace**, by Roland Bainton, Abingdon.

See also ADVOCATE

Drama

Religious expression began in the dramatic telling of stories. For the ancient Greeks, drama and liturgy were inseparable. Our mothers and fathers in the faith shared the drama of salvation in the desert. The middle ages also saw drama as a servant of the faith. From the morality plays to the excitement of the liturgy, the point of contact between the historical faith and people's lives was drama.

Yet, today there is little awareness of the power of the drama of salvation in most Christian communities. Your church may have done little to utilize drama beyond the bathrobes of the children's Christmas program. Drama author, Gordon C. Bennett, and others keep reminding us that drama is immediately at hand for every situation. The youth group is a fine place to encourage a renewal of this honored form of presenting the story of salvation.

Readers' theater is one of the easiest ways of bringing drama to the group. This technique is drama at its simplest and most accessible form. In readers' theater no one has to memorize lines. You don't even need a published script. Youth can take biblical stories and other existing material as the basis of the drama. The rewriting of the story can be done to provide different parts for several people. Copies of the readers' script need to be made.

Imagine what would happen if you developed a small group of young people who had an interest in drama. Ask the group to prepare short readers' dramas to be the centerpiece for worship at the next four meetings. As you encourage this process, the readers will become quite good. Now they can be invited for a Sunday morning presentation or perhaps a visit to a service at another church.

Almost every community has talented

drama people who usually have no outlet for their gifts. In a small city of rural Australia, a talented drama teacher utilizes a unique presentation. She draws upon people from the congregation at her church's early morning family service by asking them to join her in the center of the room. Then she sets the story situation and asks volunteers to take the parts.

One Sunday the story was about Moses and the burning bush. A young girl played Moses and a teen was God. The leader switched the roles when she realized that the young man stuttered— Moses had been a stutterer. After she had reversed the roles, the teacher read the story line by line. The actors then added their own dialogue to the actions. The outcome was amazing! The stutterer did not stutter! The young man questioned God about the meaning of the bush and his commission. (The bush was an actual dried limb with bright cellophane woven into its branches.) The drama was coached and developed as it was presented!

You might also want to try some of the standard plays. These take more preparation time and intentionality. Yet, once a group gets excited about the possibilities of this form of expression it will not be hard to get commitment. A youth group can really be drawn together in a unique way as it works on such a project.

Youth who feel self-conscious in appearing before others with their own words and expressions of emotion can be aided by being able to appear as someone else in a dramatic presentation.

One of the most important contributions you can make to the group is to find occasions in which they can share their art. It is vital for performers to perform. There are many groups in the community who will be happy to have a program.

Resources
1. **Twenty Ways to Use Drama in Teaching the Bible**, by Judy Battis Smith, Abingdon.
2. **Creative Drama in Religious Education**, by Isabel Burger.
3. **Religious Drama, Ends and Means**, by Harold Ehrensperger.
4. **Discovery in Drama**, Paulist Press.
5. **Reader's Theatre Comes to Church**, by Gordon Bennett, John Knox Press.
6. Contemporary Drama Service, Box 457, 1529 Brook Drive, Downers Grove, IL 60515.

See also CLOWNING, DEBATES, HUMOR, MIME

Drinking

The No. 1 dangerous drug in the United States is alcohol. It alters moods, depresses the central nervous system and induces physical and psychological dependence.

Drinking is a way of life for many youth and adults. The guidelines are simple: Drink before you have to do something unpleasant. Drink after you have completed a task, any task. Drink on special occasions. Drink when there are no special occasions. In other words, drink when you are up, drink when you are down.

It is not hard to follow that logic and drink all the time. Many do.

Drinking is a way of life encouraged upon many of the young by their parents and older friends. Since hard drugs are an unknown experience for many adults, they reason that alcohol is certainly better than drugs. And even if drugs were not involved, many adults still reason that alcohol is just a part of growing up.

But alcohol is an extremely addictive drug. Drugs of any kind affect the person to consider using other types. Lax attitudes toward drinking have escalated the problem considerably.

The result: There are more teenage alcoholics than ever before, more teenage drunk drivers, more teenage drinkers attempting suicide. The National Institute on Alcohol Abuse and Alcoholism states that there are 3.3 million American teenagers with a drinking problem—19 percent of the youth population.

Regardless of how you feel about your own drinking, you should develop a position of how you feel about drinking by youth. They will test you, and you will need to be consistent in your response. Incidentally, they will also quote other leaders who have a variety of positions (an honest reflection of the state of confusion). A few leaders even take their groups out for a beer or something stronger after a meeting, totally aware of the legal and moral ramifications involved.

Even though drinking is an undeniable youth problem, the members of your group will probably be hesitant to give the issue major programming attention. Part of the reason for the hesitancy is that drinking is socially acceptable, heavily promoted by media, regarded as a symbol of sophistication and success, and most amazing of all, seen as a totally private matter. We are all aware of drunk drivers whose "accidents" kill several persons, who lie in a hospital for weeks and propose a drinking party to celebrate their getting out of the hospital. (This is sophistication, success, social acceptability, private?)

Youth do not want to be seen as different from the crowd, especially as more holy or moral than others. (They know other persons will do everything possible to pull them off that pedestal.) Youth also want to avoid setting themselves up as judges of other youth.

Therefore, youth would rather ignore

programs on drinking and drugs. The usual dodge is, "We get so much of that in school." But in many cases all they get on the subject are scare tactics, which convince the youth that they need only to play it smarter than the persons used as examples. Totally lost in this exercise is important data on the deteriorating effect of drugs, including alcohol, and the mental, emotional and bodily changes.

Also lost is information related to the loss of perceptive ability caused by drinking and drugs. No one wants to go through the remainder of life knowing that their negligence caused someone's death or disfigurement.

One entry point to the subject is to deal with why persons feel that they must drink. The group will need to deal with the pressures, the desire to conform and other conditions that lead to drinking. Together the group may discover numerous alternative ways to relax, celebrate and dissipate uneasiness.

For instance, George wanted to probe the implications of drinking with his youth group. They did not openly talk about it. However, the members of the group were upset over the accident which took the lives of three teens the previous week. They had slipped away from school. Their overturned car contained several wine and beer bottles. George suggested that they focus the forthcoming retreat on this topic. The teens were slow to respond. Then he shared some of the approaches which would be used. They would play a simulation game ("Pill"), hear tape segments from teen drinkers and drug users, explore biblical teachings and role play how they could help other teens with this problem. It was a fantastic weekend! The turnout was surprisingly large for this kind of event. In the midst of deep sharing, several youth people admitted that they had alcoholic

parents. The group surrounded these teens with love and care.

This kind of study can be a rich moment by which you and your youth can explore the forces which show themselves as drinking or drug abuse. Why must we get high? What are we running away from? What are we embracing when we turn to the pill or the bottle?

It will be helpful to know the availability of alcohol treatment and counseling agencies and resources in your community should the need arise.

Resources

1. Cassette kit: **Teen Talk, Kit 1: "The Prevention of Addictive Diseases Among Youth—Alcohol and Drugs,"** by Dennis Benson, P.O. Box 12811, Pittsburgh, PA 15421.
2. **Alcohol: Our Biggest Drug Problem**, by Joe Fort.
3. **Did I Have A Good Time?** (Teenage Drinking), by Marion Howard.
4. **Why Our Children Drink**, by Edmund and Jovita Addeo.

See also DRUGS

Drugs

"My son got hooked on drugs by using my tranquilizers." The middle-aged woman found it hard to make this public confession. She had to speak because the room of adults had been feasting on an orgy of judgment and criticism about the drug problem which had just been made public in their community. This parent wisely revealed the connection point which links every problem among youth to an aspect of the adult culture.

The youth drug ethic is formed in the legal, adult world of chemical usage. Just scan the drug ads in any magazine. All the copy seems to suggest that every manifestation of tension or pain can be relieved by a drug. One is never en-

couraged to look at the source of these irritating symptoms. Taking a strong pain reliever does nothing for the roots of despair and tension. "If drugs will bring me instant help, then I can take other drugs to combat loneliness, boredom, confusion or anger." It is the ladder of cultural ethics which provides the foundation for youth drug usage.

There are many examples of the complex drug situation in America. Millions of people use illegal drugs like pot. Many users are no longer youth. Folks who now are moving to the top of the professional and business mainstreet fuel their leisure time with grass and smooth out their working day with pills.

Yet, it is always the young who are most exploited by drug abuse. It is a combination of immaturity and surface needs which breaks down their lives.

How does your group of "good kids" deal with the drug environment around you? Are any of these teens experienced with pot or pills? What can they do to touch the lives of those floating in the cloud of drug detachment? The "Reefer Madness" (an old anti-drug film) approach of scaring kids with misinformation does not work. The church suffers because we have often taken the proper stands on abusive behavior for

the wrong reasons. Therefore, our statements of concern and guidance seem suspect.

The best approach is to equip your folks with the rationale behind their ethical position on the use of drugs and alcohol. If they chose abstinence, why? You will be pleased by the reasoning which can develop in this process. Why does Christ lead us in this decision? This becomes a probe of the historical faith and not just a recital of the parents' opinions.

In the course of your work you will be drawn into situations where someone has been caught or admits that he or she is using drugs. You have won a significant step toward helping the person by the fact that you have been given this confidence. You are the link between the person and the path to health. It is important to separate your feelings about drug usage from what the person is saying to you. You need to listen rather than give speeches about drugs. He or she may know more about drugs than you do. You can provide a new context in which this person can explore what all the confusion in his or her life means.

In the award-winning radio special,

"The Crystal Roller Coaster," there is a portion of the show where teens talk about their drug views. "I use lots of pot, man. I think that it is great. Nothin' wrong with good weed."

"How much do you use?"

"Ten or twelve joints . . . I smoke before school and during the breaks."

"Why?"

"Because . . . I don't know . . . it is boring . . . The teachers don't care."

"Have you noticed any changes in your life when you use a lot of grass?"

"Yeah . . . it is great . . . I mean . . . I don't feel so bad . . . Things aren't so terrible."

"Things are bad?"

"I can't stand it, man! My whole world is awful."

"Grass makes it better?"

". . . Not really. No, I am still bad, man. Do you think I am doing too much stuff?"

"How is your relationship with friends and others?"

"I don't know. I don't seem to talk with them at all. Am I getting too deep? What can I do?"

We have found that merely by walking with people involved with drugs, they will find the uncertainties and questions. They know that something is wrong. *Encounter* rather than *confrontation* is your strongest means of helping people who are struggling with a drug problem. They know your values by the fact that you are not into drug usage. Your witness is your grasp on your world and your ability to walk with persons outside your values. This kind of strength is valued by those lost and confused.

You will want to link yourself to a solid drug rehabilitation program. There are many different approaches. A reputable psychologist can help you. You must move carefully through this area. There are many groups which have questionable methods for reaching the addictive personality. One challenged view is to displace the addiction with an emotional one for a strong authority figure. Sometimes they invite teens to get "high" on Jesus. This sounds nice. However, authentic discipleship demands something more complete than substituting Jesus for a drug.

Peer pressure, wanting to remain a child (fear of responsibile maturity), and cynicism about the world (helpless to change evil) are often cited as other factors contributing to the addictive personality. Addiction is all of these and more.

You may also have to cope with drug usage which does not appear abusive. How do we draw the line between proper and improper involvement with drugs? Can we draw such a line? This will be one of your most sensitive areas of exploration. Yet, it is also the point where the Christian faith becomes flesh and dwells among us.

Feel free to confess your own confusion and struggle. Your teens will appreciate a faith anchored on honesty which shares the journey of faithfulness.

Resources

1. **Reaching Out: The Prevention of Drug Abuse Through Increased Human Interaction**, by Gerald Edwards.

2. **Understanding Drug Use: An Adult's Guide to Drugs and the Young**, by Peter Marin and Allan Cohen, Harper and Row.

3. **Drugs and Youth: Medical, Psychiatric and Legal Facts**, by Coles, Brenner, and Meagher.

4. **Is This Trip Necessary?**, by Philip and Lola Deane.

5. **Teen Talk, Kit 1: "The Prevention of Addictive Diseases Among Youth—Alcohol and Drugs,"** a three-cassette study, by Dennis Benson.

See also DRINKING

LIST OF DRUGS
Medical uses, symptoms produced, and

NAME	SLANG NAME	CHEMICAL OR TRADE NAME	CLASSIFICATION	MEDICAL USE
Heroin	H. horse, scat, junk, smack, scag, stuff, Harry, joy, white lady	Diacetyl-morphine	Narcotic	Pain relief
Morphine	White stuff, M	Morphine sulfate	Narcotic	Pain relief
Codeine	Schoolboy	Methylmorphine	Narcotic	Ease pain and coughing
Cocaine	Corrine, gold dust, coke, Bernice, flake, star dust, snow	Methylester of benzoyl ecgonine	Stimulant, local anesthesia	Local anesthesia
Marijuana	Pot, grass, tea, gage, reefers, Mary Jane, mezz, roaches, weed, haircut	Cannabis sativa	Relaxant, euphoriant, in high doses hallucinogen	None in U.S.
Barbiturates	Barbs, blue devils, yellow jackets, phennies, peanuts, blue heavens	Phenobarbital, Nembutal, Seconal, Amytal	Sedative-hypnotic	Sedation, relieve high blood pressure, epilepsy, hyperthyroidism
Amphetamines	Bennies, dexies, speed, wake-ups, lid poppers, hearts, pep pills	Benzedrine, Dexedrine, Desoxyn, Methamphetamine, Methedrine	Sympatho-mimetic	Relieve mild depression, control appetite and narcolepsy
LSD	Acid, sugar, big D, cubes, trips	d-Lysergic acid diethylamide	Hallucinogen	Experimental study of mental function, alcoholism
DMT	AMT, businessman's high	N,N-Dimethyl-tryptamine	Hallucinogen	None
Mescaline	Mesc, chief, coral beans, San Pedro cactus	3,4,5-Trimeth-oxyphenethylamine	Hallucinogen	None
Alcohol	Booze, juice, etc.	Ethanol, ethyl alcohol	Sedative-hypnotic	Solvent, antiseptic
Tobacco	Fag, coffin nail, etc.	Nicotinia tabacum	Stimulant-sedative	Sedative, emetic (nicotine)
PCP	Angel dust, cadillac, cyclones, hog, stardust, wack	Phencyclidine	Anesthetic	Animal anesthesia

their dependency potentials

HOW TAKEN	USUAL DOSE	EFFECTS SOUGHT	LONG-TERM SYMPTOMS	PHYSICAL DEPENDENCE POTENTIAL	MENTAL DEPENDENCE POTENTIAL
Injected or sniffed	Varies	Euphoria, prevent withdrawal discomfort (4 hrs.)	Addiction, constipation, loss of appetite	Yes	Yes
Swallowed or injected	15 milligrams	Euphoria, prevent withdrawal discomfort (6 hrs.)	Addiction, constipation, loss of appetite	Yes	Yes
Swallowed	30 milligrams	Euphoria, prevent withdrawal discomfort (4 hrs.)	Addiction, constipation, loss of appetite	Yes	Yes
Sniffed, injected, or swallowed	Varies	Excitation, talkativeness (varies, short)	Depression, convulsions	No	Yes
Smoked, swallowed, or sniffed	1 to 2 cigarettes	Relaxation, increased euphoria, perceptions, sociability (4 hrs.)	Usually none	No	Yes
Swallowed or injected	50 to 100 milligrams	Anxiety reduction, euphoria (4 hrs.)	Addiction with severe withdrawal symptoms possible convulsions, toxic psychosis	Yes	Yes
Swallowed or injected	2.5 to 5 milligrams	Alertness, activeness (4 hrs.)	Loss of appetite, delusions, hallucinations, toxic psychosis	Yes?	Yes
Swallowed	100 to 500 micrograms	Insightful experiences exhilaration, distortion of senses (10 hrs.)	May intensify existing psychosis, panic reactions	No	No
Injected	60 to 70 milligrams	Insightful experiences, exhilaration, distortion of senses (less than 1 hr.)	?	No	No
Swallowed	350 milligrams	Insightful experiences, exhilaration, distortion of senses (12 hrs.)	?	No	No ?
Swallowed	Varies	Sense alteration, anxiety reduction, sociability (1 to 4 hrs.)	Cirrhosis, toxic psychosis, neurologic damage, addiction	Yes	Yes
Smoked, sniffed, chewed	Varies	Calmness, sociability (time varies)	Emphysema, lung cancer, mouth and throat cancer, cardiovascular damage, loss of appetite	Yes	Yes
Injected, sniffed, smoked, swallowed	Varies	Euphoria, non-communicative	?	No	Yes

Earthball

It's big, bouncy and a lot of fun. Use the earthball to intrigue your group.

Earthball is one of many names for a massive, overwhelmingly large ball (approximately 8' in diameter) that is a natural for church recreation. For one thing, it is so big, dwarfing anyone, that the childlike qualities in all of us have a field day. You can roll it around from person to person or group to group. You can toss it around (just so one person is not left to bat it back, since its airborne weight makes it dangerous on wrists). And you can play an abnormal baseball or volleyball game with it, or any variation of a hundred other games you and the group might construct.

With care, persons can be lifted onto it. Be careful not to let a person slide across and fall off the other side.

This unusual, absurd object draws players like flies to a picnic. Some persons will play with it by the hours, mostly rolling it and bumping it around. The strength of the better constructed ones seems eternal.

As with a parachute it is useful for drawing groups together. And strangers to the group will often come across a field to where a group is playing with an earthball not only to experience the usual fun but to check out the intriguing group that is playing with it.

Its advantages usually outweigh the disadvantages (it is expensive, must be kept away from streets and poison ivy, needs an older type of vacuum cleaner or other air source to blow it up). A less expensive, lighter weight weather balloon is available but is less sturdy than the earthball. Both are available through most recreation supply stores.

Resources
1. You can purchase an earthball from **World Wide Games**, Box 450, Delaware, OH 43015 or **New Games**, P.O. Box 7901, San Francisco, CA 94120.

See also BUBBLE, PARACHUTE, WEATHER BALLOON

Easter

The high point of the church year for the Christian church is Easter. Christ's triumph over death is the once-for-all-times victory for all who follow him.

For youth, Easter can be a singularly impressive day because of the many involvements they will have in the cele-bration of this happiest of all times. In all probability, this day will begin at a very early hour as people prepare for the sunrise service, one of the most unusual worship experiences of the year. When else is the congregation willing to worship at that hour in that setting? The sunrise service is quite a moving and commanding event, regardless of the number of times a person has attended. The music and order of service during this time is usually unequaled in feeling during the rest of the year.

Many churches have a breakfast at the church following the sunrise service, and often the youth are either in charge of this meal or help with it.

The church school hour and the morning worship also have an expres-

The celebration of Easter is a time when a creative, youth-planned event can be impressive and powerful.

siveness on this glad day. There is usually plenty of color and joyful music. The kind of excitement that youth might wish for on other Sundays is often prevalent on Easter. Brass choirs, bell choirs, children's choirs, increased attendance, baptism, confirmation class reception and other special ingredients make this a true celebration of worship.

Since this day is often in the beginning of spring, many youth groups have a special celebration of their own in the out-of-doors in the evening, perhaps a picnic and some games. As the day nears its end, the group members can share with each other how they feel as they reflect upon how Easter donates its gifts within their faith journey.

The youth in one community took this foundation and moved in exciting new directions. Remember that these special Christian days give you permission to stretch the usual worship patterns. For instance, a group of Pittsburgh folk decided to utilize the shopping center mall, the contemporary marketplace. It would be an interdenominational witness to Christ. They utilized the early Christian symbol of the butterfly. In fact, they actually built a huge tunnel-like cocoon. Using chicken wire and tissue, they gave the impression of a combination cocoon/tomb through which the worshippers passed. People saw scenes of hope and resurrection as they walked through the structure. They were given balloons as they left the cocoon/tomb which were released in the parking lot as a demonstration of Christ's resurrection.

This special season is bursting with possibility. The physicality and the spirituality of this moment of salvation cries out to be felt and experienced. Release your young people on this day of Good News.

See also CHRISTMAS, JOURNALS, NEW YEAR'S EVE.

Ecumenical

This term is drawn from the Greek word meaning "a universal dwelling place." The concept has often been associated with one organization or a bundle of particular programs. In fact, we look to the biblical idea of the room in our God's home where all the faithful are called to break bread, serve, celebrate and have fellowship. This does not mean organization merger or even common understandings about the Good News. We are beginning at this source as we look at youth ministry. Young people must experience the fact that they have spiritual roots and a kinship with all believers.

It is a very positive experience for young people to meet with other Christians as Christians. The richness within each tradition must be understood, enjoyed and shared. Some adults will get quite nervous when you suggest that your youth should attend an event like the National Christian Youth

Congress organized by GROUP Magazine. "They will be with all those other church young people." Praise the Lord that they are! There is nothing for them to fear. Yet, be kind and understanding when confronted by these good folks.

They fear for the young of their church. Assure them that this experience will not cause the young people to lose their faith. It can only be strengthened by the faith of 3,000 young people in prayer, study, worship and service. Show them the program which features leadership from their own tradition along with that of others. Point out that you will be with the young people. Explain that you will have time to prepare the young people and also time to debrief the experience. In fact, you might even invite this person to accompany the group to the conference or congress. When you return, have one of the young people offer a personal report of what happened. You may even want to have your young people present a report in worship.

Ecumenical relationships are most likely to be useful to groups when they share common goals, and this cannot be discovered until groups are willing to venture out to see if such sharing is possible.

Many programs for youth are offered in an ecumenical framework. The two primary reasons are the common concern for youth ministry and the greater efficiency that comes from combining resources. Whether such programs are right for your group will depend upon many factors, not the least of which is the value of establishing faith links across former dividing lines.

It is possible to get carried away with cooperative youth ministry to the point of neglecting the local church program. Some communities plan an ecumenical youth program once a month, and there is a temptation for each church to let that one event carry all the youth ministry needs. Another temptation is to rotate the programming among the churches to the point of never permitting the youth group of a particular church to discover its own unique potential.

In the same way, each youth group needs to recognize its roots and its significant unique insights of faith. However, the group also needs to recognize its place as a part of the body of Christ universal. Easter, Christmas, World Day of Prayer, World-Wide Communion Sunday and other such times remind us that we are part of a wider body of believers, in which it is not important that we continually say, "We are of Paul or we are of Apollos." Youth, who are increasingly citizens of a global village, need to claim their birthright as international brothers and sisters in Christ.

Resources
1. **When Faith Meets Faith**, by David Stowe.
2. **Christian Faith and Other Faiths: The Christian Dialogue With Other Religions**, by Stephen Neill.

Emotions

One of the trickiest parts of youth ministry is being sensitive to the myriad of emotions that continually race through a youth. Many of these emotions are brand new to the youth, who does not know how to identify them, control them, mask them or ignore them, much less recognize their origin.

There is a temptation for adults to assume that since they lived through those years, they can correctly appraise the emotions of youth, label them and channel them in the correct directions. A better definition of manipulation could

Emotions youth face can be a positive force in their lives . . . if they learn to recognize and control these newly found aspects of their personality.

probably not be found. This short-cut approach to dealing with emotions can be disastrous.

An outward expression of an inward emotion must be recognized as an extremely complicated reaction to life that generates heightened nervous reflexes. The world may be seeing an excited flurry of laughter and body movement, but the person may actually be experiencing excruciating pangs of fear toward what is perceived as thwarting confinement.

As with a young child who can register a bad case of flu and accompanying high temperature one minute only to have it completely disappear an hour later, so a youth can experience extreme contrasts of emotion within an amazingly short period of time. Adults have usually fallen into more sustained emotional patterns (grudges or rage can be held for days, fear can remain indefinitely), and it is difficult for some adults to comprehend that youthful feelings can quickly flow from hate to love to revenge, often toward the same person!

Occasionally, a youth will test an adult's emotional anger or jubilation either to see how well they can pull it off or to survey the other person's reactions. Other times the emotions stem from new bodily functions, and the youth sits helpless as streams of tears flow down the face or uncontrolled shaking torments his or her frame.

Since the youth years are full of emotional buildup, it is important for positive "release" experiences. Recreation really can be re-creation for youth when it transfers a healthy distribution of emotional energies into uplifting and rebuilding patterns. Singing, sports, work projects or even dancing can enable persons to burn off pent-up knots of tension as they help establish new relationships with groups and individuals using the same burst of adrenaline.

The youth leader need not be a doctor of psychology to understand a youth's intricate emotional patterns. It is enough to know that they are ever present, often in explosive arrays of short duration, and that they can strike innocent bystanders.

There will be times when emotions overtake the individual youth and strong feelings of jubilation, fear, remorse, separation and other intense inner buildups will make it impossible to proceed with anything else. At such times a strong support base is needed to comfort and to listen to the person as he or she deals with these very real problems or victories. The tendency often is to discount the validity of the emotions, but unless individuals have a chance to confront what they mean and where they seem to be leading, it will be difficult to attend to any other matter. For instance, you as a leader of a group may sense a feeling of suspicion or fear as a particular project is approached, and you may not discover without some exploration that a prior experience has left the group wary of a repeat.

The youth advisor's most immediate concern is that surprising moment when the emotional floodgates open. What should you do when a person starts crying or an angry outburst explodes in the course of a discussion or worship service? It is easy to sit back and figure out a response a week after the meeting. When emotional lightning strikes, draw upon your initial feelings. Most mistakes we have made during the past few years have come when we did not follow the sixth sense within us.

The discussion was heavy. The weekend had been going very well. The 14 teens were probing the Spirit of Christ. They were following the emotional moments of his ministry. It was amazing how closely they could relate their own lives to his! At one point they were talking about the moment when Jesus' friends had deserted him. One teenage girl started crying. Pete, the youth leader, was stunned. He felt tears in his own eyes. This scared him. "Let's hold hands." The circle drew close to the sadness and pain in the room. There was silence for a couple minutes. Then a teen started speaking about his own feeling of desertion when his parents divorced. The girl stopped crying and started comforting the boy. The circle was soon strong and the pain had passed. When Pete thought about it later, he was amazed to realize that he had only directed the group's care to the girl and said nothing!

No one can help you by giving you the proper responses to these kinds of emotional moments. You are called to trust your own emotions as they meet those of the young people. Your support system will help you to keep on an emotional level.

Youth are to be loved, emotions included. Youth need friends who forgive their outbursts, listen as they search for reasons behind what they feel, and provide an environment where they feel secure enough to express their rage and frustration. The youth need to experience both discipline and heartfelt emotions.

Resources
1. **Living With Your Feelings**, by Barry Bailey, Abingdon.
2. **Emotions: Can You Trust Them?** by James Dobson, Regal Books.
3. **From Rock Bottom to Mountaintop**, by Bill Stearns, Victor Books.
4. "**Masks—How We Hide Our Emotions**," a filmstrip by Human Relations Media.

See also BLUES, DESPAIR, FRIZZIES, MOUSE BREATH, ZITS

Encouragement

"We have put a band together. Would you mind coming out to hear us? We are playing in my garage." We have received many such calls over the years. The callers are teens struggling to become better. They know that the invitation is extended to someone who will be a great audience. The church has a vital role in providing a context where youth can become better at whatever they are seeking.

Many now-famous musicians could never get a start in most communities today. Local audiences usually demand that the hometown group play and sound like the famous bands. If a performer wants to be original or play something which is currently out of vogue, there is no place to practice his or her art. The world only wants what has become successful. Note how the opening band at large concerts usually gets booed. But six months later the rejected band is often the headliner.

The church was once a major patron of the arts. It was a place which appreciated the creative folks of the day. Youth ministry has an important role and much to gain from an interest in those who are refining their skills. These folks need an audience. We can anticipate their growth before it becomes evident.

We have also found great resources for the local congregation in the midst of the creative artist community. They can give us their art while we give them our acceptance and, sometimes, our content.

While visiting a pizza parlor, Harold, an Episcopal priest, came to know a trio which played there. The priest asked them to set the gospel lesson for Christmas Eve to some original music. They met several times. The music they

Adults play a vital role in encouraging and nurturing young people's gifts and interests.

offered was perfect. The trio also made some fine suggestions to enhance the presentation in the service. On the night of the worship experience, they asked him if they could receive communion. If we accept the gifts of others, they will receive our offering.

Youth ministry needs those folks outside of our community. We need the creativity and restlessness of this part of the body. Church youth are incomplete without young people outside of the congregation. The performing artists can especially offer gifts for the fullness of faith experience.

Resources

1. **Experiential Education**, by John and Lela Hendrix, Abingdon.

See also BELONGING, COMMITMENT, LOVE

Equipment

"If our church had a gym, then we could do something to help these kids."

"Do you remember that church where they had the leadership traning school? They had a videotape deck. Now, if we had that, Sunday school could really be nice."

"If we just had . . . a stage with first class lighting . . . a good PA . . . a pool . . . a pool table . . . our own camp . . . a bus."

Sound familiar? We've all thought and said some of the same things.

And it is logical—without the right wrench, some bolts are next to impossible to budge. It's hard to bush hog (cut weeds) without a tractor. Can't fly many planes without radar these days.

The only problem with those examples: Youth ministry is not logical! Churches with every audio-visual item or teaching gadget you ever wished for will painfully tell you that fancy equipment is not what makes the difference.

Scores of enormous, beautifully built gymnasiums sit vacant week after week; rust has gotten to untold video machines before they were used half a dozen times; wonderfully equipped stages are vacant.

At the same time there are churches with 75 persons in their total membership, and all 30 of their youth turn out each Saturday morning to practice basketball behind the high school for their church league play. There are church school classes operating with borrowed slide projectors, old popcorn poppers, and battered ping pong paddles. And, of course, there are thousands of churches of every size making use of every piece of equipment they own.

Having super equipment does not mean better programs. It would be so simple if it did. But dedicated persons who love other persons seem to be able to perform miraculous ministry without or with equipment. They know how to borrow, how to help persons to learn how to make, rebuild, modify.

Adaptation is in itself a valuable thing to learn as our world deals with the scarcity of resources. It is also valuable to learn that people are infinitely more important than things.

All of this is not to suggest that equipment is unimportant. It is just not the most important creature in the classroom. And it has been far overrated.

Okay, what are the alternatives if your budget is low? How about borrowing? As you notice items that would be helpful to the youth program, could any members of the congregation own them, such as: a slide projector (an unbelievably versatile machine), cassette recorder (unlimited possibilities), camera, sports equipment (some of which might be kept by the group), lighting (photography buff), land, remote cabin for retreats, whatever? A bulletin announcement can work wonders.

Public libraries have a surprising amount of equipment and materials available for loan, including films, records, slides, projectors, pictures, tapes, cassettes. Regional resource centers of denominations also have impressive stockpiles of resources waiting for your request. It is also amazing how many services and resources can be obtained from community agencies, industry and government.

See also CABLE, FUND RAISING, MATERIALS, RESOURCES

Ethics

The church is the perfect setting in which youth can deal with ethical issues. All public and many private schools cannot enter the areas of morality and ethics, especially as they relate to religious convictions. No other group within the life of the youth can face head-on those decisions of what is right and wrong.

The youth group is the place to ask tough questions about life, faith and the future.

The church should deal openly with any dilemma facing individuals and society to search for what is the best Christian response. It is extremely valuable for youth to learn how to apply their faith to any problem they are currently facing or will be facing in the future. Within the supportive community of believers, youth can ask those rough questions and face those troublesome dilemmas. They can reason and probe those reaches where faith still applies and sustains.

Adult leaders will also be challenged to do some stretching and trusting. If the youth group reaches a stage where all of the youth feel that they can bring out some of their deep problems and questions, the frankness may startle some adults. On the other hand, youth dilemmas may do nothing more than amuse the adults or bore them. Whatever the reaction, it is important for the adults to support the youths' searching. It may be difficult for the adults to resist an urge to bring the discussion to a sudden, neatly wrapped conclusion that cuts off more needed pursuit. Some of the questioning will not be totally resolved at the end of each time together, and that may lead some members to concentrated probing with other persons and resources.

The group may not be willing to be open and honest at first. Time may be required for a trust level to be developed, and perhaps a more relaxed setting such as a camp or a weekend retreat may be called for. Campfires, long rides in a car or bus, hikes in woods, fishing expeditions and similar activities often provide natural conditions for persons to share concerns with others who are willing to help.

Groups will also need to wrestle with such decisions. Try tossing out this challenge: ''Our group has just been given $50,000 to spend in a meaningful ministry to other youth, the only stipulation being that we have to unanimously decide within 30 minutes how to spend it. Let's quickly divide into 3 or 4 teams to think through major needs. Report back in 10 minutes and we'll see if we can agree on how to use the funds.'' (If you want to make the process a little more difficult, suggest that each team must agree to its priorities and send a person to a center table to negotiate with persons from the other teams. You might further add that $1,000 is being taken away for each moment the entire group cannot reach consensus.)

Most of us would rather not make decisions that affect changes in our lives and those of other persons. Pose some current difficult questions to your group and poll their responses. When there is intense disagreement, join those who

agree into teams and debate with the other teams. As the process ends, discuss what was occurring within the thought process of the participants. Did the issues get lost in the midst of our side's attempt to win? Did the competition cause us to think less of the other team members as capable persons? Help the group to pull away from the issue of the debate and think through how they came to their conclusions. Where can we turn when we are overwhelmed by the urgency or awesomeness of making a decision?

The group will probably realize how valuable it is to have a supportive community that will listen to problems and be there to fall back on. This realization may be enormously helpful to these youth in years to come when very real ethical decisions appear to have them cornered.

Whatever the dilemma, with God's presence, the Christian community can be of ultimate help to others.

Resources
1. **Growing Up Moral**, by Schaff, McCoy and Ross, Winston Press.
2. **The Christian and His Decisions**, by H. Smith and L. Hodges.
3. **Love, Power and Justice**, by Paul Tillich.
4. **Moral Man and Immoral Society**, by Reinhold Niebuhr.
5. **Christ and the Moral Life**, by Knud Logstrup.

See also CONFLICT, DEBATES, VALUES CLARIFICATION

Evaluation

One of the most helpful resources when planning any youth ministry event is a record of people's reactions to the last similar event held by this group. Without such a record, the planning often turns into one of those games of, "Well, I think the attendance was 30, but then again it could have been 50." "Yeah, and didn't we serve ice cream, or was that at the school party?" And our memory has ways of playing tricks on us as to whether the whole thing was a flop or a success.

That's the nice thing about having a written evaluation on file. When we look over the comments that were made during and shortly after the event, a lot of the details start coming back. When we see Todd's suggestion, "Next time, don't forget the agendas," we are already on our way. Or we think about the proposed schedule when we notice that a number of persons noted that "We could have had a better retreat if we had stayed until Sunday."

As you plan your evaluation process, think of what you would like to know to help you plan the next event. Try to keep the questions open enough so people aren't locked into saying "yes" or "no" on a similiar future event. Allow them to suggest different events, varied approaches and improved planning.

You may wish to ask open-ended questions, such as:

The part of the retreat I liked best was . . .

If something had to be omitted, I would leave off . . .

Specific activity evaluations are helpful:

The way I would rate:

	Super	So-so	Terrible
The opening address	____	____	____
The closing recreation	____	____	____

Another rating scale:

The Meals	1 2 3 4 5 6 7 8
	Yuck Yum

A blunt question about the next event:
The speaker I would like to have next time: . . . .

Using an evaluation process also helps individual participants pull together what they've learned. It can help them to think through the event and realize which parts were meaningful.

You may wish to add some questions for this purpose, such as:

The most important learning for me this weekend was . . .

I was most challenged by . . .

There are no right or wrong answers on an evaluation because the people providing the answers are experts. They know their reactions better than anyone else.

The evaluation process need not be as formal as filling out a questionnaire. Many times it can be as simple as "How would you change . . .?" or "Would it help if I gave you some of the Bible passages we will be using the next week?"

Some sort of evaluation should be conducted regularly to keep in touch with the group. Asking the group for suggestions often forms something of a convenant between each person to work toward the mutual objectives.

See also FEEDBACK, SUCCESS

Evangelism

If there is any group in the church that can spread good news to others, it is youth. When young people begin to realize the power and love of Christ in their lives, they do not hesitate to spread it to everyone they meet.

Wise churches include youth in their evangelistic outreach. Not only do young people contribute significantly, but they gain much from sharing spiritual insights with older persons. Without this contact, it is easy for youth to conclude that what they feel is unique and adults would not understand.

Youth often need help in learning how to articulate their faith. Once their school and neighborhood friends realize their spiritual commitment, there will be many difficult questions to answer. ("Does your church really believe in.............?") Giving youth opportunities to speak at events in the local church will help them to become familiar with important words and concepts.

Some church leaders have looked at membership trends and decided that it is not worth their time for the growth of their church to try to reach youth. (After all, they say, youth move on to other churches as they get older and go to work in other cities.) What a fallacy! Based on membership alone, church leaders should realize that they receive the results of other churches' evangelistic efforts. And, almost without exception, a family with children of any age will not join a church where there is not a good youth program.

Membership trends are not the real issue anyway. The crucial issue is that youth desperately need to hear and experience God's love for them. Christ's command to all of us to reach everyone in the world relieves anybody of being able to make choices.

Martin Marty reminds us that the historical, mainline churches are invita-tional at their evangelistic core. We invite everyone to partake of this fellowship of Christ.

See also BELONGING, HOSPITALITY, MALLS, NEWCOMER, OUTREACH

Exchange Programs

Exchange programs mean learning to live with different looks, tastes—even different ways of expressing our faith.

By far the highlight of the youth years for many persons was participating in a youth exchange program in which they lived in another country for a fairly long period of time. That period was a time of exploration—searching out the challenging facets of another culture, seeing one's own country through the eyes of a foreign nation and coexisting with persons of a different political and religious persuasion, testing the values of a different monetary system and laying traps for where truth comes down for you is possible in this kind of inter-cultural experience.

One of the most famous of the exchange programs is the International Christian Youth Exchange, which operates as a copartnership in about 20 countries among many denominations. It stresses the Christian affiliation and seeks to place students in Christian families in all countries. Older students

often live in dormitories of various institutions. A flat fee covers the program's expense, host families contribute for the student's upkeep and host churches donate money for the students in their midst.

Returnees as well as persons currently engaged in the program can offer excellent insights to youth groups. You can receive more information by writing to 74 Trinity Place, Room 610, New York, NY 10006.

Expectations

It would be an interesting experience to be able to observe the various expectations that different persons have for the youth group. On a given day, you might see:

1. A parent who hopes her daughter will meet a "fine young man" in the group.

2. Another parent, who hopes the group will learn how to do a great job this year during Youth Sunday. He would like for the group to do a Christmas play as he did when he was a youth.

3. A youth, who is happy as long as there are plenty of people to play volleyball this week.

4. The minister, who would like for the group to have more members, do more projects.

5. The janitor, who suspects that the youth are getting into his closet to smoke. He hopes each week that the group will not mess up the polished Fellowship Hall floor.

6. The children's leader, who lives for the day when the youth next door will be quiet, setting a good example for the younger persons in the church.

7. A youth, who would like to be a youth group officer and have some good programs for a change.

8. An adult leader, who hopes the group will simply make it through the evening with everyone enjoying it.

The list could go on and on. The point is that no one program could fulfill the unreal list of expectations that float around in the minds of the persons near the youth program.

From time to time, it might be useful to ask persons to express their expectations for the group. These could be handed in on paper (unsigned) and transferred to newsprint so that everyone could see the possible and impossible expectations. The wilder the hopes, the more the group might be stretched to think in untried ways to see if some rewarding hopes might be reached.

The survey might be expanded to include recorded interviews with the expectations of persons not normally considered: the neighbors of the church building, youth who might consider attending, the music staff, newcomers to town. A spectrum of expectations might offer much to the planning meeting as plans for the year are considered.

See also EVALUATION, RISKING, SUCCESS

Failure

When you risk for others you will sometimes fail. But failure opens fresh opportunities for success.

The youth ministry "expert" was invited to the seminary for a special one-day meeting. The professor who had extended the invitation was very firm on what he wanted. "Present your theory of youth ministry. There will be seminarians and youth from their youth groups." The guest suggested that they do something more energetic. "Why don't we send the youth into the streets with audio cassettes and have them do interviews? This will give them a sense of the city and will equip them." The teacher was shaking his head. "We have done all that stuff. We want solid input and reports from the seminarians."

With much misgiving from the guest, the day unfolded as designed by the Christian education professor. It was terrible. The speaker accepted the crushing focus of failure. Two weeks later, the guest received a letter from the professor with the judgment that the guest had failed. "Everyone in the class agreed that you were terrible. They had never seen anyone be received with less enthusiasm. You were just plain bad."

The guest wrote a letter of reply. "Dear George: Thanks for your feedback. You and your students were right about how bad the day was. I was very bad. I did not do that which the young people deserved and needed. However, I do hope that you and your students went one step further in your evaluation. You all agree that I failed. The important point is that we are all bad sometimes! Nobody is good every time. I hope they remember how bad I was when they have a significant failure. Perhaps they can then smile and be encouraged to go on to the next time."

Sometimes you simply don't know if you have failed or not. You may have one goal in mind and something very different takes place. Often the real accomplishments of our work cannot be known by either party until much later.

Emily was teaching an experiential course. The high school students were discussing the tension in their lives. She took a box of corn flakes and shook out a few into the hand of each student. They were asked to look at the flakes for a few moments. "How does that handful of corn flakes represent something about your life?" One student threw the flakes on the floor. He got up and stood at the window for a few minutes. Then he left before the class had finished. Emily stopped another teacher after the class. She was very upset. "I did something terrible. It was a mess!" The friend listened and asked a few questions. "What did the fellow who left do in other classes? Why do you think he acted this way? I think that you were able to touch something deep within him. Be patient and see what happens."

A couple weeks later the boy who reacted so stongly spent the hour telling the class how his whole life jumped out before him. He talked about the drugs he had used and the way he had thrown away so much of his life. The corn flakes and Emily's invitation had broken down the wall surrounding him.

There is a certain spirit which must guide you in your creative ministry. When you risk for others, you will sometimes fail. However, your folks will come to support you at the very moment things fall apart. An older man stopped at the church door on his way out of the service. He put his hand on the young minister's shoulder. "I didn't get anything out of what you did this morning. However, keep at it!" Your teens will sustain you when they know that you face the possibility of failure for them and the gospel.

The most important response to an obvious failure is faithfulness. You have to hang in there and continue the good fight. Perhaps you are giving the teens the most important gift you have in your willingness to shake off the mistakes and face the future. They do not see many adults who can admit failure and move on with strength.

It helps to note the places where the failure took over. Why did you fail? This query will help you avoid the same mistake in the future. How can you recycle failure into something positive? It is hard to answer those questions. Some people cope well with failure while others are destroyed by the collapse of a task. It is up to you to determine what the role of failure will play in your life. The "failure" of Jesus became the victory for all of us.

What about youth failure? When do you let youth fail? There are times when you as an adult leader will foresee potential failure that you could prevent, but you are not sure if you should intervene. It is not an easy situation, since people learn by mistakes (when the mistakes are not devastating). While each situation must be judged on its potential harm and helpfulness, a rule of thumb is whether the long-range good is better served by your intrusion or by letting the teen fail. Sometimes an adult will foresee disaster and be wrong, either by incorrectly perceiving the danger or the ability of the youth to make last-minute corrections.

There is no way for the leader to correctly analyze every situation for the ultimate good of each person, and there must be a constant exercise of determining small, inconsequential errors or misjudgments and large, devastating disasters that should be avoided at all costs. We cannot know the future, but we can know and seek the counsel and direction of the God who does. His guidance can help us to better perceive the persons and the actions involved.

Resources
1. **Man's Search for Himself**, by Rollo May.
2. **Man's Search for Meaning**, by Victor Frankl.

See also DESPAIR, FAILURE, SUCCESS

Faith

One of the primary functions of every youth activity in the church is to enhance the development of personal and corporate faith. It is the pivotal link with God's action throughout history, the sovereignty of God throughout the world today, and the culmination of God's plan for the future.

Faith is to claim our rightful place within that history, present and future, both as individuals and as a group. God's call is both to individuals and to groups of persons whose response is undergirded by strength and direction.

Nothing you do as a leader and as a member of your church's youth ministry is more significant than enabling all the individuals in the group to realize the astounding fact that the One who created all of the universe is concerned about each person and has life-fulfilling opportunities awaiting their affirmative response.

Equally significant, one of your primary functions is to help the group realize its profound importance as a part of the body of Christ, able to minister and serve.

An enormous misconception of youth ministry is to consider youth as the church of tomorrow. Youth are a vital part of the church of *today*. The youth group is the church at work. Whatever group God chooses to work through is obviously very special, and the youth group can repeatedly be that vital access to God for many persons.

Another fallacy is to consider the youth group as separate from any other part of the church. It is not a body unto itself. It derives life from the rest of the church body and it pumps dynamic life back into that body.

It has been suggested that *faith* is both a noun and a verb. We receive faith as we use it, live it in daily mundane or critical ways. We show faith in our existence as we rely upon God's power working through us, looking back to the unbelievable ways he has entered our lives in the past and looking toward even greater fulfillment of unfolding dreams in the future.

Take some time and talk with your group about your faith. Talk about where you have been, how you got here. Talk about the joy with which you live each day. Talk about your faith in an unlimited exciting future within God's will.

See also RISKING, THEOLOGY OF YOUTH MINISTRY

Faith Development

Following the discovery of Swiss psychologist Jean Piaget that persons pass through certain recognizable and predictable stages of mental development, and the discovery of Harvard University's Lawrence Kohlberg that there are similar predictable stages of moral development, James Fowler and others recognized that these stages correspond in amazing similarity to faith development stages. While a person may be at one stage in his or her mental development and another in faith development, the individual proceeds through these stages in order and never skips one. It is also possible for people to stop at any one stage and never progress even though decades of their life may pass.

Youth leaders will benefit from exploring these studies further since many of the critical changes occur during the youth years. Activities we plan for youth groups can be extremely significant in helping youth to expand their developmental horizons. Some of the influential factors in faith development appear to be: understanding and acknowledging the beliefs of persons quite unlike themselves, learning to give themselves to causes where there does not seem to be personal reward, and learning that they have worth.

Resources

1. **Developmental Journey**, by Mary Wilcox, Abingdon.
2. **Moral Development: A Guide to Piaget and Kohlberg**, by Ronald Duska and Mariellen Whelan.
3. **Life Maps: Conversations on the Journey of Faith**, by Jim Fowler and Sam Keen, Word Books.
4. **Moral Stages and the Development of Faith**, by Jim Fowler, Religious Education Press.

See also AGE LEVEL CHARACTERISTICS, FAITH, VALUES CLARIFICATION

Fall Celebrations

Celebrations are a major part of the lives of God's people. The secular society (if we make such a separation) has found various religious celebrations very helpful for sales. Yet, we often have difficulty enjoying that which is ours. Youth ministry is an important place for people to appreciate this special dimension. Young people can be the means for others to meaningfully experience these celebrations.

Thanksgiving grows out of the American experience of being fed during times of difficulty. One group in Texas provided an exciting celebration during their church's morning worship service. As people entered the church for worship, they gave each person a stainless steel spoon. The teens retained the regular liturgical format. However, at the prayer confession they asked everyone to look into the spoon. The image of each person is upside down! Worshippers were asked to reflect how their lives were turned over by sin. After this confession, they gave the words of assurance from scripture and asked them to look at themselves in the other side of the spoon. The image was restored!

For the prayer of intercession (for others), they asked everyone to put the cold, empty spoon in his or her mouth while slides of hungry people were shown.

The teens had wanted to serve communion on the spoons, but they weren't able to get the adults in charge of worship to go along with it. Their idea was that the people would experience the message of worship once again when they sat down to eat and handled a spoon.

Ed McNulty, a minister and Christian media specialist, has created one of the most exciting models for a fall celebration. Using the inspiration of Harvey Cox's book, **Feast of Fools**, and many other sparks, he conducts his famous "Feast of Fools" event on Halloween night. Drawing upon the middle ages and the biblical sense of being a fool for Christ, he encourages everyone in the congregation to come in costume for this celebration.

This is an evening in which the king becomes a servant and the slave is transformed into royalty. Simple food is served (drumsticks and baked potatoes).

There are several centers developed to enable people (young and old) to make things to be used in the concluding worship service. For instance, one group developed a huge cross out of boxes and pictures from magazines. During the worship experience, Ed presented a 15-minute sound and slide experience. The young people read the script while the pictures and music were shared. The show depicted the history of other fools for Christ (Martin Luther, the Apostle Paul, John Wesley, Martin Luther King). The script was written as a dialogue between characters from a popular TV show.

Ed has found that creating this kind of event is a perfect component of the church's confirmation class. Class members can participate in this sort of creation as a way to experience the community of faith by using their gifts and being open to new forms.

See also CHRISTMAS, EASTER, NEW YEAR'S EVE

Family

This word is shop worn. Crazies who grouped in drug-laced, sex-oriented packs often called themselves "families" in the late '60s. Cults and religious fringe sects also drew upon a sense of belonging to give their movements a family label.

On the other side of the coin, religious traditions have been frightened by the breakdown of the nuclear family unit. They seem to be saying that the only kind of acceptable living configuration is the "ideal family:" a home-based mother, a working father and a nice batch of homebred children. This is a fine composition. However, it is no longer the common pattern in the United States. Only 15 percent of the households in America now are patterned like the nuclear family. Whether this is good or bad is not really the point. You just can't be caught like many clergypersons

who carry on from the pulpit with the assumption that the folks they preach to are living in one of these model families. This is not the way things are.

The young people in your group are now living in different kinds of family structures from those to which you are probably accustomed. How does this reality alter or influence your shape of youth ministry? You probably have several young people from divorced homes. Others in your group have mothers and fathers who both work. A few will be living with a stepparent and siblings from another family. A couple of your youth may be from single parent homes. Some youth may be adopted.

This change in family structure offers youth ministry a fantastic opportunity for theological probing of what the faith offers. We are the kin of God through the life, death and resurrection of Jesus Christ. This spiritual family gathers around the Word and sacraments as a family.

Where are the attributes of our life together in this youth ministry kinship? Families love, forgive, encourage, fight, heal and endure. Your youth ministry could be built around these themes too.

One of the hopeful probes concerning the new shape of the family in society is that of the extended family. The concept is built around the traditional quality of life together: care, understanding, commitment, forgiveness and support. This model for the family draws upon spirit rather than blood to keep its body alive. The husband and wife may not be limited to caring for their own children. They may also welcome a retired person from the community as a member of the family. Remember the rash of newspaper items from families advertising in the want ads for "an adopted grandparent"? People from these families were seeking the older person because of the geographical distance that separated them from blood-related older people. Such extended families may also invite single young adults into their circle. Young children love the young adult brother or sister figure. The single person also needs the covenant family relationship.

One church developed an adopted grandparent program. Once a year the children in the church would make different things in church school. They would place these items in the front of the worship center. During worship older adults would go to the front and pick out an item. Then the child would come forward and claim the adult. They would make a covenant for the next year. As a result of one covenant, one man picked up the young person every Saturday. They worked together in his woodworking shop.

Maggie Kuhn, one of the founders of the Gray Panthers, reports that one of the organizations in her community has enabled a special program for creating covenant families. They found that many older people would lose a spouse and then have to sell their homes. They also learned that many graduate students in their city could not find good housing. By matching a couple of young people with an older person, they could create a small family which lived and ate together. There were over 80 of these families in the Philadelphia area.

Family situations are important to the youth advisor because he or she will only have a limited time with each young person. The family life of your youth has a direct bearing on the theological life you create and explore with your folk.

Resources
1. **Understanding Families With Young Adolescents**, by Lawrence Steinberg, Center for Early Adolescence.

See also NUCLEAR FAMILY, PARENTS, SINGLE PARENT FAMILY

Feedback

All of us have heard the ear-piercing sound that comes from public address system speakers when the volume level for a microphone is turned up so loud that the microphone picks up its own sound. That instant cycle is called feedback because the microphone hears itself. The term has been transformed by group process lingo to describe the need individuals and groups have for hearing an honest reaction of what they have been saying or doing.

This is particularly true for youth ministry. Regular feedback is necessary for youth leaders to find out how things are going, if there is general agreement with the direction the group is progressing. The youth council may feel that it is planning well for the life of the group, but a simple process of feedback may reveal the discontent of several members.

It is important for those in charge to know how to use the feedback once it is obtained. The worst response is the normal one—to take the feedback personally and let feelings get in the way of hearing the message as a genuine suggestion for improvement. Neither is it good to take the feedback as a literal pronouncement of the final word since the feedback itself may be a temporary, fickle emotional comment. Preferably, the feedback should be taken as a reading of that moment, and should be compared with other such readings. The leadership should listen for what is fed back in order to make appropriate changes in its youth ministry.

Resources
1. **Developing the Art of Discussion**, by John Bushman, Judson Press.

See also COMMUNICATION, EVALUATION

Festivals

These special events usually take place out-of-doors and are generally less structured than a youth conference, but more organized than a concert. A festival is a model for gathering large numbers of young people in a spirit of celebration.

The idea of this Christian festival-celebration came to a group of ministers from a cluster of United Presbyterian churches as they struggled with the problem of developing a relevant and meaningful gathering for high school young people.

The genesis of the Christian folk-rock festival titled "Dawn: The Beginning of a Personal Odyssey" came from this conversation. "Odyssey" in this instance referred to the journey every Christian takes with Christ.

Young people and adults from 30 churches planned and brought the festival to life. The time was a beautiful Sunday afternoon from 1 to 7 p.m. The site was the county fairgrounds. Five thousand young people from a nine-county area took part.

The program included an endless stream of musicians who either played on a central stage or did intimate "sets" in nearby smaller buildings. The festival's success rested largely on the caliber of the talent. The musicians were relevant, committed and skilled.

This rock festival and celebration, as might be expected, came under some fire from city and county officials as plans developed and were made known. Several park permits for previous rock festivals planned by local radio stations had been cancelled at the last minute. But when park officials reviewed the plans for "Dawn," they permitted the festival to continue. However, tickets (at one dollar) had to be sold in advance at

Many youth point to festivals as turning points in their lives.

A group of high school students interested in introducing this kind of worship into their church extended the team's workshop.

One musician, after completing his stage performance, let a crowd of 75 experience a mix of secular and sacred sounds and sights. He flashed slides on the side of the barn wall and sang.

Five hundred high school students in the agriculture building expressed their approval with applause, shouts and the stomping of feet, as a Christian rock band played their heavy rock and sang, "Give Christ a Chance." Mime Dan let his body express man's quest for understanding, while later his lips articulated his concern for peace as he talked with 25 students.

As the tired festival director stood beside the stage, a couple of barefooted, barebacked students moved up beside him. Their faces and backs were burned from the afternoon sun. "Hey, thanks for the day. It was really something else." The director smiled and the students moved on.

During the special folk celebration which concluded the festival, a county policeman said quietly as he watched the mass of people worshipping: "I guess we were too worried about this event." He looked over the cars, vans and mounted police. "We have had no trouble at all. It was a very good day."

churches in the area. This meant that people apart from church groups were not encouraged to drop in. And the advertising had to bear the religious emphasis of the event, which discouraged the general public from coming. This narrowed the original idea of a broader outreach for the festival.

The day of "Dawn" was bright and clear, even so. The 100 "marshalls," who had been prepared ahead of time at a series of training events, provided support for the entertainers or mixed to give the event cohesiveness.

The starting time of 1 p.m. was close to church dismissals and made a lot of the people late. But the crowd kept growing, since the design for the festival made it easy to enter into the happening whenever people came.

One crowd gathered before the stage to catch sounds from the center stage. Others wandered from barn to barn to take in the rap sessions and mini-concerts. Some of these sessions broke into instant workshops. A team from Chicago, for example, talked about their experimentation with music and liturgy.

Resources
1. **Banners, Banners, Banners**, by Robert Anderson, Christian Art Associates.
2. **The Banner Book**, by Betty Wolfe, Morehouse-Barlow.
3. **Catch the New Wind**, edited by Marilee Zdenek, Word Books.
4. **Feast of Fools**, by Harvey Cox, Harper and Row.

See also DANCING, FALL CELEBRATIONS, NOVELTY DANCES

Finances

Make youth group finance an integral part of the planning process.

Every youth leader needs to know the group's financial arrangements. What is this year's youth budget? Are there traditional budget items? (Church school curriculum, food for fellowship meals, retreat promotion, etc.) Are there other sources of funding? (Contributions, grants from committees for certain items.)

Some churches encourage fund raising projects; other prohibit them. The leader should determine his or her church's stance on fund raising.

It is important to account to the church for what was spent. Rarely is this requested, but it is very helpful for interpreting what happens in the youth program. The church should also know what it has the privilege of supporting. Rarely do churches request that permission be granted for larger expenditures, but the support of an administrative body can be most helpful in case there is ever any question.

Leaders sometimes decide to support the program with their own money. Almost without exception, this is unwise. Despite the assertion to the contrary, the leader often begins to feel exploited. The leader may develop resentment toward "less giving" sponsors. The youth hesitate to suggest items or programs that cost much because of the complexity that personal financing creates. Persons begin to see this program as the sole ownership of one sponsor. The church has no idea of the cost of the program and may not be able to maintain it if the person resigns (which often happens when so much emphasis is placed on one person or family). Worst of all, the congregation is denied the opportunity of participating in one of its most significant ministries.

A budget can be most helpful for letting everyone see the sources of funds, the expenditures and the fact that accurate accounting did take place. The budget should be a servant of the group, not vice versa. When changes are called for, the group should be made aware of the fact and take necessary steps to change the budget.

A sample budget might be as follows:

INCOME
Contribution from the church
Membership contributions
Projects (itemized)
Donations for refreshments
Donations for personal remembrances
Miscellaneous

EXPENDITURES
Resource materials
Audio-visuals
Travel
Refreshments
Council retreat
Resource persons
Recreation equipment
Personal remembrances
Parties
Room decorations (pictures, painting, etc.)
Newsletter
Project development
Special equipment (materials for clowning, media, drama, etc.)
Miscellaneous

See also FUND RAISING

Friends

Those who study the growth patterns of churches find that most people come to a new congregation because they have been invited by friends. Martin Marty, professor of church history at the University of Chicago, reminds us that the strongest gift of the historical Christian churches for outreach is that of being invitational. People are called into community as they become our kin and friends.

This is the body created by the love of Jesus. We are beckoned to be friends. This assumption is also shared by those who have studied the growth of youth groups. New folks come along because they have been invited by friends. Acceptance by others is important to our survival in a hostile and alien culture.

Accepting this friendship thrust on a superficial level can be dangerous. Social acceptance has a dark side that exerts great pressure. This dynamic explains why some youth smoke and use drugs. At least, it can be seen as one aspect of peer pressure. Christian friendship has a set of qualities which surpasses the friendliness of society. Our understanding of friendship has a strong inclusive quality. The youth group is a place where the loner, the racial outcast, the troublemaker, the child of divorce, the jock and the cream puff (school high achiever) belong.

There is a sense of covenant relationship in our friendship context. We are modeled after the friendship model seen between God and his people. If there is a breach of friendship's responsibility, the results are predictable.

Christian friendship is much more durable than the world's version of friends. Dating couples can break up, neighbors can move away and interests can change without the relationship being destroyed.

All of these ideals do not just manifest themselves without nurture. A consistent aspect of all youth ministry is the continuous exploration of the meaning of Christian friendship. The moments of strain on friendship must be taken seriously. There is time to gather around a misunderstanding or a lover's quarrel. In the rehearsal of these momentary problems we are probing the basic

The youth years are all-important for learning how to make friends and be a friend.

quality of our life together as Christian sisters and brothers.

As the first four calls unfolded on the talk radio show, it was clear that friendships would be the topic of the night. The host patiently listened as the young girls poured out their pain at losing their boyfriends. "He won't speak to me anymore. What can I do?" Each person was treated seriously. These moments of coping would establish life patterns of befriending others. The fifth call was quite different. The voice of an older woman was shaky. "My problem is much different from those who called earlier. I figured that if you listened to them, you would listen to mine. My husband was drinking. He accidentally killed my baby . . . He buried it himself. The police caught him. He is now in jail. I don't hear from him any more. I had a nervous breakdown. They took my children away from me. I love my husband and my children. What am I going to do? . . . I am so lonely and lost." Befriending is an endless process which encompasses our experience with Christ. How we receive and give friend-

ship never ends.

Don asked the youth group members to spread out around the floor. He turned the lights down. The group listened to the Carole King song, "You Got a Friend." He then read selections from John 14 and 15 ("I have called you friends") and played the song once again. The teens were asked to imagine a friend's face. "Look into his or her eyes. Do you see a worry or problem? Is there something the person needs?" After a guided fantasy, the youth shared their feelings about friends. It was a moving experience. Then they focused on the kind of friendship members of the group had with each other.

Friendship is very complex and demanding. The youth group is the best place in the world to explore it.

Resources
1. **My Brother Dennis**, by Dennis Benson, P.O. Box 12811, Pittsburgh, PA 15421.

See also HOSPITALITY, NEWCOMER, OUTREACH

Fund Raising

"If we only had some money!"

Many youth cabinets have spent hours worrying about this topic. Churches have been slow to give youth groups any budget. They have generally encouraged their young people to raise their own money.

Some churches have turned to the community for support. By running special events (lawn sales, candy sales and dinners), they have traded their time and energy for the money. Another pattern draws almost exclusively on the giving of the members themselves.

Some youth do not have the option of giving money. They are best positioned to trade their time and labor for the financial gifts of others. This opportunity is filled with all kinds of dangers. It is amazing to see what some groups do to raise money. They will sell things which are not needed and questionable. Their activity will be totally out of keeping with the nature of their fellowship. It is also quite easy for youth to be set up as agents of pity. They offer a service or product which has no merit. The appeal is their cause. The adults outside the church will be asked to buy or give because the youth is an appealing or sincere person.

It is unwise to get your youth into this kind of bind. There are some questions which you must answer as you face the possibility of raising funds for a particular reason. What does the cause say about the fact that you are Christians? Who will benefit from the money? Is it totally self-serving or caring for the needs of others? Does the cause combine both concerns?

What does the product or service being sold say about your nature as a faith community? Does the product promote bad health? (Sugar, fat or other ingredients of questionable value). Is it an item which seems to support a wasteful view of contemporary lifestyle as opposed to a simpler lifestyle?

A youth group in Ohio developed an exciting project to raise funds for a

A truly effective fund raiser is creative, realistic and accomplishes personal or community-wide good.

summer trip to the shore of Virginia. They had worked for several months organizing the participants into troupes of performers. They had a clown unit, a juggling unit, a musical group and a recreational activities cluster. They would provide a beach ministry when they arrived on the coast. They were preparing to minister once they were there.

In order to raise the needed funds, they developed an interesting service/ product. They obtained a number of free metal drums which they converted into compost units. They researched the process of building a compost pile, mimeographed a set of instructions, and offered to deliver this unit to folks in the community. This offering provided the money they needed and strengthened the recycling of garbage, which helped the environment.

There is a real sense in which youth fund raising can be placed within the context of the whole church's ministry and stewardship. How do we urge youth to give of themselves as individuals and at the same time encourage them to work within the whole community of faith?

Resources
1. **Fund Raising Projects with a World Hunger Emphasis**, by Paul Longacre, Herald Press.
2. **Try This One**, Volumes 1 and 2, edited by Thom Schultz, Group Books.

See also FINANCES, GOAL SETTING, PRIORITIES

Goal Setting

One of the most effective planning methods is built on the concept of reaching goals that have been developed and agreed upon by the group. Agreement signifies implied participation.

During the goal setting process, members may have named numerous goals they would like to see the group achieve, then narrowed the number down to two or three goals that are realistic for the set time period. As these priority goals are established, they are described in realistic terms.

It is imperative that the process also deal with methods for reaching the goals. These intermediate stages of arriving at the goal are called objectives, and they can be seen as the journey of the group as it marches toward success. The parts of the objectives are called steps.

Examples of realistic goals:

GOAL 1: By June, our group will have grown to 35 regularly attending members.

Objective 1: We will establish a membership committee.

•Step 1: The group will nominate persons on October 15 at the retreat.

•Step 2: This team will be trained by the Smiths, our advisors.

Objective 2: A party will be held during December to honor new members.

GOAL 2: By December 31, we will have collected $500 toward world hunger.

Objective 1: Each member will learn about the hunger problem through a special newsletter, announcements and a sermon during congregational worship.

Objective 2: Each person will be urged to pledge to this cause during November.

Such planning is usually encouraging to youth, who often desire to see rapid results. As the short-range parts of the goal are achieved, the momentum is energizing.

Writing out goals and agreeing to

them builds confidence in the group and usually encourages teamwork. Individual concerns can be dealt with as the wording is perfected.

Goals help to identify what the group is and what it stands for. As goals differ from year to year, the membership realizes that its own character determines purpose, effectiveness and results that affect many other persons.

Resources
1. **Goal Setting; A Guide to Achieving the Church's Mission,** by Dale McConkey, Augsburg.

See also BALANCE, PLANNING COUNCIL, YOUTH COUNCIL

Goodbye

There are times when you as youth advisor or someone else important to the youth leaves. Parting is always hard. We have talked about the grief of death in another entry. Yet, saying goodbye is also a special occasion for Christians. Be sure to take time for the celebration of this passage rite.

The folks who are left behind experience a mixture of feelings. Some teens have never had to experience this kind of separation from someone they valued greatly. If they hold the feelings inside, they may experience waves of rejection, anger and despair. They may feel that you are rejecting them. It doesn't make any difference whether this feeling is based on fact or not.

One of the powerful aspects of the Christian faith is that it compels believers to confront the painful passage points of life. This is possible because such a recital is the care and love of God known through the community of faith. What does the departure through a move or death mean in terms of this community? It is a time when we can

both acknowledge our pain of loss and our hope of eternal communion as members of the body of Christ. Both sides of this coin can be appreciated and celebrated.

One youth advisor left his work after three years. He was finishing college and wished to attend graduate school in another state. The 75 youth decided to celebrate his departure with a worship service designed and conducted by them. It was an amazing moment. Teens who had never taken part in a service were leading the congregation through a very moving and deeply religious celebration. There was a flood of tears. The tough guys in black leather jackets could cry because the youth advisor was doing the same. The advisor then gave each person a small cross. He took time and faced each person. A short charge was given to each one and then they hugged.

After a few weeks teens drove over to the university and visited their former advisor. Letters went back and forth. The air of grief had been cleared and the situation was set for the next youth advisor.

Group

This word appears with great regularity in this book. It is probably one of the best ways of describing the collection of teenagers which meet in church basements, living rooms and Sunday school rooms each week. Its members are gathered for a lot of different needs. They come with many different gifts— most of them not recognized or appreciated by the teens themselves. In some settings, they form a group from many different school systems.

In all of these configurations, they only become a group through their experience as part of the community of Christ. You should help them to recognize this fact. The Christian youth group is not just another social organization. It is called into this relationship in order to have fellowship, study, serve and worship. This means the youth will be challenged as a group to do ministry as well as receive ministry.

Resources
1. **40 Ways to Teach in Groups**, by Martha Leypoldt, Judson Press.

See also BODY, COMMUNITY, GROUP BUILDING, ICE BREAKERS, LARGE GROUP VS. SMALL GROUP

Group Building

Individuals do not automatically become a cohesive group just by gathering in the same room. And once a group, they do not stay that way without constant attention to the intra-group dynamics that take place.

Throughout the youth group schedule a number of support aids should be planned to help the teens to realize some of the potential they have for becoming a group. It is good to include assurances that they are indeed functioning as a group as well as recognition of what they accomplish as a group.

Here's a brief outline for initiating group building exercises with people who do not know each other:

Opening—

The individuals should be introduced to each other. This is usually easier if the introduction process lets individuals first meet individuals, then small groups of persons, and finally the full group in some experiential way (singing, humor, recreation, a meal). Name tags are a must (the more intriguing and colorful, the better). Exhibits and displays help people to bump into each other (touch is helpful). Registration is good for giving everyone the same frustration experience.

Maintenance—

Keep tabs on how people are feeling. A second introduction period is necessary. Referring occasionally to schedules points out what has passed (group history) and reaffirms expectations. Announcements reassure participants. Regular large group recognition is helpful.

The final event should bring together the best of whatever happened throughout the event. It is best when everyone's contributions can be included. The group's progress should be highlighted. Refer to the next such event, and include everyone (proof positive they were good participants in this event).

Resources
1. **Encyclopedia of Serendipity**, Serendipity House, Box 1012, Littleton, CO 80160.
2. **GROUP Magazine**, Box 481, Loveland, CO 80537.

See also COMMUNITY, GROUP MAGAZINE, HOSPITALITY, SERENDIPITY

GROUP Magazine

In a day when many producers of materials for leaders of youth are cutting back or suspending publication, this magazine, and its related projects are experiencing growth. The magazine meets the needs of quite a diversity of persons and denominations because of its well-written articles on crucial subjects.

GROUP comes in two different subscriptions: one for youth and one for leaders of youth.

The magazine sponsors a number of national gatherings, including the annual National Christian Youth Congress, which attracts over 2,000 youth and their adult leaders, a mid-winter skiing conference which always fills to capacity, and various summer workcamps around the country.

A number of useful books and booklets are also produced in conjunction with the magazine. Drop them a line at Box 481, Loveland, CO 80537.

Group Media

Don Roper and others who work in the context of Third World people of faith have championed this fresh concept. The term *group* suggests a small collection of folks who are intentionally together for the purpose of sharing and growing. *Media* are simply the means by which something is communicated to us or we communicate to others. People have assumed that the word *media* refers only to electric means of communication. But our bodies, our voices, our art forms are all media.

By latching these terms together, we put the control of communication in the group members' hands. This emphasis means a great deal to the person living in a society which does not have resources for expensive audio-visual materials. It also permits the person in another culture to use media resources from a different value system. This sense of control and responsibility is a gift to the industrialized nations also.

The group media concept suggests that the youth group is the context for creating new media forms. The students are participants in the development of vital communication forms from their lives. This shift in outlook has vast implications for youth ministry. You are called to enable your folk to create valid communication means. This may mean that only a part of a film is used. Young people in your group may add the gifts of music, mime or cooking to the program.

This concept is more radical than you might imagine. Almost all of the use of media in the church and secular community is based on consuming the message and form of the media producer. This means that the pastor's sermon, the filmmaker's movie, the poet's sonnet or the public prayer is designed to be swallowed as prepared. Group media assumes, on the other hand, that the participant will reshape everything utilized in the group. It also is based on the premise that the leader will nurture the contribution of the group members.

This has not always been the case. For instance, youth advisors often use films in their youth group programming. Their goal seems to be that of selling a specific pre-determined message to the group. However, group media calls for an experience which believes that the Holy Spirit guides people as they work on the meaning of truth for a given moment.

Timothy was faced with a difficult situation. He is a fraternal worker in Ghana. At first, his students presented him with a situation in which there was no paper or other formal teaching/learning resources. Other teachers in the school assumed they could do little because they didn't have curriculum material. He decided to use the material they had on hand to enable them to learn and communicate. Using leaves and sand, he urged his students to create a miniature biblical village. They used their own materials for communication. How do you find new teaching/communication uses for existing resources?

Such an exploration into the world of media in this way will change the attitude of young people as they encounter the secular media world. You will have given them the power of transformation. Their faith can now change everything they confront in the mass media wasteland.

Resources
1. **Gadgets, Gimmicks and Grace: A Handbook on Multimedia in Church and School**, by Ed McNulty, Abbey Press.

See also MULTI-MEDIA, RECYCLE THE-OLOGY

Handicapped Folks

For some years, the government has been using legal pressure to provide public facilities for handicapped persons. As a result, fast food and entertainment establishments are more sensitive to handicapped folks than institutions like the church. Most of the places where people worship are inaccessible to people who have trouble being mobile. Where do you put a wheelchair in most sanctuaries without setting the person in the aisle or apart from the congregation? However, buildings don't blockade the handicapped; it is the attitude of believers which handicap physically and mentally limited folks.

For instance, Bonnie is an exceptional person. She has two masters degrees and provides an important ministry with children. She works from a wheelchair—polio attacked her years ago. Her biggest handicap has been people

who have told her that she couldn't live a meaningful and faithful life. Unfortunately, she has found that Christians, young and old, are some of the hardest folks to face. They either want to explain the pain and suffering of her life with the assurance that God wants this or they have pity for her.

The handicapped person does not need cheap theological shots or the dehumanizing aspect of charity and pity. The person of faith is drawn into the life of another because he or she needs what that person also has to give. Christianity is a ministry of mutuality. If you can't determine how your youth are ministering to you, then you'd better evaluate yourself carefully. If you feel that you alone are saving all those "poor kids," you are using them in the worst way.

It isn't surprising that people don't want to accept those kinds of hand-me-downs. Paul and Ananias teach us how Christians are sinners in need of the other (Acts 9:10-19).

Sam had been fighting back. He was quarterback on the football team when a hunting accident paralyzed him from the waist down. His best friend had shot him. The youth group had to adjust to all kinds of stress. Sam was part of the group. Sometimes he wanted help; other times he rejected it. How could the group help and not condescend?

Youth can be very cruel to those who are strange or different. Just recall how people at school have talked about those "weird" classmates. They are exhibiting a trait the late John Lennon called "crippled inside." It is fear, inexperience and insecurity which breeds ridicule of the handicapped. Yet, the person of faith is faced with the awing judgment that the Messiah is the one who is "uncomely, bruised, twisted and not beautiful to look upon." Perhaps the means of understanding our salvation rests with those so rejected.

You should intentionally bring the handicapped into your sphere of ministry. They can't find you. You and your youth must find them and help them be part of the community. When your group is invited to visit a home for handicapped folks, brainstorm with your group ways that the two groups can interact with each other. What are you really offering and what are you ready to receive?

There are many youth who have been judged "crippled inside" by society. They may reside within your community in group homes. These "halfway" houses provide homes for youth who suffer from a variety of problems. How can your youth include them in your circle? What fears arise in youth and adults with such a consideration?

Resources
1. **Help for the Handicapped Child**, by Florence Weiner, McGraw Hill.
2. **Creating the Caring Congregation: Guidelines for Ministering with the Handicapped**, by Harold Wilke, Abingdon.
3. **Ethical Issues in Mental Retardation**, by David and Victoria Allen.
4. **New Life in the Neighborhood: How Persons with Retardation and Other Disabilities Can Help Make a Good Community Better**, by Robert and Martha Perske, Abingdon.

Heroes

Some people claim that we are living in a time of anti-heroes. These media personages seem to embody all the negative attributes of the culture. They are heroic losers. However, many young people do look favorably upon achievers. These media projects are disposable and not really models upon which one bases his or her life. The attributes of the media-enhanced persons are the

While teenagers generally are not interested in traditional hero models, they are interested in various contemporary hero figures.

attraction. How does a young person make a connection between the distant hero and himself or herself? Sometimes religious reactors don't help in this process.

In his classic article, Markus Barth suggests that Sunday schools tend to reduce the biblical message to "westerns" (The Cowboy in Sunday School," Religious Education, March-April 1962). The good and bad people of scripture are sorted out for the young. The heroes wear white hats and the bad guys wear black. This, of course, misses the point of biblical theology that the good and bad are intermixed. David is both a hero and a heel. It is this duality which makes God's forgiveness so much more amazing and applicable to a younger or an older person. Mister Rogers captures the essence of this biblical theme in his song "Sometimes People Are Good, Sometimes People Are Bad."

The Bible is caught in an uneasy relationship to the task of youth ministry. There are so many dangers in the selection and use of biblical material. What do certain stories say to certain age groups even when they are presented in a creative way? Professor Dale Goldsmith critically strikes out at the misuse of biblical material when he accuses Sunday schools of teaching religious "literature." He contends that the tendency to stress certain Old Testament passages with children and youth results in the retention of "the most bizarre and theologically irrelevant stories." Such exercises in the religious literature approach reveal that youth advisors are trying "to develop good people rather than demand theological decision."

On the other hand, there are some fine opportunities to build on this interest in heroes so the average teen can develop his or her own personhood. Some folks in Michigan created a week-long course which focused on heroes. The high school youth taught the course for fourth and fifth grade students. The first week featured cardboard cutouts of Superman and Wonder Woman. They asked the students to come up with characteristics of these heroes, which were listed on the non-printed side of the cardboard figures. The students were given individual biblical passages which described characteristics of Jesus. These were listed and differences between the two lists were discussed. The children discovered that Jesus could do things which the super heroes couldn't do. He could heal and love. He could also give up his life for others.

The next week the teens invited an older person in the church to share stories of her life. She had faced depression, death, war and cancer while keeping her faith. The youngsters were asked to think for the next week about how they are superheroes as Christians.

The following week they made scrapbooks about the super-qualities they had as Christians, which were shared in worship. The minister had been preaching a series of sermons on the same theme.

Resources
1. **Celebrity: The Media As Image Maker**, by James Monaco.

Holy Spirit

There always seems to have been a swirl of confusion and controversy around believers' attempts to respond to the facet of theology known as the Holy Spirit. Christians have either been afraid of this doctrine or they have embraced it with such compulsion that all else about the faith has been excluded. This kind of polarity is, of course, ridiculous. It would be funny if there hadn't been such a painful history of Christian brothers and sisters attacking and judging each other over this issue.

The Holy Spirit is a hard concept for the young (and old) to understand. How do we explain the idea of Father, Son and Holy Spirit when we worship God? It is helpful, and simple, to explain this mystery by talking about the three attributes of one reality. In confirmation classes we have used the analogy of a person looking in a three-way mirror.

The real point of focus as you work with youth concerning the Holy Spirit is the context in which this theological truth is understood and experienced.

The biblical presentation of this approach of God to us is the community of faith. In the second chapter of Acts we find the family of Christ together in one place. They are very close through love. It is at this point that the Holy Spirit touches them and creates the church of Christ. It seems that the biblical occasion of the Holy Spirit's presence is the people of God. The purpose and reality of the Spirit is the community. This is no

elitist, individualistic gift. In fact, the source of the church, the whole church, is the Holy Spirit. This means that all of your young people can claim this great reality.

We are talking about something much more than an ecstatic thrill. There is certainly the emotional moment as part of the manifestation of the Holy Spirit for some people. However, we are talking about something much deeper and inclusive. The very heart of our faith and life is the Holy Spirit. It is the majesty and depth of the Spirit which enables us to take the leap of faith as we struggle to be faithful in a world of temptation and persecution.

Youth need to claim this rich reality without being forced to conform to another's experience. The young person who often feels that he or she lives in an alien environment can particularly appreciate that the Holy Spirit is a comforter and advocate. If this promise enables the young person to know that nothing can separate him or her from God's love, the awareness of the Holy Spirit assures the teenager (and adult) that he or she has roots and belongs to the family of the saints. When he or she prays, the whole church of Christ is present through the Holy Spirit.

See also JESUS, RECYLE THEOLOGY, THEOLOGY OF YOUTH MINISTRY

Hospitality

This intangible spirit is the key to authentic and successful youth programming.

Alfaretta, a lady in her late seventies, is a serious student of Greek New Testament. This active laywoman daily studies the biblical material in its original language. One of her great discoveries is the significance of a Greek phrase which means "be at or upon the same place." It appears when the church receives the visit of the Holy Spirit (Acts 2). As Alfaretta chases this term through the New Testament, she finds that it is the "togetherness" context which becomes the occasion for the Spirit. This is truly where hospitality exists.

The youth group seeks to be more than a setting for "friendly" people. It is the communal cradle in which the spirit of faith can be nurtured.

One youth group dealt with the problem of being a collection of strangers by intentionally choosing specific young people to be hosts. Once a month the group staged popular programs to draw youth from outside the group. At these gatherings, the hosts openly worked to provide a setting in which they could be "in one place." They invited individual youth to join them for a small group study at another time. The planning cluster leaders knew they could not accomplish close hospitality with a huge crowd. However, they could sow the seeds of acceptance for the next experience.

How do youth and adults who feel uncomfortable provide a context of hospitality? This may be the most important challenge facing your group. The New Testament suggests (Acts 2: 39-42) that the gathered folk studied, worshipped, broke bread and went out to serve. It is not the use of "ice breakers" that creates community. It is the warmth of intentional acceptance which melts the alienation of strangeness.

See also ATTENDANCE, BELONGING, EVANGELISM, FRIENDS, NEWCOMER

Hostility

Issues which try the spirit of many sensitive Christians are on the increase. Many things around us have changed for the worse. Yet it is hard to gather more than a handful of people around any given concern. At least, social causes do not seem to have many visible advocates. This leaves those who are the children of the social gospel without a context or community. The poor, old, disenfranchised, jobless and lost have fewer persons to bring these concerns to the attention of the country and the church.

The anger and frustration caused by these and many other conditions will appear in different ways. The rate of murders within families and senseless acts of terror are increasing. There will be a great deal of hostility as the economy and social changes threaten the freedom of many youth. The dream of a sports car and fine clothes appear to dim considerably in the latter part of this century. How will this frustration be expressed? On campus, young people move to a privatism. Students seek their individual sex, drugs and religion. As a veteran campus worker notes, I can understand teens raised during the Korean War. They spend their lives with trivial matters because they didn't know any better. I feel sorry for the current teens. They live in triviality and selfishness, but they really know that people are being tortured, starved and murdered. How can they live with this dishonesty?"

How can the frustration from an uncertain future and a confused present be given an outlet? Your youth ministry must focus in this area of hostility. This is hard work. Sometimes you will only be able to bring feelings into the open which will find no answers immediately.

Judy and John were unable to have children but wanted to be parents. There were no children available for adoption.

A social worker with whom they worked asked if they would consider being foster parents. They welcomed a 12-year-old boy into their home. He did

not speak and no one knew the source of the blockage in communication.

These two folk worked for nearly a year to bring Tommy into the world of communication. One day at dinner Tommy suddenly exploded in an outbreak of hostility. He threw dishes and attacked both Judy and John. They fought to restrain him.

He was taken from their home. The couple was crushed at the thought that their love had ended with the boy's breakdown. But at the next meeting with the social worker, they learned that just the opposite had happened. "You helped Tommy break through the wall around him. He let out some of the anger he was carrying from his earlier home life. Only your love freed him to work at it."

Being upset and concerned about the issues and problems encircling us can wall us into an enslaving cocoon or these feelings can give us the strength to work for improvement. One of the most significant ministries that the youth group can perform for its members is to provide the loving arena in which hostile feelings can be expressed. When it is possible, the entire group can be activated to be part of the solution.

Resources
1. **Caring Enough to Confront**, by David Augsburger, Regal Books.

See also CONFLICT, REBELLION, TOUCH

Humor

The pastor opened his sermon with voice impressions of superheroes. The congregation was stunned as the bigger-than-life characters seemed to fly off the comic pages and into Sunday morning worship. By the time he reached his Superman imitation, the worshippers were rocking with laughter. The children and youth particularly enjoyed the service. They remembered his message about the contrast between biblical heroes and those in the popular culture. This moment of humor in the serious business of religion is unfortunately quite rare. Perhaps much of God's humor is found among the young. They enjoy the bubbling delight of the faith.

Nelvin Vos, author of **The Drama of Comedy: Victim and Victor** (John Knox Press), compares the experiences of comedy with the religious experience. In the act of comedy we become both victim and victor. The Christ form embraced both the loser (Chaplin's Tramp) and the winner (W. C. Fields' punch lines).

Two youth advisors developed a five-session unit on the gift of humor. They had played many fun games and had many laughs with youth; however, they wanted to make the connection between faith and humor. They planned a course of five sessions by using contemporary comedy and the Bible. They quickly developed an outline for the course:

Session 1: "Laughing With Important Others: You and I" [Acts 2:41-47]. On this evening the leader showed several cartoons clipped from the Sunday comic page, the Bible and a doll. A volunteer read Acts 2:41-47.

"We have heard what God has done for us," announced one of the leaders as he played a portion of an album titled, "An Evening with Nichols and May." The group exploded in laughter as they heard the struggle between a mother and her son on the phone. The leader asked the group, "What kind of reaction do you have to this conversation?" One teen hadn't smiled. "That's my mother."

A middle-aged woman who was helping with the group that evening piped up, "That's my son." A long and painful discussion followed as the group shared the joys and problems of parent and child as they grow apart.

Ed then played a comedy piece by comedian Steve Martin. It described his poor treatment of his mother. More discussion followed. Comedy posters and other comedy material added fuel to the discussion.

The high school students and adults studied the biblical passage as they reflected on the connection points between them. The session concluded with the "passing of the peace:" One person after another grasped his neighbor's hands and said, "May God smile upon you this week." Each person was asked to bring a funny joke to be shared at the next meeting.

Session two: "Laughing With Things: I and It" [Mark 12:41-44]. After reading the passage, the students shared the jokes they had prepared. The Beatles' song "Eleanor Rigby" was played several times during the next half-hour while the people tried to project into the lyrics what they had known from their own experiences and those of others.

Then Ed and Tom showed the film "Chairy Tale." In this simple movie, a man tries to relate to a chair. The leaders vigorously shared their views about this difficult interaction. The high school students next reflected on how

As Christians, our laughter is as significant as our tears.

Mark 12:41-44 spoke to their relationship with material objects. Before the session ended, the leaders asked members of the class to pair up with someone else. For the next session they were encouraged to work out a joke which could be presented as a dialogue between two people. They then passed the peace.

Session three: "Laughing With Ourselves: I and I" [Matthew 16:21-28].
During the opening experience members read the passage and told their jokes. The old Simon and Garfunkel song, "I Am a Rock," played over and over as teens made collages by tearing materials from magazines as a response to the song's example of someone alone. The students shared their collages with the group.

The leaders showed "That's Me," an old film about two lonely people who try to relate to each other. During the first showing of the movie the sound track was turned off and people shared what only their sight had revealed to them concerning the gap between these folks. After discussing their insights, the film was shown again with the sound. The biblical input was discussed at this point. The session closed with the passing of the peace. For the next session, everyone was asked to find a bad ethnic joke about his or her own nationality.

Session four: "Laughing With Frightening Others: I and Them" [Acts 9:10-19]. After reading the passage, the leaders encouraged the telling of ethnic jokes. There was nervous laughter during this sharing. A question was raised: "Why are groups of people so easily viewed in these stylized ways?" Students told stories about their grandparents and how such jokes hurt.

Ed showed the film, "Two Men and a Wardrobe" and asked the question, "How did these two men become so separated from the world about them?"

Tom played Bill Cosby's story about his brother, Russell. Why could almost everyone in the group relate to this childhood story so easily? Why did it transcend ethnic groups? After passing the peace, the students were asked to bring jokes about God to the next session.

Session five: "Laughing With God: I and Thou" [Exodus 3:1-10]. The jokes about God were shared: Were they really disrespectful? What made them funny? The leaders showed "Chairy Tale," a film used a couple weeks earlier. How was this film a parable for our relationship with God? After a lively discussion, a Jonah and the Whale routine by comedian David Steinberg was played. What had been exaggerated to make it so funny? What was also true about the humor?

The group then reviewed the Exodus story. What is funny about humans from God's perspective? Each person in the group received sections of the evening newspaper along with the instructions, "From God's viewpoint, what looks funny and sad about our actions as reported in the story you hold?"

This course may seem bold to you. We are not suggesting that you lead the same event. However, we do believe that you have a great opportunity to link all of youth's experiences together in your ministry. As Christians, our laughter is as significant as our tears. You will find that humor keeps your young people from taking themselves too seriously.

Humor is also a good way of growing as persons of faith. Marshall McLuhan suggested that humor affords us our most appealing tool: "It does not deal in theory but in immediate experience and is often the best guide in changing perceptions."

Humor will help you catch the conscience of youth.

See also CREATIVITY

Hunger

The question isn't if youth are willing to take part in world hunger programs; it is how they are to become involved.

In a world which has plenty of food for everyone, it is a disgrace that hunger is so evident in every part of the world. This disparity has long been a concern of the youth of the world, and they have been willing participants in hunger projects for decades.

The whirlwind of enthusiasm does not solve the problem with one evening's program or hunger walk, though. A one-shot program does contribute, but it is most crucial to help youth to realize that they should make a long-term commitment that involves long- and short-range projects, continual education, prayer, political and industrial involvement, and a long list of other commitments.

How can your group help out?

Research helps. Sometimes it is overwhelming and guilt-producing, but we do need to search out the facts in the causes of hunger. The research may lead us to multinational corporations and business entanglements that seem so far from our reach and ability to influence. Even more fearsome, the culprit may turn out to be massive systems, such as national policy and tradition, which are as elusive as air. But the more we search, the more we begin to discover that corporations and traditions always center around people, and people are changeable. Whole systems have been known to turn completely around when the right letters were written, the right film was made, the right person was contacted. We don't have to start from scratch since a lot of research has been completed and some of the clues for answers are available.

Work helps. Hungry people are fed as a result of rock-a-thons, UNICEF collections, and shipments of food and clothing. Our efforts may seem so infinitesimal in light of the massive starvation we hear about, but they are steps in the right direction. Note too, our efforts are much greater when we convince others to work with us.

Hunger awareness helps. The organized fasts help us to comprehend slightly the anguish of the world's starving persons, and they urge us to work harder. Statistics and reports of the specific problems help us to better direct our efforts. Sometimes posters make us uncomfortable enough to quit ignoring the problem.

Political and social action helps. We can not expect our elected and appointed officials to do all the caring concerning hunger. Our voices and actions must keep the government aware that we want our resources shared with those in need. Public display of our concerns are often the only way to attract attention to the long neglected fact of hunger in our neighborhoods and global village. Sometimes boycotts are the only communication link we have left.

Prayer helps. We must be in tune with the One who created us as well as the world's resources. We must ask God how we can best make use of all that we have at our disposal to restore life to persons for whom hunger is robbing their minds and strength.

Jesus the Christ mentioned hunger too often during his ministry for us to ever ignore it. To us is left the miraculous responsibility of sharing the abundant life. To the starving person, the abundant life includes food.

The young people gathered around the circle. They had just seen an eight-minute movie narrated by music star, Harry Chapin. He confronted the teens with everyone's responsibility for the problem of hunger. His words cut and challenged. In the middle of the group was placed a bowl of unpopped popcorn and a corn popper. The leader passed out pieces of unpopped corn to each person. They were asked to focus on this symbol of food. Members of the group shared their thanks for the meal which had meant the most to them during the past week. Slides of hungry faces haunted the rough wall. "Share some thoughts as you look at that child's face.

What would the piece of corn mean to her?" The sharing was very moving. The pieces of corn were collected. The youth advisor placed them and others in the popcorn maker. The corn began to pop and the fresh aroma filled the room.

"Let's have a popcorn prayer. Each person say one word in prayer as we go around the circle." The first round focused on a prayer of confession. The leader then gave each person one piece of freshly popped corn. "Hold it and look at its beauty. Smell your corn. Can you imagine the delicious taste you are about to experience? Let's offer our popcorn prayer of thanksgiving." The chain of prayer words went around the group several times.

"Now let's taste and see how good God is to us."

These folks were going through a special "hunger" study weekend. There are many exciting designs for such growth events. The hunger meal in which some eat much and some eat nothing is a youth group favorite. There is probably no better focus of study and action than the hunger question.

Resources

1. **Predicament of the Prosperous**, by Bruce Birch, Westminster Press.
2. **Youth Group Activities**, by Craig Cramer, Discipleship Resources, Box 840, Nashville, TN 37202.
3. **What Do You Say to a Hungry World?** by Stanley Mooneyham.
4. **Small Is Beautiful, Economics As If People Mattered**, by E. F. Schumacher, Harper and Row.
5. **A Covenant Group for Lifestyle Assessment**, by Bill Gibson, Discipleship Resources, Box 840, Nashville, TN 37202.
6. **Rich Christians in an Age of Hunger,** by Ron Sider, Inter-Varsity Press.

See also FUND RAISING, GOAL SETTING

Ice Breakers

Youth workers and advisors have known for a long time that it is necessary to "break the ice" which forms around the coldness of people who don't know or trust each other. In the past few years a number of exercises have been developed to draw isolated individuals into a community of fun and trust. These simple techniques tend to be games. Some of them look gimmicky. Perhaps they are. The use of exercises, ideas and other techniques is never an objective matter.

Every teaching or communication approach depends on the leader's attitude in terms of its authenticity. If you believe in your youth and the possibility of an idea, it will have integrity. This means that you cannot just leaf through idea books and use suggestions without considering a few matters. Who are your youth? What are they ready to experience? Will this idea add to their humanity? For what reason am I tempted to use this item? Do I feel comfortable in using this method? Am I hesitant to use this approach because I am afraid of the risk? How will this approach fit into the program's goals? Would I participate in the game myself?

If you can develop this kind of sensitivity, most ideas will work for you. You might find yourself taking a plan and changing it to fit your situation. You are the only person who can determine if something will work with these teens at this time.

We urge you to push past the discomfort of risk. It will always be there when you journey with others in the quest of a fully realized faith.

A youth advisor team in Virginia developed an exciting means of getting young people from several youth groups to communicate with each other. They built an ice breaker into the meal. They were serving sandwiches, pickles, chips, etc. The participants had to follow a person-oriented menu to assemble their dinner:

Seek a Person	If You Desire
1. you have never met (name and age)	1. bread
2. whose family name begins with the same letter as yours	2. peanut butter
3. who shares the same month of birth	3. ham
4. who is in the same year of school	4. bologna
5. who has brown hair	5. mayonnaise
6. who has the same shoe size	6. mustard
7. who is wearing blue	7. cheese
8. who is sixteen	8. pretzels
9. who is fifteen	9. potato chips
10. who has red socks	10. pickles
11. who has blue eyes	11. lettuce
12. who is under six feet feet tall	12. a beverage

Another easy way to break the ice among a large youth meeting is to create "puzzles" made up of participants' names. Each person is given a sheet with the name as he or she registers. They must hurry around and get people to sign their names on the sheet. This forces people to get the names of others. It mixes the teens in an activity of fun.

One of the simplest mixer techniques was developed by a teacher who couldn't get her junior high school Sunday school class into small groups. They were very uncomfortable with each other. One morning she passed out jawbreakers. After a couple minutes, she asked them to break into smaller groups for a discussion of the biblical passage. "Stick your tongue out. Go into the group which has the same colored tongue."

You will be able to design your own processes to get folks into community.

Resources

1. **Recycle Catalogue I** (700 indexed ideas) and **Recycle Catalogue II** (600 indexed ideas), P.O. Box 12811, Pittsburgh, PA 15241.
2. **Try This One** and **More. . .Try This One**, GROUP Books, Box 481, Loveland, CO 80537
3. **Idea Books**, Youth Specialties, 1224 Greenfield Drive, El Cajon, CA 92021.
4. **Guide for Recreation Leaders**, Fakkema and Bannerman, John Knox Press.

See also GROUP BUILDING, NO-LOSER RECREATION

Identity

If someone stopped you on the street and asked you to tell who you are, you would probably give them your name (if the request seemed reasonable enough at the time) and then walk off, assuming you answered their question. But names, occupations, addresses, family information, even hobbies and personal tastes are not really who we are. To be sure, all that is a large part of it, but our identity has more to do with our dreams, fears, loves, the persons and groups we invest ourselves in. When we finally get pushed to the wall, our identity is found in the power in whom we have ultimate trust.

It is rather difficult to explain our true identity to another person. When we consider the difficulty of accurate communication, we usually go for the easy stuff. . .the names and addresses.

Explaining true identity is almost impossible for youth. Even their names and addresses are parentally endowed and restricted. The school, community and society add their own controls and definitions to the point that it sometimes seems their identities are kept from their reach. To ask youths to tell who they really are can be devastating.

This is where a church youth group can be a liberating transformation for the youth. Initially, the group gives an additional corporate reference point which is chosen by the youth, and soon it adds a dimension of freedom when the group and the individual are given choices about future directions. Leadership roles are there for the volunteering, commitment possibilities are there for the investing, and friendships are there for the risking and sharing. Ultimately, the youth may discover in these exchanges that he or she can be brought closer to the One who offers the unlimited future of their dreams, along with all the necessary strength it will take to get them there.

The probing for identity will often arise in youth programming and many times it will be a sore place to touch. The group can be an invaluable environment for the individual to use in the frightening process of discovering who they are.

There are numerous exercises that

can help youth to begin to probe their own identity: even the simple process of choosing colors and symbols for decorating a name tag, an animal to represent who they are, or a weather forecast for the way they view life. Any of these can start an internal examination of identity. A group leader can help each person discuss these choices with other persons.

A difficulty in discovering your own identity is having to deal with the different identities most of us maintain with different persons. This can be troublesome to youth who often feel that a person should remain the same regardless of the situation. But the more young people are helped to be sensitive to pressures that individuals must meet, the more they are able to understand the ways various persons can comprehend. This can lead to an understanding of how the powerless of the world must speak one language to themselves and friends but a totally different language to those in power.

Christ always sought to have his identity linked to those in need. He reached out primarily to those who were willing to grow and be changed. He shared his identity with them. This identity is one that we all share, the gift of life we receive from the One who calls himself, "I am who I am," the ultimate identification.

Resources
1. **You Are Promise**, by Martin Marty, Argus Communications.

See also BODY, SELF-IMAGE

Insurance

Unless a group has unlimited funds, there is wisdom in obtaining adequate insurance for a group and its mode of transportation prior to every trip and event. Indicate all the probable activities and known conditions of the group so that coverage will be realistic. You do not want to be caught following a tragedy with a policy that does not include certain present activities and conditions.

Don't skimp on liability or medical coverage. The cost for extended coverage is usually small, and costs encountered in accidents and tragedies can be astronomical. Incidentally, persons will definitely sue churches, including church leaders.

In most states it is advisable for the church to be incorporated so that you as a leader are acting on behalf of the corporation and not as an individual. This will allow the church's coverage to extend liability coverage for you. Of course, irrational, irresponsible or vicious acts could warrant separate charges.

Obtain from your insurance agent the contact phone numbers and names of other agents along your intended route. Whether or not it is requested, it is also helpful for the agent to have your contact numbers and persons along your route.

It is also wise to construct a form for all participants (youth and adult) to fill out information that could be invaluable later. You will need medical information (known medical problems, allergies, blood type), contact information (parents, guardian or next of kin, along with various phone numbers for different times of the day and week), handicaps (including swimming ability, any problems with various means of travel, reactions to various medicines), and any other information that you can foresee needing.

Insurance coverage may or may not require that you have two additional information forms signed by participants, but they may prove to be most beneficial to you. One form is simply a permission form to participate in the

PARENTAL CONSENT FORM

Name . . . . Phone . . . . Birthdate . . . .

Age . . . . School & Grade (this year) . . . .

Address . . . . City . . . . Zip . . . .

SIGNATURE OF PARTICIPANT

. . . .

To Whom It May Concern:

I, ..., Parent or Guardian of . . . ., do hereby request that the above named child be permitted to attend . . . . the date of . . . . I agree and consent to having the staff members and counselors, under whose auspices the program is conducted, and any other worker in the program approved as parent to secure any emergency medical care or treatment that may be necessary for my child during the entire outing, including the trip to and from their destination. I further assume all responsibility for the decisions so made, and the emergency care or treatment so secured by my child.

Signed . . . .

Relationship to Participant . . . .

Do you have hospitalization insurance?   Yes ☐   No ☐

Name of Insurance Company . . . .

Policy Number . . . .

Emergency numbers to call are:

Home . . . . Work . . . .

AUTHORIZATION TO TREAT MINOR

We, the undersigned parent(s) or guardian(s) of . . . ., a minor, do hereby authorize adult workers with youth of the . . . ., as agent(s) for the undersigned, to consent to any examination, x-ray, anesthetic, medical or surgical diagnosis or treatment and hospital care which is rendered under supervision of any physician or surgeon licensed under the provisions of the Medical Practice Act on the medical staff of a licensed hospital, whether such diagnosis or treatment is rendered at the office of said physician or at said hospital.

Dated . . . .

Parent or Guardian . . . .

Address . . . . City . . . .

Telephone (home) . . . . (office) . . . .

Other number for emergency contact . . . .

INSURANCE

event which acknowledges the parent's or guardian's awareness of the specific event and the participation intentions of the youth.

The second form is a little more complicated and varies in value from state to state. This is the form to authorize medical treatment under emergency conditions when parents or guardians cannot be contacted within the time available before critical medication or other measures (anesthetics, x-ray, examination, surgery, etc.) should be administered. Often the form includes the phrase that the treatment is to be "rendered under the general or special supervision of any physician or surgeon licensed under the provisions of the Medical Practice Act on the medical staff of a licensed hospital, whether such diagnosis or treatment is rendered at the office of said physician or at said hospital." Obviously, it is to be expected that in any emergency the parents or guardians (next of kin, in case of the adults) are to be contacted concerning preferred procedures. But when time does not allow and such persons cannot be reached, the physicians and hospitals can be legally prevented from taking the corrective measures they have at their disposal without some legally acceptable document of consent. It may be helpful to clarify what the law in your state says as well as those of the states in which you may be traveling.

In essence, these forms and this insurance coverage is a basic attempt at taking care of each other the way we would prefer to be cared for.

Interest

Athletics and theaters call it "box office;" broadcasting calls it "the ratings."

Regardless of what you call it, the issue is whether young people choose to return to your youth group.

First off, we can all probably agree on one thing—it's grossly inhuman to think that a volunteer leader in a non-profit institution which has no attendance requirements should have to even consider whether his or her leadership abilities are outdrawing all of the available alternatives for the youth's time and attention.

But somehow we get caught in the hard-line style. Did teacher A keep up attendance better than teacher B, or better than last year's teacher A? Maybe teacher A just doesn't have "it" anymore. Susan and John said last week they were never coming back to Sunday school because teacher B was so boring (or talks too much or is so serious or is no fun). "I wish our advisor was as young and had a neat van like the advisor at the church across town," might be heard in the church halls.

With all its harsh inequities, the

system of evaluating leadership abilities by observing student interest is kept basically to monitor the group's comfort. Without such a system, there would be no way for students to register complaints about unhappy situations in which they are caught. So the leader is pressured to keep the group happy.

There seems to be little way to eliminate these pressures. Each leader has to search for his or her own way to live with them. However, one of the most available ways to deal with these pressures is to share them with others. Share them with those who supply your support system (whatever committee or group is responsible for the ministry of which you are a part), the pastor and with the youth. To do this, you can be intentional about the interest level by engaging all of these persons in a continual process of evaluation and feedback. From time to time all persons related to this program of youth ministry, including the parents, should look at the mutually agreed upon goals and objectives and then evaluate how well each of the efforts of those involved are helping to meet those goals.

Make no mistake, evaluation is going on all the time. The important feature is to turn that into positive action so that the future will be better than the past. It is necessary to encourage participants to enter the process and be as honest as possible about how they see their expectations being met. Some persons may not be totally open in a verbal sharing session, so regular efforts at gaining reactions on written surveys is extremely helpful. It is important that attention is paid not only to the words that are shared but what is being said behind the words (at times, they can be contradictory).

For example, Ted was extremely dedicated to his regular teaching responsibility. Since we had a three-year rotation plan for teachers, he was look-

ing forward to his full tenure. But his class members had other ideas. An observer could set a clock each week by the time that the superintendent was met in the hall after class by at least 10 of his regular 28 students. And each week it was the same complaint—he was boring, he lectured to them, he kept them too long. The situation did not change for the next year and a half until Ted rotated out. It was then that we asked the group just who they would prefer as their teacher. It was no contest, they wanted the young lawyer with the fancy sports car. He almost didn't take the job till we told him that he was the unanimous choice of the group. Within six months, the scene changed dramatically. Attendance had fallen to seven or eight, and Ted's former critics now realized that his quiet weekly time with them had been genuine and its intensity for him had often touched the group very deeply and they had not been aware of it at the time.

Ted's situation is not unique. Many excellent teachers and youth leaders go about doing their jobs in simple, unspectacular ways that do not bring rave reviews from the students. In fact, most of us can remember leaders that we had when we were younger, and it was not until years after we had been with them that we had begun to realize how much they contributed to our lives.

However, as comforting as this long-range view might be, most of us as leaders are troubled when we sense that our leadership efforts are not appreciated at the time. The students might be right. It could be that our methods are inappropriate and need reappraisal. Our content might be more suited to our own interests than our student's needs.

There are numbers of resources being released daily to help stimulate student interest, and we should regularly check them out. Vary your teaching approaches. Share the leadership. Listen to the real needs of the students. Leadership courses are being offered for us to update our skills and insights, and we need to discipline ourselves to participate. Leaders need to be replenished. The day we think we know it all is the day we cease being one who can give, since we can no longer receive.

After we've prepared ourselves as best we can, we need to keep alive that flame of learning, growing and becoming that leader we need to be for this particular group. Knowing that we are in the process of becoming can give us the confidence to withstand the unfair rating system that scrutinizes our contributions.

See also ATTENDANCE, BOREDOM, BRAINSTORMING, DISCUSSION, MOTIVATING YOUTH, NEWCOMER, STORIES

Inter- generational

"Those oldies look like bone city to me."

"I don't like hippies and punks!"

It is easy to label folks whose ages make them different from us. We all do it. It makes complexity much more comfortable to face. Yet, when we look carefully at the interwoven needs and gifts which different generations have to offer, it seems as if some giant plot must be afoot. What else could make the young and restless shy away from the wise and secure? Why would those unable to be a part of the future not give their insights and experiences to encourage the young who are the future?

The ancient Greeks talked about the "forth thrust" which interlocked the young and old. The youth were encouraged to stand on the shoulders of the aging in order to reach higher on the ladder of wisdom and goodness.

There are many reasons why the glue which holds together the continuity of age groups has failed. Some people accuse the media mix of delineating subgroups by age for marketing purposes and therefore underscoring the differences between age levels. The products and personality in the media marketing system are tailored to appeal to specific age groupings. For instance, the preteen can be harvested for money by appealing to the bundle of needs he or she has at that point in emotional development.

The evolution in patterns of family life has also been cited for the high level of distrust between the young and the old. Grandparents no longer have daily access to their grandchildren. Teens cannot escape from a family hassle by spending a couple days with grandparents, who live across the street.

Most of the present educational system no longer is based on an apprenticeship model with a significant adult model as master of art, trade or intellectual skills. Many youth have no idea of the kind of job their parents do, or the duties that are involved in that job. In other words, the teen does not really participate with adults who are giving their personhood. There certainly are many teachers in school. Some of them are significant who share the art of living, thinking and being. Yet, most educational systems do not emphasize this aspect of learning.

Maggie Kuhn, one of the founders of the Gray Panthers, has worked hard to break down age barriers. "In my home, I had aunts, uncles, cousins and friends who were always there to read to me and care for me. They made me feel accepted and important as a person. It was an extended, intergenerational family. Where else should this concept be nurtured than in the church?"

The communication gap narrows when adults and youth share common goals and dreams.

The community of faith is centered in the ministry of all members. We are here only because the elders of the tribe have gone before us. But the witness of courage and hope provided by our elders will continue only because of those who are the youngest among us.

Faith is also caught and passed on through families of believers. This process of faith building is really the apprenticeship style of living and growing. Church bodies have tried to adopt all secular educational systems to make theological learning more systematic. Yet, our religious roots scream out to continue the process of having the oldest in the tribe pass the bread and cup to the youngest.

When we come to programming this theological stance, it is easy to fall into a number of traps. Every Christmas season the youth choir whips out to the retirement home for a concert of favorite carols and hymns. This is nice. However, the challenge facing the youth advisor in every youth outreach opportunity is to make sure that the action doesn't become a one-sided act of charity. The older folks appreciate the singing. However, they have even more desire for conversation between themselves and the young visitors. They also like to see youth all year 'round. All mission outreach from the faith community is based on an awareness that we go out in order to receive what the other person has to give to us. Intergenerational ministry is an act of mutual ministry.

Many groups have found wonderful gifts from the very old during visits to care facilities. One group in Kansas City took audio cassette tape recorders and interviewed these senior citizens. (See *Interviewing*.) Two of the youth found folks from their own church in the home! In a moment of inspiration, they asked these folks to offer short prayers of thanksgiving. They had the minister play them during the worship service on Sunday morning. The congregation was deeply moved by this ministry from a portion of their congregation who was ill, close to death and without money.

This sensitivity of the young people also enabled the old to realize that in the family of God everyone still has something to offer. Their prayers were honorable and needed contributions to the worship of God.

It is wise to develop intentional intergenerational events that include several aspects of sensitivity:

1. The young and older persons should be involved in a relationship and activities which permit them to contribute something to others.

2. The gifts and limitations of each side of the age gap should be considered.

3. The setting which provides the proper timing and environment is very important.

4. There must be a planned continuity in the relationship so that it doesn't have the appearance of a one-time program.

5. The content of the activity might well focus on something outside everyone's experience.

6. Build in debriefing opportunities— together and apart.

Imagine a camping experience built on intergenerational participation!

Resources
1. **Generations Learning Together**, by Donald and Patricia Griggs, Abingdon.

See also CHILDREN

Interviewing

This is probably the most important transaction between strangers. We are familiar with the interview which got us that job or college entrance. Mass media have also featured the sharp interaction between the reporter and the famous person. However, the interview method as a growing and rich exchange between two people is a possibility for every youth and adult.

It is vitally important that an audio cassette tape recorder be used for the encounter. While it was once believed that people froze before a microphone, this assumption is totally untrue. People are only afraid of a microphone when it is being held by a frightening person. The interviewee reacts to the person

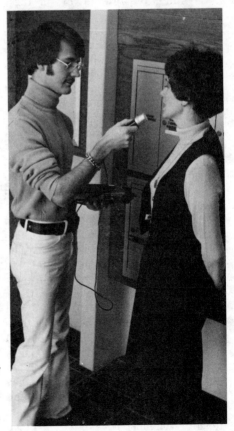

doing the interview, not to the tape recorder. In fact, the possibility of being the subject of a recording adds stature and importance to the transaction. The ordinary person is suddenly important. It is an absolutely affirming experience.

This opportunity is particularly helpful in youth ministry. We have often sent young people into the streets to talk with strangers. Their task was simply to gather the stories of others. We sent them out in pairs. (It is almost too threatening for many to undertake the experience alone.) Each duo was equipped with an audio cassette tape recorder with a hand microphone. The built-in microphone may be useful for recording meetings, but it is useless for recording quality interviews. The students should also use good quality tape and have full power on their batteries.

The street interview must pass through several steps in order to work. For instance, Eddie walked up to an old lady and pushed the microphone into her face. He asked a question without any prelude. She responded by slapping him in the face! The first step must be the *contract*. This is a formal label for a very warm and vital action. The interviewer approaches a person and announces his or her name, explains the reason for the interview and gives assurance that the interviewee's name will not be used. If you say you are from a church, the people tend to give "religious" answers. These comments may be fine, but it is much more authentic to have people share such beliefs on their terms. You want them to tell their stories in the most comfortable and real manner. It is surprising how eager folks are to share. Many of the stories will come from their own faith values. Once they know who you are and what you are doing, a strange thing happens: they switch their fear from you to themselves. "What could I say of importance?" You must move to the next step

at once.

The second step in the street interview is the *encounter*. This is the hardest part of interviewing. It forces you to listen! The good interviewer (or Christian communicator) is the person who listens to others. The person facing your microphone will open doors to their world—you must be alert to follow these invitations. A young pastor was doing this kind of interviewing as part of a workshop. When he returned to the group, he played his conversation with an elderly woman. After hearing the encounter, he realized that she kept mentioning how she missed her farm. As she gave a clue to her pain, he would change the subject and ask her about another topic.

It is hard to listen while you are worrying about what you are going to say next. The sensitive street interviewer works to focus on the person who is sharing his or her life. These strangers read your face and the motions of your body to discover if you are really interested in them. You are naked before another in an encounter like this.

It is helpful to ask questions which cannot be answered incorrectly. "If you had 15 minutes to live, how would you spend that time?" "If you were invisible, what would you do?" "If you could have a perfect day, what would it be like?"

A group of young people in one church interviewed everyone in the congregation over a six-month period. They asked three questions: "If you were God looking down on this church, what would please you the most?" "If you were God looking down on this church, what would you change?" "If you were God looking down on this church and community, what would you have us do that we have not yet done?" They then invited the church to attend a gathering at which they played segments and showed slides. They broke the meeting into sections and had small group discussions about the questions. It was a joyous celebration.

The third step in the interview is the *conclusion*. This seems obvious. However, it is vitally important to affirm the person for taking this risk of sharing. I have sometimes even played a minute or so for those who have never heard their voice. You may not agree with the statements or opinions expressed, but you can honestly affirm the experience of telling their story to another.

This model has been extremely valuable for youth groups. Many youth have found that the process of receiving the story from another is much more loving than just going to a retirement home and singing. By using the tape recorder, youth are able to accept the most prized gift that a person has: the story of his or her journey.

Interviewing is also a critical technique if you are just getting your bearings as a youth advisor. Take several weeks and interview every young person in the church. Give them this quality time to explore their world with you. Two things will happen as you take 30 or 40 minutes with each young person. You will learn a great deal about these special persons. No one will be better informed about your youth than you after such a probe. The second major result of this one-on-one experience will be that each young person will know that you are the kind of adult who listens. This may be the basic attribute that the youth advisor or youth worker has. The microphone in the hands of a sensitive person of faith becomes a means of grace.

For a 90-minute audio cassette on the creative use of this medium and interviewing: "Cassette/Cassette," $7.50 from P.O. Box 12811, Pittsburgh, PA 15241.

See also COMMUNICATION, LISTENING, RISKING, TAMING

Jesus

Jesus means a great deal to Christian young people. They can latch onto his love more easily than just about any other aspect of faith. In fact, most will be puzzled when you talk about the Trinity. Jesus is so real and accessible to those who are confused and unsure about so many things. However, it is important to introduce your folk to the whole spectrum of the gospel! We have a very rich story of salvation. This full message comes at us in many different ways. We not only meet the human Jesus, but we also know his divinity.

Mentors in the faith have reminded us that theology is like a giant wheel that has many spokes. If each spoke represents one of the aspects of the faith, then the wheel must keep turning. Our needs tend to stop at one spoke as we let one part of the gospel speak to us. The community of faith is so important because it helps us see the complete wheel through the faith of others. One of your jobs is to keep the wheel turning.

The "Jesus freaks" of the early '70s were a good example of a group with a narrow theological focus. It was good that they found Christ. However, they were often unable to understand the complete gospel. Taking only part of the good news and excluding all other attributes of the faith becomes heresy. Followers of a partial faith often seem to either fall away or become a sect.

The church has also often fallen victim to a myopic view of the historical faith. For instance, some churches have focused so closely on intellectual religion that members have been forced to discover the spiritual aspect of the faith in other groups. On the other hand, groups which only celebrate the Spirit tend to be short on other historical aspects of the faith.

It is good to strengthen the understanding young people have concerning their faith. Jesus is a wonderful place for them to know God. Yet, you must gently lead them into a faith which embraced the fullness of Christ (servant, prophet, priest, king).

Resources

1. **The Miracle of Jesus for Today**, by James Bailey, Abingdon.
2. **The Life and Teachings of Jesus**, by Charles Laymon, Abingdon.
3. **He is the Still Point of the Turning World**, by Mark Link, Argus.

See also CHRISTMAS, EASTER, HOLY SPIRIT, RECYCLE THEOLOGY, THEOLOGY OF YOUTH MINISTRY

Job Description

"How do I know what I am really supposed to be doing?"

The answer to that question should be of utmost importance to you and those with whom you work. Misunderstandings about basic job expectations and limitations can grossly affect you personally, your efforts and the results of those efforts.

You may have been recruited by an individual or a group, and the approach may have been, "All you have to do is. . . ." But sooner or later, it will probably occur to you, to those who recruited you, and to those who will work with you that no one is completely sure what you agreed to do, let alone what you understood the person or group to have interpreted for you to do.

Before you assume a new position, you should request that a written description of your objectives be prepared by those who are responsible for the program of which your work will be a part. This description should include as much information as is known about: your length of service, the scope of your duties, the persons (or titles of persons, since the same individuals will rarely remain throughout your service) to whom you can go for help (any kind of help), goals and expected outcomes of your efforts (what constitutes success or failure in the minds of those responsible for this program), any budgetary considerations, and any other significant information related to your work. It is wise to write the description around your unique abilities as well as the specific challenges of the job. Copies should go to all persons related to your work. (Yes, it is even good for the entire church to see such job descriptions.)

The fact that this is in writing gives everyone a chance to see for themselves what you were asked to do. Of course, understanding of the wording is open to individual intepretation, but this is usually less of a problem when the relationship has been committed to a mutually agreed upon written statement.

A review of the job description should take place annually with a time period in which you can influence revisions.

See also FINANCES, GOODBYE, YOUTH MINISTER

Journals

One of the most exciting techniques available for youth ministry is that of writing dialogue journals. Ira Progoff (**At a Journal Workshop**, Dialogue House Library, 45 West 10th St., New York, NY 10011) is a pioneer in this field. He conducts workshops around the country and has written several books on the subject. One of his methods is to ask his students to write personal dialogues with someone living or dead. It could be their father or Jesus. The two criteria for choosing the person are: 1. He or she is important to you; 2. There is the possibility in the relationship of going beyond the point which now exists.

The journal writer must first write a terse focus statement describing the situation and the relationship as it is now perceived. This can be significant events in the history of the person with whom he or she will have a dialogue. This is the writer's attempt to capture the other person's journey.

The participants are then encouraged to be quiet as they develop a dialogue script. The writer speaks through writing and then listens as he or she writes the other person's response. This sounds strange, but the responses are stunning. The dialogue should be written in short sentences without judgments. This process will last with much energy for nine or ten minutes.

The participants can be in separate rooms. They are encouraged to read back the dialogue to themselves and note the emotional response created by certain parts of the dialogue. When the group gathers, no one should be forced to share anything if he or she feels it is too personal. Others can share their emotional responses or even read the dialogue aloud if they wish.

This is an excellent method for reflection time at a weekend conference or event. In fact, we have found that using

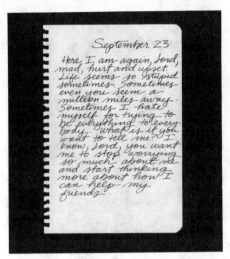

Journal writers are usually surprised at their insights and sensitivity when they read past entries.

some aspects of the dialogue writing works extremely well for events with a large number of young people. At one such gathering, 3,000 young people were given notebooks and encouraged during worship times to write responses to different kinds of concerns. At the closing of the worship service, the youth were encouraged to share some reflections from their journals. We had placed ten microphones in the aisles. The response was a powerful experience.

Some youth workers spend time counseling young people. They have found that daily journals are often helpful in enabling young people to cope with their problems. Instead of the adult doing the reflecting to help the youth cope, the teens are able to read the journal and discover their own insights with the counselor. It is significant that the early church used the written word to bring us the Gospel. The testimonies of the saints of every age are important to all.

See also COMMUNICATION, ROLE PLAYING

Junior High and Senior High: Together or Separate?

This issue is one of the most debated youth ministry questions in many churches. There are as many reasons for keeping the two groups together as there are for separating them.

Generally, it is easier to maintain one group. Fewer leaders are required, less space is needed. Fewer resources. Less time. The youth and adults may prefer a larger group even if there is an abundance of leaders, space, resources, time, etc.

However, when a person looks carefully at the enormously different needs of 7th graders and 12th graders, it becomes rather apparent that the program is more responsible to the needs of youth when there can be at least a junior high group and a separate senior high group. Where the number of participants is high enough, another preferred grouping is: 7-8th grade, 9-10th, 11-12th. Another possible grouping is: 7th grade, 8-9th, 10-11th, 12th.

Most early teens are experiencing what might be termed a second birth. Different glands are beginning to

function for the first time; physical growth spurts in various directions leading to awkward movements and vocal changes; the body has shapes it did not have a few months before. All those changes take some adjustment. And though we as a society give a newborn child plenty of time and encouragement for acclimation, we do not give an early adolescent a moment to deal with these new and strange developments. Instead, we expect this person to accept adult responsibilities and perspectives, as we withdraw our touch, verbal support and patience.

A good early teen program needs to provide time: time for giggling, time for groping around issues without needing to come to immediate conclusions, time for uplifting affirmation which needs to come in a zillion different ways. That obnoxious word *adolescence* means between, and therefore it applies to young teens because there needs to be some supportive space for making this important transition.

On the other hand, older teens generally know a few things about who they are. They need to think through several directions that are open to them for the future. The momentum comes from within. There is a rush to check out ideas, insights, ways of doing things, lifestyles, bases that might be reliable. The demand is for handles. Hopefully, there can be solid relationships.

A good late-teen ministry lends exposure and evaluation, exploration and rationale, searching the far reaches of the universe and the inner self, rejoicing and reflecting, mysteries and models, meanderings and meanings, and future probing.

Certainly, there are great combined youth ministry programs that are able to provide well for all the various needs of the wide variety of persons called youth. Some of them work because of the unbelievable attention and commitment of their adult leaders who make sure that there really is a special youth ministry program tailored to fit the needs of each youth.

However, in most churches, the best constructed program includes separate programs to fit the unique needs of the early teen and the late teen.

Resources

1. **Communicating With Junior Highs**, by Robert Browing, Graded Press, 201 8th Avenue S, Nashville, TN 37202.
2. **The Exuberant Years: A Guide for Junior High Leaders**, by Ginny Ward Holderness, John Knox.
3. **Growing Up Forgotten**, by Joan Lipsitz, Transaction Books.
4. **Early Adolescence: Perspectives and Recommendations,** National Science Foundation.
5. **Junior High Ministry**, by Wayne Rice, Zondervan.

See also AGE GROUP CHARACTERISTICS, COMMUNITY, CULTURE, LARGE GROUP VS. SMALL GROUP

Keeping Current

How can I work with youth? I can't stand their music. It's been 20 years since I was in high school."

"I really want them to think that I keep up with the times. I've grown a beard. I try not to wear out-of-date clothes."

The adult leader does not need to act or dress like a youth. However, it is helpful if the adult leader can keep in touch with youth culture.

Some adult leaders drop in at the local high school occasionally, not only to see various youth (most are grateful for that interest; some do not like it) but also to familiarize themselves again with the feeling of being back in school. They go to a few ball games and volunteer to chaperone dances.

An adult does not have to like youth music to listen to it from time to time. It is not necessary to identify every artist on a youth radio station, nor even to like the music. What matters is that the adult's finger stay firmly planted on the pulse of youth culture. It really does mean more if an adult leader can refer to some phrase or concept in current culture than to continually refer to a form of culture that occured before the youth had a chance to understand it. (Yes, much of significance was said, sung and worked for in the 1960s, but it is unfair for adults to engage in one-upmanship by nostalgically pointing to that period.)

Many newspapers list the top songs in the city and nation for that particular week. Checking that over occasionally could be helpful.

Casual research into youth films, television programs, concerts, and other cultural ingredients should be pursued. Again, there is no need to become an expert. Simply have a sense of what is happening in the lives of those young persons with whom you minister.

See also CULTURE

Language

Adult youth workers often admit that they are horrified about the language the youth use. They are upset about the words (profanity, swearing, limited vocabulary, vindictive and abusive phrases), the tone (hostility, paternalism, constant upmanship), the patterns (using "you know" for commas, repeating, abrupt abandonment of discussion participation, overworked phrases with obscure meanings) and total absence of terms for whole fields of knowledge (religion in particular),

Poor language is reason for concern, though the situation may not be as serious nor as permanent as might be suspected. At best, words are simply tools that we employ for telling another person about a belief or a feeling that we have. Actually, words are less than that. First, we have to decipher how our past conclusions and current feelings come to bear on a topic before us. Then we carefully choose the most appropri-

ate verbal symbols that will convey all that information to whomever is near us. Those verbal signals must approximate the ideas, feelings and personal feelings we intended.

Youth have had little time and opportunity for learning those precise verbal skills. They are far less inhabitants of a verbal world than most adults were at the same age. Youth spend considerably more of their time with visual teaching methods in school and with TV and its pictorial symbolism than did previous young people.

Therefore, when pushed to express themselves, youth must grab for the closest words. They punctuate those words with as many phrases as possible to provide a little extra time to scramble for acceptable terms. Then they try to emphasize the message with a number of emotionally-laden phrases to ensure the package. The same speech delivered 10 minutes later may have come out quite differently, particularly if the time could be used in preparation.

Don't take the words youth use too literally. They are probably words that are handy at the time. The words may be chosen to check out your reaction or try out their sound within the unique setting. The young person may express an idea heard from someone else, and he or she wants to hear how you would have responded to the other person. Or the youth may have had an unusual insight, which he or she may not agree with at all, but he merely wanted to test your response regarding its viability.

Even though language is difficult for young persons, don't think for a moment that youth are any less interested in accurate communication skills. Quite the opposite is true. They very much want to learn to express their innermost convictions and they value anyone who can help them learn how to communicate well.

Christian youth are aware of their need for help in learning the language of the faith. They do not seek the worn-out terms or the pious utterings with which to clobber opponents in a debate, but the terms and concepts by which they can articulate a meaningful faith.

The wider the variety of study and discussion offerings, the more able the person will be to compare his or her conclusions at the present time. A biblical word study is immeasurably valuable, especially if the group is stimulated to trace down some of the Hebrew and Greek words with their rich and inclusive root meanings.

Resources
1. **An Introductory Theological Wordbook**, by Kendig Cully, Westminster Press.
2. **A Theological Wordbook of the Bible**, by Alan Richardson, Macmillan.

See also COMMUNICATION, X-RATED

Large Group vs. Small Group

Both small group intimacy and large group energy are valuable ingredients for any youth group.

Both small youth groups and large groups have advantages and disadvantages. Experiences can take place in one that are very difficult in the other. It would be impossible to claim one is better.

One of the luxuries of the group with few members is its flexibility for movement, scheduling, resourcing, space requirements and leadership needs. There are groups across the nation with three members that have a great time doing an amazingly wide variety of activities. Sometimes these are all the youth available. Of course, there is the danger that a small group will grow so close that they will not reach out to other persons.

The benefits of a large group are the abundance of skills and energy, ability to conduct a variety of programs and projects, ready support for speakers and other leaders and increased planning resources. Numerous groups have regular attendance in the hundreds of persons and support a multitude of sophisticated and intriguing programs. Usually, the large group will need to break into smaller groups quite often in order that the members can interact on a more personal basis and establish more intimate rapport.

The church with few members often feels that it cannot have a worthwhile program because of limited participation, but that does not have to be the case. When significant ministry begins to happen, the importance of numbers seems to be overlooked—that is when the importance of each person is valued and that can happen with a group of 500 or five.

Within the multi-millions of persons on the globe today, God cares for each one as if that person were here alone. A caring youth ministry will attract numbers—but it will also focus its concern on individuals.

See also BALANCE

Lifestyles

One thing for sure, youth are definitely conscious of the fact that the world's resources are fast depleting. It is a regular ingredient in their school studies and conversations, since youth hope to inhabit this planet for several decades.

The response has been quite varied. Some youth are determined that they will not get caught without enough financial resources to buy their way out of any future shortage, and they cautiously plan to enter into the most lucrative vocation they can locate. Others are learning from many adults that one response is to ignore the problem and live for the moment, utilizing any form of entertainment at hand. Quite a few youth are learning to value the resources they

Get it fast, eat it fast and move on.

now have, to live in such a way that they consume and pollute the least they can, and to seek to learn more about nature's coordinated plan so that they can support it.

Each of these is a lifestyle response. Each has some conscious and unconscious elements that are assimilated from family, community mores, peers, media and personal reflection. Youth group discussions are also very instrumental in lifestyle choice.

Of course, lifestyle is more than just an economic alignment. Lifestyle includes how we use our leisure time, how we relate to family and friends, political preference, religious affiliation, clothing, and on and on. Many parts are changing constantly, but there is a sense in which the basics seem to get locked in during the teen years or shortly thereafter and the embellishments do not stray too far from the basics.

An active youth group that helps its members to encounter various lifestyles can provide an extremely valuable laboratory for each youth to make the

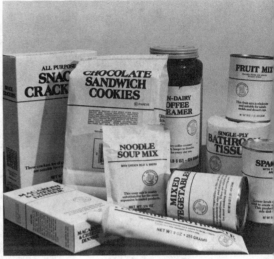

Some Christians see wealth as a gift from God. Others see it as a curse. The Bible asks us to be responsible with what we have.

choices with as much concrete knowledge and reference as possible. For instance, many youth groups have traveled to engage in work projects within a totally different culture than the one they have known in their own community. The contrast can help the youth to realize that this different culture, which may have seemed illogical and unwise earlier, can have validity for those who live there each day and have had to adjust their actions to surrounding conditions.

It is too easy for us to judge everyone's lifestyle by the one we have chosen for ourselves. Only if we could live within another person's body for a length of time could we know the pain and pleasure that has led them to where they are. We need not support another person's lifestyle to acknowledge the integrity that led this person there.

In the final choice, our lifestyle is our response to God's love for us. It is our way of living out the gift of life, forgiveness, love and support. One of our greatest joys in youth ministry is to help youth to comprehend the magnificence of those gifts as they make choices concerning their style of life.

Resources
1. **Living More With Less**, by Doris Janzen Longacre, Herald Press.
2. **Traveling Light: How to Keep Things From Owning You**, by Pat McGeachy, Abingdon.
3. **99 Ways to a Simple Lifestyle**, edited by David Taylor, Doubleday.
4. **No More Plastic Jesus: Global Justice and Christian Lifestyle**, by Adam Finnerty, Orbis.
5. **Enough Is Enough**, by John Taylor, Augsburg.
6. **Good News for Rich and Poor**, by Harvey Seifert, United Church Press.
7. **A Planet to Choose**, by Alan Miller, Pilgrim.
8. **Repairing Christian Lifestyles**, by Clapp, Brownfield, Seibert, Box 2050, Bloomington, IL 61701.

See also PORTABLE MINISTRY, TAMING, WORK PROJECTS

Listening

In a world of clashing sounds and persons screaming at each other, few of us really listen to what individuals are saying. Church school teachers are often so busy "getting through the lesson" that they fail to hear the human cries for help from their class for concerns other than those on the day's agenda. Parents sometimes fill the air with non-stop verbiage toward their children without pausing for a second to compliment them for their significant forward steps. Youth often give up in despair when their best friends and parents offer only mouths instead of ears also.

Almost always, persons have to *learn* to listen. It is not the same as being quiet or not talking. Listening is an active learnable talent.

Listening means literally to tune one's attention to hear the innermost concerns of the other person(s). Listening is chasing after another's thoughts and feelings.

Persons tell you a lot about themselves by their clothes, mannerisms, body language, what they carry with them, their speed of movement, hair style, jewelry, who they are with and many other ways.

And they also communicate by speech. Again, listening is not just piling up another person's words and making conclusions based on the height of the word stacks. Listening happens when we constantly check out our reception by putting their words and actions and what we understand about their feelings into our own words. We then ask them to check to see if we really did hear and comprehend what they said.

We may find it helpful to use some of the following comments as check points: "I think you are saying to me that Miss Johnson has really made you angry." "Now are you saying you like going on a retreat or that you like the idea of retreats but that you don't want to go on this one?" "You seem undecided. Am I correct?" It is absolutely necessary for the listener to regularly check signals to seek clarification in case any missed reception might have occured.

Our active listening should enable the other person to feel free to explain positions completely and explore alternatives. Our listening says that we support and love that person, though not necessarily in agreement or approval with him or her. We are signifying that someone else in the world knows how they feel and cares enough about them to hear them clearly. Often, others do not want our approval as much as they want us to recognize and appreciate their opinion in its related detail and supporting logic. What matters is that someone knows (a very significant biblical concept!).

See also COMMUNICATION, CIRCULAR RESPONSES, DISCUSSION, FEEDBACK, SERIOUS SUBJECTS

Local Church Government

It is crucial to find out what group makes the ultimate and intermediate decisions regarding youth ministry in the local church. Usually, an appointed committee is responsible for the program (leadership, approving functions, budgeting, etc.) and an elected executive or administrative body is ultimately responsible for all major decisions (approving hiring of staff, new directions, building facilities, etc.). Sometimes a church has a youth council composed of persons related to every program being offered in youth ministry (fellowship, scouting, choirs, church school, etc.) to oversee scheduling, guidelines, philosophy, using facilities and so on.

In all probability, some of the adult youth leaders (and hopefully, many youth) have been appointed to these decision-making bodies. Representation by young people is imperative to keep the channels of communication open. The youth need to hear the reasoning

behind the decisions that are made, and the committees need to hear the concerns of the youth.

Use this simple rule of thumb: Whether or not your group needs permission from the governing group for every function, ask for approval any time there might be a question of propriety. It is better to proceed on a certain program if you have the backing of the supporting group behind you. Then if there is a problem, you and the youth group are covered.

It is always easier to request permission prior to a success than after a failure.

See also JUNIOR HIGH AND SENIOR HIGH TOGETHER, PASTOR, PLANNING COUNCIL, TASK FORCE, YOUTH COUNCIL

Lock-in

Almost all of us have secretly desired to live in a gigantic house (at least for a day) and be able to play all over in it with our friends. Imagine playing hide-and-go-seek in millions of dimly-lit spaces! For the youth group, a massive church building is a dream come true since all the former adult restrictions (not running in the hall or sitting on the counter tops) might be lifted. Our own mansion.

A lock-in provides some of that excitement, childhood wonder and the potential for a group to experience a new dimension of fellowship. Normally, a group will gather at the church building near dinner time (the meal may or may not be included) and lock themselves into the building until mid-morning the next day (breakfast usually is included).

A lock-in should be planned carefully, else it can become a horrendous experience for all involved, including the neighbors and the police. The youth may regress temporarily and seek to do

Young people will get to know the church building and each other very well through an overnight lock-in.

everything they wish for their own pleasure. It can be destructive both physically and to the future prospects of the group.

A lock-in can be one of the highlights in the the life of the church. It can be an enriching experience of realizing the depth of love between group members. There can be a moving realization that the future direction of the church is already coming into the hands of the youth, an acute awareness of the faith inheritance waiting to be claimed, and the awesome reverence one can feel in a place where so many persons have worshipped over the years.

Rarely will anyone sleep much during a lock-in. Sleeping is not really its purpose. However, few persons have the ability to stay up all night, and every attempt should be made to allow for a generous amount of sleep.

Lock-ins can be meaningful periods of worship and study. Many groups use these occasions for pursuit of a special topic. A favorite has been a study of world hunger by viewing films, experiencing hunger simulation games, covenanting to participate in a fast, and contributing their energies on a project to benefit those victimized by local or worldwide hunger.

Playing and learning can be combined. A treasure hunt can be conducted throughout the building by giving clues that will teach various insights about objects within the structure. ("Clue 3 will be found behind clergy numero uno" means that they should look behind the picture of the congregation's first pastor, the picture being found on the wall of the fellowship hall.) Upon return, the group could describe its discoveries.

A lock-in is an excellent time for various church leaders to drop in informally to be a participant or share some insights. It can encourage a new appreciation for the congregation and the building in which it worships. ("I know this building in ways that no one else does," one girl responded.)

See also ICE BREAKERS, NO-LOSER RECREATION, REFRESHMENT, RETREAT

Loners

Isolation, self-imposed or otherwise, is a dangerous and difficult state for most young people. The boy who wears the same shirt for six weeks while the kids in the class keep a score on the board for each day he does not change it is faced with an obvious unhappy situation. There is something wrong in this kind of dynamic. Almost every school and church has these kinds of rejected folks. Both the isolaters and the isolated are part of the youth setting.

Often youth groups in churches do not want the new loner. The teens may be so close with each other that they are afraid the new person will upset their closeness. Of course, they never look at it in this way. Does your group experience situations where a new loner will come once and never come back? "He wasn't very friendly." "I don't think he liked us." Such statements do not cover the facts of the case.

Many folks are loners at one time or another. We (the authors, Bill and Dennis) have been in such positions. In fact, we are often the stranger when we lead workshops. It is sad that most church groups hold back their hospitality until we prove to them that we are acceptable. If this happens to those who are invited, what happens to the loner who has no assurance of eventual acceptance?

Most youth advisors get at this potential problem by becoming the bridge relationship between the loner and the group. You can easily model hospitality by being hospitable yourself. However, you are not the social director for a cruise. The task of being invitational to the stranger falls upon everyone. Most teens will carry into your group the high school's social patterns. Unfortunately, most schools have tight tracking patterns which clearly classify each person according to a specific pecking order.

Vernon found that the tight school system in his church situation was heightened by the fact that the young people came from six different high schools. He reached out to these clumps of loners and strangers by doing something that the school clubs could not do. Worship became the major focus of his youth programming. He drew upon the communion aspects of worship. They were one in Jesus Christ and this could be celebrated in the liturgical moment. One week he took the young people into the darkened church. He had them find

Youth groups can create a climate that will let loners know that they are wanted.

isolated spots in pews and on the floor. He had them lie on their backs. He then used music of isolation ("I Am a Rock," etc.) and projected slides on the ceiling. The service moved them from isolation into a circle of hands where they talked in the darkness about their greatest challenge during the past week. The session closed with the singing of "Blest Be the Tie That Binds." Vernon turned the lights up slowly. They then went for refreshments. He said the interaction at the end of the worship was a thousand times warmer and more real than it had been at the beginning of the evening.

There will always be certain persons who cannot be fully incorporated into the group. Yet, you can create a model and a climate for those loners to know that they are welcome to attend when they are ready.

Resources
1. **Loneliness: Search for Presence**, edited by Hugh Willoby, Convention Press.
2. **The Pursuit of Loneliness: American Culture at the Breaking Point**, by Philip Slater, Beacon Press.

See also COMMUNITY, FRIENDS, GROUP BUILDING, NEWCOMERS

Love

The pursuit of love in all its forms is one of the most powerful attributes of youth ministry. The electricity of love is so confusing among youth because it is so ill-defined.

Many layers of love swirl around the lives of the young adults in the process of becoming. A love of self flickers in the eyes of the young. They struggle to discover what makes them lovable. They give a lot of attention and energy to this inner-directed probe. The good feeling about self is threatened easily.

The young person also has a flickering love for parents. Young folks test this source of love in many different ways. Yet, this focus of love is important because it gives the teen assurance of his or her own worth.

The third interplay of love is the romance of loving another person outside the family circle. The biggest, and the safest, area is the love of those of the same sex. Friends are very important. There is often a great deal of intensity wrapped up in this peer love. It provides security when so many other aspects of love are being challenged and tested. We have often seen the negative aspects of this kind of peer power. In order to retain the acceptance and love of these important people, teens often conform in dress, language, behavior and viewpoint. Yet, the value of male bonding or sisterhood cannot be denied. It is one of

many love relationships which anchor a teen's life.

The most explosive dimension of this third level of love is that of a romance with a person of the opposite sex. Suddenly, a new depth of loving is awakened by another person. This can be an explosive experience because many struggles take place.

Self-love and peer love are wedged into all kinds of mythological views of love. The youth group is a prime spot for the "boy-girl" romance. It can be humorous and moving to watch. You will also find such brush-fire relationships dangerous and disrupting. The heat of new love can quickly freeze into anger and despair. It will be a girlfriend or boyfriend who will bring that new person to the group. The acceptance of this stranger will be important if he or she is going to survive the short life of the romance. The youth group is the unique place in which young men and women can relate without the need for love pairing. It should be acceptable, but unnecessary.

A fourth layer of love is the romance of relating to significant adults. This experience goes beyond key adult family figures. The young teen often first becomes attracted to a sports figure or pop performer. This is the time of personality posters and teen magazines. The media marketing people develop this area very carefully. Just note the letter columns in the fan magazines. The editors use these columns to discern the interests of the readers in order to keep on top of this rich source of consumers. This experience of remote love figures is a form of modeling which has always been present in human development.

The mass media have added intensity to the process. The bigger-than-life personages are more immediate and more unreal. The marketing push demands a certain disposability of these pop

An effective youth ministry helps young people deal with the issues of love, sex and dating.

figures. The young teen is encouraged to change models often. Most fans do not want to pattern their lives after these distant love characters. Certain attributes (freedom, style, strength, physical attractiveness, etc.) are the points of appeal.

Another dimension of this fourth layer of love is the romance of relating to an adult figure. This person can be a teacher, coach or adult at the local church. The youth advisor or youth minister can easily become this figure. In fact, an effective youth ministry develops a real sense of love between the youth and the adult leader(s). If the adult does not understand the dynamics of this romance, he or she can confuse the possibilities in the situation. The teen's love for the youth advisor can be directed back to the person as he or she grows. If this is seen as a personal love experience by the adult, serious problems can follow. The adult is charged with the responsibility of being in touch with his or her needs. This is imperative so that the advisor can separate the layers of his or her love needs from those of the young people.

The context for all these layers of romance is the love of God. This gift of faith encompasses all love quests. It is the wholistic nature of God's love which makes each of these love expressions valid and important.

What do you do if you are a male college youth worker and a young girl in the group asks you to be her date? What is your response if you are a female and a young guy stays after the meeting to tell you about the breakup with his girlfriend? "I don't want to live without her."

It may be in these small moments of walking with youth in their journey of romance that they will come to know more fully the love of God.

See also SEX, SEXUALITY

Malls

The shopping mall has become the hang-out for suburban America.

These sprawling collections of stores are appearing everywhere. Once the playground of suburbanites, they are now to be found in the cities and rural areas around the world.

The shopping mall is a magnet for young people. It has become an old-fashioned street corner. The dead summer season finds huge collections of youth hanging around the mall. This hanging around has resulted in some nasty situations. The merchants will often relate collections of youth to shoplifting and other distractions from their businesses. In many states, the mall complex is legally private property. This means that the responsibility for policing these facilities seems to fall upon the shoulders of merchant organizations and other powers which run these shopping centers.

Adults from the community are also upset by groups of bored youth in the malls. They point to the drug paraphernalia available in the stores and say that the mall is a breeding group for all that is bad with the young.

But the malls can become the center of an exciting ministry. For example, a group of Australian young people developed a special ministry to other teens who hung out in the shopping center. Using the clown ministry method, they created interest and activity centers. They found that other teens were very responsive. On another occasion, the same group was involved in a family week celebration which featured nightly presentations in the mall. They discovered that many of these "hanging around" teens were from divorced homes who responded warmly to family-type presentations.

In some communities, churches have cooperated to provide special mall youth ministries. One such interfaith group in Pennsylvania even sponsored a mall worker who focused on teens in the mall. The group developed a job bureau which helped match those who needed help with those who needed work.

How do we relate our youth ministry to the rhythms and new life forms of today? It is often hard to answer such a question because the local congregation has not dealt with the question of reaching those outside the church.

In many cases, adults in the church see the primary goal of "youth ministry" as getting all the youth in the congregation involved in the group. However, the mall outreach symbolizes the challenge of touching the lives of those who are not within the faith community. If you know that the gift of the faith is for all those young people being battered by a senseless and lost culture, you will want to wrestle with the kids lost in the mall maze.

See also EVANGELISM, OUTREACH

Materials

The publishers call it *curriculum*, but most people call it either materials or books. Consequently, there is a multilingual person in every church who has to learn how to fill out a curriculum order blank, put the returned order on the shelf for youth materials, and tell the leaders, "Your stuff is here!"

What do you do with the "stuff"? Well, some conscientious leaders keep it neatly piled in a special place for the entire period it is to be used and then return it still unused but well preserved and protected.

Some are terrified of it. They assume that you have to use all the suggestions

—and they could never pull that off. But there are others who try to follow every recommendation diligently regardless of anything the class might do to head off this herculean effort. Really.

Let's be realistic. The author's foremost task is to develop the material's subject matter. But that writer never met your group and has no idea of the things on your group members' minds. No set of suggestions will ever perfectly form that link between the topic and your group. That's your foremost task.

It may be that on a given day, the material will serve you best by simply helping to suggest other areas for study. At other times, one group meeting may use up three or four days' worth of suggestions. Sometimes four or five paragraphs of the first page of a six-page lesson are enough.

Regardless of how you or your group finally decides to plan for your time to-

Youth ministry materials. Use and adapt what you can to meet the demands of your unique situation.

gether, it is still wise to check through what the materials have to offer. Most denominations go to great effort to put together a set of materials that systematically study the Bible, basic beliefs, major questions about life situations and other significant subjects. It is this overall plan that can give you the most help. While most of us can prepare our own meetings for several weeks, we tend to fail by following only current points of interest and completely ignoring the long-range learning needs of the student. As with a school system that carefully builds one part of education on top of something else, we need to see our contribution in terms of what has been taught before and will be dealt with later. A well-planned curriculum can do that.

Of course, there are a number of independent producers of youth ministry materials. These vary greatly in quality with many of them trying to compete with the denominational materials by claiming to be easier to use. That point is debatable. Many of these publications are shallow in theological content and are overly sensational in their approach to most subjects.

Some persons and churches write their own materials. While this can be an educationally profitable exercise for those involved in the writing and production, it is time consuming, expensive and duplicates other persons' efforts. It may be void of variety unless constant evaluation takes place. On a limited scale, though, every leader will need to develop unique approaches for his or her group to accomplish learning goals. Many leaders keep notebooks and files of materials they have found useful in the past and can be used again.

See also CURRICULUM, INTEREST, RESOURCES

Media Awareness

Commercial media is all around us, but too often all we notice is the programming, not the forms of media themselves. Most of us rarely stop to think about what the different media do to us. The print media (magazines, newspapers, etc.) and the electronic media (radio, TV, records, etc.) occupy an enormous portion of our time. Many surveys tabulate that one-third of our waking hours are spent with the electronic media alone.

Of course, when the content of a TV program or a pop song enrages the audience, it is easy to be aware of media's power and potential. At those times groups will call stations, sign petitions and want immediate disposal of that which disturbs them. However, the media's strongest impact comes from the subtle messages that are distributed year after year without our being aware of their presence. This includes everything from consideration of content as well as commercial bombardment, sensationalism, exploitation (Ever notice what happens to a true story that is turned into a TV presentation?) to outright manipulation.

Media's growing presence can make us take those subtle messages for granted and accept them without question. Yet, our response should be just the opposite. When something grows as fast as television—cables encircling our world, video cassettes, large screens, satellite dishes for the backyard—we should constantly ask ourselves whether this presence is helpful. We must ask such questions as: *Who controls what is presented? What is happening to our free time, our time for family interchange, our creativity? What is happening to our sense of community?*

The church can be a valuable community servant by being a responsible media evaluator, not one that censors and bans programs but one that helps persons to make wise choices in using media by applying their faith as the crucial deciding factor. Study groups should be encouraged to analyze the content and motives behind the presentation of current media, particularly magazines, TV and records. The church can highlight that which is best in media and hold up for rebuke that which is the worst.

Resources
1. **Electronic Media: How Dear a Friend**, by Bill Wolfe, Discipleship Resources.
2. **Music and the Young**, C-4 Resources, P.O. Box 27, Sidell, IL 61876.

See also TELEVISION AWARENESS TRAINING

Mentor

This concept is more complete than the term teacher has become in our society. The ancient student was attached to the lifestyle of someone who was a master in his or her field. Mentor was the master under whom Telemachus of **The Odyssey** studied. The disciples chose Jesus as their Lord and mentor—and he chose them. You are a mentor, model, teacher of the youth in your ministry. This is a very freeing role in which you give away all your wisdom —and how you came to these understandings. The apprentice gathers in all that the master has to give. Once the apprentice learns everything possible, then he or she is free to execute the act of living, thinking or performing.

There are mentors for you also. See those who can help you grow in the art of youth ministry. A person with a special gift may be your mentor for that

You are a mentor, model and teacher of youth in your ministry.

particular area. There are mentors everywhere. In some aspects of your life together with teens, *they* will be your mentors! This quality transaction is the very source of Christian growth.

The college students gathered around the visiting media person who had just created a six-projector media event for the students attending chapel. Using his body, slides, film clips and a mixture of sounds, voices and music, he had created a reflection of the human mind being overwhelmed by the sensual bombardment of the world.

Five students took the guest to the snack bar. They talked long and hard about media. Before he left, they proposed that they spend a month with him as media apprentices.

These folks spent the time working with him as he produced weekly radio and television shows. They prowled the streets interviewing people for a series of ten-second radio spots he was developing as an experimental approach. The four men and one woman assisted their mentor in every part of his work. One of those students is now making a major contribution to the field of theological media. He has been responsible for creating a major program for understanding television's impact of values.

Imagine the implications of this style of learning for youth ministry! You can arrange these kinds of relationships between teens and significant adults who have gifts to share. This might involve teaming youth with adults who are currently in work positions that the youth are interested in, either a vocational interest or a personal interest (auto mechanics, home economist, aviation). There is no better method of learning. This style may be the best way to counter the "dropout" attitude of many teens who are not challenged by school or the church. Think of just about any art form or skill and you will find a name floating into your mind.

See also ADVISING, ADVOCATE, SUPPORT SYSTEM

Mime

Youth grow up in a world brim full of sounds that range from the clock radio that wakes them to the tape player that stays on after they have fallen asleep. Perhaps this is a reason why many youth turn to cults and other groups that require silence and meditation.

This noise explosion may also have contributed to the increased interest of youth in mime, an extremely visual, non-verbal mode of communication that trusts its audience enough to maintain an exchange of ideas and emotions through body movement and facial expression. More than any other form of communication, the person becomes the message.

Television and film have helped to make this a day when highly visual and emotional stimuli are needed to elicit a response. As media consumers, youth are intrigued with the strong impact of seemingly simple mime presentations. Equally intriguing is the luring dynamic of symbolism that mime can create with the audience's imagination.

All of us use mime in varying amounts in our daily routine. We signal to other persons using our faces and bodies. We wave with our hands, point our thumbs down to tell our disapproval, point to our watch when we want others to be aware of time. Thus, it is natural to expand this to develop an elaborate system of conveying our feelings.

This ultra-human involvement is a perfect activity for youth. They can be aided in their own self-discovery by trying out other personalities, learning to mimic humorous common occurences, investing skill and energy through demanding practice schedules and sharing inner feelings by acting them out.

Expenses for materials are minimal. Props are not necessary since they are constructed in the imagination. Little makeup or costuming is required. The scripting is done either through personal creation or by using passages from the Bible. On occasion, music can be helpful, though not necessary.

As religious expression, mime is quite potent. Parables can be enacted. Teachings can be powerfully illustrated, describing the common absurdity (and hypocrisy) of our responses to the gospel message. Character creation of biblical personalities enables the scripture to have more personal relevance through living out the story. The sense of awe and wonder that we sometimes have lost in our day can be recaptured through the total investment of a person in such enactment of our relationship with God.

Resources

1. **The Mime Book**, by Claude Kipnis, Harper Colophone Books.
2. **Mime Journal**, edited by Thomas Leabhart, Grand Valley College, Grand Rapids, MI 49505.
3. **Mime News and Mime Directory: International Mimes and Pantomimists**, by August Freundlich, 200 Crouse College, Syracuse University, Syracuse, NY 13210.
4. **Mimes on Miming**, by Bari Rolfe, Panjandrum Books.
5. **Mime: A Playbook of Silent Fantasy**, by Kay Hamblin, Doubleday.
6. **Mime: The Techniques of Silence**, by Richmond Shepard, Drama Book Specialists.
7. "An Introduction to Mime," a filmstrip by Reid Gilbert, Contemporary Drama Service, Box 457, Downers Grove, IL 60515.

See also DRAMA, PUPPETS

Mission

A youth can accomplish a multitude of worthwhile endeavors, but unless it can keep alive a spirit of mission to others, it will experience only a fraction of what it means to be members of the body of Christ. Mission and service to the needs of the world are the lifeblood of Christian discipleship for any age group.

This realization seems to be more true for youth than other age groups.

Mission is that overpowering awareness of the magnitude of God's gracious love which causes the individual or

Spiritual maturity is advanced when your group becomes caught up in a spirit of mission.

group to respond by seeking to be an agent for helping others to also claim that gift for themselves. It is a process of becoming a servant to share that which makes life meaningful for us.

Geography and expenses and time and numbers of volunteers lose their relevance when the surge to engage in mission develops. The gigantic obstacles can be felled by the mission-minded Davids with their slingshots.

Some youth groups contact missionaries whom their churches support to find out some of the major needs in the countries they serve. One such response came back from the field saying that a couple of motorcycles were needed to make some of the rounds in Brazil easier. Nothing could have matched the imagination of the group better, and they quickly turned the congregation and community into a support system not just for the motorcycles but all the helmets, clothing and fuel that the missionaries would need for many years to come.

Many groups have chosen to send themselves to provide mission help— some to Mexico to rebuild churches and homes, some to Appalachia to teach summer Bible schools, and some to lead recreation and to tutor in mission projects just around the corner from the church building.

The location of the mission need not be some far-off land or even an economically neglected part of your own town. Many youth groups have realized that they also have a mission to those persons just like themselves who live next door, persons for whom life has no meaning. Several such groups have developed radio programs to broadcast a message of hope and support by using music and comments that the youth themselves select and deliver. The stations join with the youth in making this mission happen.

One youth group picked out a downtown vacant lot and asked the owner if they could host a downtown recreational event once a month during the summer. The owner agreed, and the police volunteered to help supervise. An enormous program was held there on many occasions, and often they included a film to be shown on the side of a light-colored building. Usually the films were entertaining but also helped the viewer to realize that God does care about them.

A significant mission can be accomplished through the mail. As the group keeps itself informed about current issues, culture and events in light of its faith, it can write to various congressional leaders, media decision makers, youth heroes, and other significant persons to communicate their concern for improvement of conditions for persons in all segments of civilization.

Mission means nothing less than giving oneself away in service. Realizing the truth of what Christ said about finding your life as you give it away, youth will gain a lifetime orientation toward meaningful service to others.

Resources
1. **See It, Do It**, by David Ng, Friendship Press.
2. **Making Mission Happen**, by Arthur Bauer, Friendship Press.
3. **Purpose of the Church**, by Richard Niebuhr.
4. **Claimed by God for Mission**, by Eugene Stockwell.

See also NEWCOMER, OUTREACH, PUBLIC SCHOOLS, WITNESSING

Module

This term has had various uses in many different fields. Decades ago the housing industry found that it was more efficient to prebuild certain parts of houses in the convenience of the shop before assembling these parts together at the building site. The electronics industry picked up the idea, and now we have large pieces of equipment that can be repaired easily by replacing or correcting a small non-functioning section.

The module idea is fairly new to education circles, and in this setting it refers to a unit of study that is offered in connection with other units. These units may last just a few minutes or several months, but usually the long-range goals involve the student in a progressive program working through basic units toward more complex ones.

In youth ministry, this concept has unlimited possibilities. Modular planning emphasizes the freedom of choice of the participants while not losing the value of necessary core parts.

In the church school class, there are numbers of concepts and truths

Modules are built upon the interests and needs of small groups of youth within the context of the larger youth group.

youth needs to understand. These might include understanding the main story of the Bible, basic Christian beliefs, the history of God's people from ancient times to today. A church, along with all those who work with youth, needs to list consciously what it feels are the basics, something that every youth should know while in church school.

In addition, and no less important, are any number of related subjects that stem out of and enhance the basics. A short-term module on Christian symbolism might be of great interest to some youth, and the freedom of choosing this above others may lead the individual to invest more into this personal interest. Other modules might include creative writing, music creation, electronic expression, what others believe, creeds, prayer, etc.

Additional interest may be generated by having a team of youth to help with the module development, involving scheduling, leadership, progression, and resourcing. It is much easier for persons to participate in something if they help develop it, especially the scheduling. The more creative it is, the

better its chances for support.

Modules are a natural in the youth fellowship group. The planning council can usually look over the coming year and readily identify certain events and insights that should be shared with everyone. It can also point out some options that may have interest for only a few persons. Some of these may need to happen prior to others. For example, suppose a group wants to take part in a summer project helping persons of a different culture. Thus, it schedules a springtime module to explore the other culture. It also schedules time for a skill development module.

On a retreat, modular planning can help the planning team to see overall objectives while encouraging compatible individual objectives. In fact, the entire retreat can be planned in modular parts so that these pre-packaged (by a smaller group prior to the retreat) segments can be encountered as the group progresses through a design it can change as it wishes.

See also BIBLE, CURRICULUM, PRO-GRAM, SUNDAY SCHOOL

Motivating Youth

Sometimes we fall into the trap of fantasizing glittering attractions that will instantly fill the youth group with great excitement and enthusiasm. It's the old carrot and donkey concept.

A different and more reliable strategy is to realize that within your group are deep wells of enthusiasm waiting to be tapped. Motivation is not a link to something external but to something deep within. It does not need to be manufactured (or fabricated, as we often assume) but simply unleashed.

Youth are at a stage in life when the future is limitless. Therefore, they are future oriented and their eyes search for possible promising directions.

The motors are already running. The challenge is to discover the best existing road or how to build a better road. The challenge for the youth worker is helping clean the windshield, occasionally pump up the tires, offer to help tune the engine.

Interest finders often help a group to realize its opportunities. Early in the year it may be helpful to have each member choose his or her interests from a multitude of possibilities (this reminds them of the many possibilities at hand). Another way is to have members write out a list of their personal interests (this has the advantage of catching glimpses of that which is utmost in their consideration at the time).

When the results of these interest finders are brought before the group, then a number of common linkages may appear for the first time.

When the group does not seem to be motivated to accomplish very much, look very closely at what their inactivity is saying. It may be telling you that they sense insurmountable blockage, restrictions and mistrust. A little delving into the past, perhaps in reference to other leadership styles, may give you some clues. The key may lie in their roles at school or in the home, or in the possibility that the group does not know each other well enough to conceive what they could possibly do together. In such cases, the group may be aided by visiting other groups or hosting active groups.

Motivation often comes through chemistry, mixing persons in such a way that their spirits can blend and complement one another. Loyalty to friends and to the group contains its own impetus for action and encourages tenacity.

See also BUBBLE, CAMPING, GROUP BUILDING, INTERVIEW, LOCK-IN, RETREAT

Mountaintop Experiences

When an adult looks back over her or his spiritual journey, it is easier to recall special events than the regular ongoing classes, services and group meetings. We remember them because they were different and extraordinary, even spectacular. We also remember them as times when insights just seemed to click, offering dramatic answers to questions that had stewed within us.

On repeated surveys over the years, seminary students indicate that they first decided to become a minister during a weekend retreat at a camp or summer conference.

For some persons, it was the unusual quiet times in a natural setting that brought about the climactic response. For others, it was unique large group singing, speeches or drama presentations.

It is important to note that for most of us, the spectacular one-of-a-kind events depended upon the regular involvement in a local group back home, and the reverse was often equally true. Neither should be overlooked to bring about the other.

Mountaintop experiences do not necessarily happen by determined planning, though many adult workers with youth appear to believe otherwise. They go to elaborate means to set up highly emotional and pressurized situations, hoping that something similar will happen to the youth as it did for them. Of course, sometimes it does. But usually, our efforts at manipulating emotions are fruitless.

A leader must always analyze the motives behind these efforts and methods. We must ask if this is an attempt to force youth into an emotional dependency upon the leader: "Ever since

Most mountaintop experiences need a sensitive transition into everyday life to remain meaningful.

that fall retreat, our youth have been skipping the worship service to sit and talk with Jim and Joan, their advisors," or some sort of a success record: "At least three youth have joined the church during each of our last five conferences, and we never fail to bring them back all teary-eyed and sleepy from our all-night prayer sessions."

The value in the mountaintop experience can be found in the growth that takes place within the individuals and the group as a corporate body. How rewarding it is when a person has the rare gift of a number of hours away from the

normal routine to deal with significant issues for them and to be mentally and spiritually stretched in the process.

The biggest danger of these experiences is leaving the person and the group on the mountaintop without a way down. Life is almost always easier, more rewarding, and alluring when we can stay away from the stressful, threatening daily decisions and confrontations. Therefore, group leaders must be very determined to smooth the transition to reality, to where "life is so daily," as one person has described it. What we experienced away from the routine must be applied and redirected to the valleys where we reside.

A final period on the mountaintop (called something like "What Next?" or "Back Home Application") can help transfer the previous learnings into useful tools for our future. These debriefing operations, as the space programs taught us to call them, help us to move our feet back down the mountains carrying with us the treasures found up above.

Your group may wish to role play some situations you will encounter upon return and try to apply your new understandings and commitment in ways that will help each person with real life challenges. Also, you may wish to help the group consider some future opportunities for those not at the event to receive similar insights and experiences. Finally, a very positive and supportive way to end a mountaintop experience is to help the group members share support for each other by pledges of ways they can be called upon.

In short, these are unique occasions when we can see above the confining valleys to unlimited possibilities for ourselves and our world. There is no way to assess their lasting value. And in response to the question all of us often ask—yes, these experiences are worth the effort.

See also EMOTIONS

Movies

The flicks are still a major entertainment medium of teens. At least, young people make the most significant contribution to the box office. Films which do not appeal to teens do not bring a good financial return and rarely make it.

The church once viewed all movies as sinful. There may still be movies that church folk consider bad influences, but film as a powerful art form has been accepted by most people.

There are two different film situations. The first occasion is in-church use. You may rent or borrow a film for an evening program. There are many sources of free movies. Local and regional libraries now stock huge selections of motion pictures. They will even order them for purchase upon request!

At one time, education assumed that audio-visuals would completely teach people. Just turn on the projector and let it be. However, it is now apparent that a discussion leader is more important than ever when a film is used.

A movie in a youth group setting is not just a message from a filmmaker which must be caught. Each person in the group has a different and valid experience as he or she watches the film. The goal facing you is to enable these scattered pieces of feeling and meaning to fit into a gathered tapestry. Often this cannot be done in a frontal manner. If the film has a strong impact, it may be hard to set these feelings into word patterns. After the showing of one powerful anti-war film which had graphically illustrated the results of an atomic blast on England, we were stunned. There was silence. A college student broke the specter of fear. "I need to hold someone's hand." We joined hands for a couple minutes. Then we started the discussion and debriefing of our feelings.

It is also important to realize that in this kind of setting you can use the film any way you desire. We have used movies in sections. We have played the first few minutes, then stopped the machine. "What is going to happen to the characters?" The projector started again after reflection.

We have also used two films at once. One screen may show Harry Chapin talking about hunger while the other features the faces of hungry people from an old mission film.

Slides can even be used to contrast

A good discussion leader is more important than ever when a film is used.

the images of the film. Try showing the movie on top of the slides! The film can be shown with a different sound track. Play a record while showing the images. Use the motion picture in several different ways at the same program.

The second setting for film usage with youth is the local theater. This is a trickier task. It is hard to find films which work well with all teens. It seems that every picture with a safe rating throws in unneeded rough language. However, it is a fact that your teens go to these shows with or without your approval or planning. If you want to deal with film as a theological art form, you will have to plunge boldly into the secular realm. There is a great deal to explore. Much of it is very good for those who want to struggle with the relationship between faith and life.

Even the most secular subjects cannot escape the person wearing spectacles of faith. These films are particularly dramatic and will usually carry strong character development. This form is especially good for discussion. Role playing and other techniques have been helpful in debriefing the cinema experience. For instance, if a story ends with the future uncertain, have members of your group take key roles and act through what will happen next. Add situations under which further development will take place.

Ethics emerge again and again in most secular films. They are ideal ways of probing the Christian's decisions in similar situations. Science fiction, western, detective, romance and adventure stories all have a place in your probe of film with youth. You are preparing them to think theologically about art and media. They are being equipped to apply the theological mindset on all of life. Many adults and youth cannot make the transition from faith to entertainment. They seem like two different worlds to many.

See also CURRICULUM, GROUP-MEDIA, MEDIA AWARENESS

Multi Media

The combination of media can be more powerful than any single medium.

A few years ago the education establishment became overwhelmed by what has been termed "the audio-visual" revolution. It is understandable how the hope of film, slides and sound recordings sprung into the minds of secular teachers. "If it can sell potato chips, it should be wonderful for science." Religious types also caught the bug. "If multi-media can sell science, it should be wonderful for theology." The process of putting together several images (slides and film) with a background of music and voices soon became one of the hottest fads. Like all techniques zealously pursued without question, the audio-visual thrust soon faded.

We are now living through a "media" fad. This differs from the audio-visual interest because it is a bit broader. The teacher and students are taken more seriously as ingredients in the learning process. We have learned that a movie or slide show in itself cannot teach. It must be the interaction between the medium, its content and the receiver which promotes growth.

Media sensibility can be an important skill for youth ministry. However, it is just one of many techniques which must be packed into your ministry survival kit. When the moment arrives which best dictates the use of a particular approach, then you will have it to use.

Technically, this means using a number of different audio-visual sources at the same time for one production. Occasionally, there are presentations using film, slides, spotlights, and different types of audio input but usually, *multi-media* refers to a sound and light show using several slide projectors aimed at several screens with a cassette or reel-to-reel tape recorder soundtrack.

The technique of some multi-media producers is to put a number of visual images on the screen in rapid succession with compatible sounds, and the viewer is encouraged to reap whatever conclusions that are inspired. Other producers are the opposite, and they give a literal soundtrack to what is seen, even to the point of including visual headings and audio narrative to accompany the visual images.

Youth are particularly fascinated by multi-media because they have grown up in a visual world where information is not necessarily presented sequentially as it usually was in the days many of the adults were in school. A TV show today may incorporate four or five major plots, many of which are not retold in chronological order. This stimulates the brain and tempts the viewer by arousing curiosity.

Youth also love to make multi-media since it is using the form of communication with which they are the most familiar. Perhaps the most significant contribution is that it encourages them to actively produce and control media which often so highly manipulates and controls their world. Participating in the process makes them aware of what can be done and to be more on their guard against it.

Ed is a serious multi-media practitioner. For instance, he worked with a high school confirmation class as it probed the meaning of baptism. He had gathered a number of old filmstrips from the denominational office. (They are almost always throwing some away.) He had purchased several boxes of "half-frame" slide mounts. This enables the young people to cut up the old filmstrips in order to get the images they need. The frame is easily slipped into the mount without glue or paste. The black film at the beginning of the strip was cut up and placed in the mounts. By using a pin, one teen was able to scratch the name of each person in the group on individual frames. These were mounted.

On a big table, Ed had placed a huge pile of old TV commercials. They were on 16mm film. Many TV commercials are now on videotape. However, the 16mm film can still be found in local stations. Ed asked his students to find sections of the film which related to the theme of baptism. These were then connected by using a simple film splicer which utilizes small pieces of tape.

Ed had one group of young people working on the soundtrack of the baptism media presentation. Portions of scripture were searched. A sound effects record with the rush of water was used. The youth in this group decided to get some interviews from adults about the meaning of baptism to mix with the scripture and sounds. One member of the group found a recording of a song about baptism.

This presentation was put together in several meetings. Additional slides from private collections and even some shots from magazines were utilized. The evening service in which the three-screen presentation was shared, a young person was baptized. It became a meaningful experience which combined the personal, electric and historical.

Such productions can utilize every ounce of skill and time that a person or group wishes to give, but it also produces rewards. It is quite a thrill for youth to view their own creation on a large screen and hear sounds they have put together on several large speakers. It means that someone has taken them and their world quite seriously.

Resources
1. **Gadgets, Gimmicks, and Grace: A Handbook on Multimedia in Church and School**, by Ed McNulty, Abbey.
2. **Multi-Media in the Church: A Beginner's Guide for Putting It All Together**, by W. A. Engstrom, John Knox.

Music

A once-popular song suggested "I've got the music in me." While this may be true, most adult leaders feel uncomfortable in their encounters with youth's pop music. Often the youth advisor or sponsor has been away from pop music for the past 10 years. In fact, the occasional brush with rock music through an essay in a newsmagazine tends to be frightening. The latest musical fads seem like light years away from the simple music of the past.

There is a temptation to generalize about kinds of music. "Acid" rock (a term heard only from those outside of music) has often been a favorite area of attack by religious folk. "If it weren't for those terrible rock stars and that drug music, the young people wouldn't be led astray." Perhaps this simplistic answer is comforting to some. However, the single evil theory doesn't hold up very well in a biblical context. The Lord God did not accept Adam's and Eve's attempt to point the blame at another for their sin. They did not slip out of their responsibilitiy that easily. God placed

the burden of choosing faithfulness on them. Music and stars don't lead young people astray. It is much sounder to call young people to be responsible for their decisions in a complex society.

Bob was a typical youth advisor—his pastor had talked him into taking the youth group. He was totally out of touch with youth culture and its music. Fear filled him those first few weeks. But he swallowed his pride, told the youth that he knew nothing about their music and asked each person to bring one song which meant a great deal to him or her. He wanted them to teach *him* about the meanings in the music. The only rule they agreed upon was that no one would make fun of someone else's favorite record.

The discussion was amazing! He discovered that the group learned a great deal about its members through the music. An "obvious" lyric was interpreted in a totally different manner when it was filtered through the listener's values and faith. It became quite clear that the young people took this trivial idiom very seriously.

Bob found that the students enjoyed teaching him something. Each person was an expert on that which he or she liked. In fact, most young people discovered they had a lot to contribute. It was quite easy to cast the concerns into a bigger realm of reflection. The themes of ethics and religious values easily entered the conversation. Bob was amazed how easily the youth could link these secular musical forms with their spiritual lives.

Some youth groups have used popular music to reach out to other teens. *The Place* radio format was produced locally as a radio show. Several teens from a local church would discuss feelings and ideas while surrounded by several songs from the station's regular playlist. The new context of serious discussion changed the meanings of the songs.

New Christians

Over 200 different groups produced this show at its height. The biggest problem the show faced was finding an adult host who would trust the young people enough to let them talk. The anxious adult often interrupted the discussion to impose questions which would give answers he or she desired.

There are aspects of popular music which are not pleasant. Every art form reflects the values of the times. This means that some lyrics are sexist and others are in bad taste. However, our goal in youth ministry is to equip our folks to make the right decisions.

The example of Ulysses can be used to reflect this style of using music with youth. This ancient hero learned that he and his sailors had to pass through straits of danger. Strange female-like creatures would lure them to their destruction with seductive music. The power of the music would drive them crazy. Ulysses put wax on his sailors ears, told his men to keep rowing and to tie him to the ship's mast. Having no plugs in his ears, he was able to take in all the sights and sounds without being destroyed.

This image expresses our goal of working with youth. There are those who tell us to put wax in our ears and not listen to the music. However, lashed securely to our faith in Christ we are called into the world to experience creation fully. We trust that our life together will give us the security of Christ so that nothing can lead us astray.

Resources
1. **Songs**, edited by Yohann Anderson, Songs and Creations, P.O. Box 559, San Anselmo, CA 94960.
2. **Music You Wear**, by Bill Wolfe, Discipleship Resources.
3. **Rock Generation**, by Dennis Benson, Abingdon.

See also CHOIRS, RECORDS

In the life of every youth group, there are moments when the spiritual journeys of youth are apparent to you. You may even see bad influences reflected in some of your folks. There will be occasions when a boy or girl has a breakthrough in faith. It may be called a "born again" experience or spiritual renewal. The young person will suddenly have a new focus on all the things you have been teaching him or her. The teen will feel compelled to share this awakening. This is a wonderful moment. Yet, it can also cause some difficulties. Other members of your group may feel threatened by the compulsion of this new Christian. At this stage in the person's life, the use of judgment and fear may seem to be important ways of reaching others. This will scare some younger teens.

You will also feel a bit uneasy that the newly-inspired youth is judging you. "Are you a real Christian?" If you can handle this irritation, you might be a bit concerned about the prayer group or other organization which led your teen to this stage.

One of the best ways of dealing with this brother or sister is to encourage further and more demanding growth. Lead him or her into deeper Christian commitment. One youth advisor was confronted with this kind of situation. The young boy carried his Bible to school and preached to everyone he met. Unfortunately, he had much to learn about the faith. The extra-church group he met with studies the Bible by flipping around the scriptures. There was no appreciation for historical and contextual biblical study. Jim, the youth group leader, suggested how his teen could become even more of a disciple. By talking to a clergyman in the community, he arranged for the young person to take lessons in New Testament Greek.

The pastor spent three hours a week teaching the biblical language to the teen and two other people. An amazing thing happened in this enriching environment. The teen learned exegesis (how to dig out the meaning of the text) from the sound historical manner.

The beauty of this model is that you are not challenging the faith or sincerity of the babe in Christ. You are merely leading him or her into a growth pattern which can build on the initial rush of being a Christian.

See also BIBLE, DEVOTIONAL LIFE, GROUP BUILDING

Newcomer

Every group wants to grow. At least, this is the most common question we receive at our workshops. "How can we get more people to our meetings? They come for the parties, but not for Bible study or other programs."

The attendance at your meetings is a result rather than a cause of your problem. Youth like to go where something exciting is happening. However, there are always a few teens who will come every week just to be with their friends. Sadly, it is sometimes their commitment to the small group which destroys the possibility of drawing other teens. The "in" group becomes very close. They find those points of community which makes them compatible. Language, jokes, songs and other subtle signals develop among these eight or ten youth. They enjoy this closeness. It means a great deal to their lives.

The stranger or newcomer finds great difficulty breaking through this tight circle. The faithful few almost resent the newcomer. They flex their unity by cutting the guest out of their communication system. Just watch what happens when the outsider visits. Does he or she sit near the others? Do the regulars cluster together and laugh a lot? It takes a very strong person to fight into this cell.

This suggests that you work on your tight-knit core as a prelude to outreach. Help them understand hospitality as a spiritual gift. Once the core group learns how to be inclusive, develop with your youth some strong programming reasons for meeting. Then get the word out to others about what is happening. One of the best ways to reach other youth is the one-on-one approach. Ask each person to bring someone else. There should then be a followup to the

newcomer. A personal phone call or a chance to serve the group can follow during the next week.

One group in Georgia has passed through the first training steps. Now the members develop imaginative ways to include others. The kidnap bus is one of their favorites. Using several vans they pick up inactive teens at their homes. They take them as honored guests to a picnic or some other fun outing.

There was a time when youth advisors would complain about youth's lack of commitment. Most youth workers now know that young people are living in a world which encourages limited commitment. We are not a culture of joiners. We go to something because the group seems appealing or we are needed. In a way, this is a helpful situation. This means that the Christian faith is being challenged to deliver the quality of its message. If our youth meetings are boring and meaningless, maybe the young people shouldn't be there! However, once we have a solid hold of our real contribution to their lives, nothing will keep them away.

See also ATTENDANCE, CLIQUES, COMMUNITY, INTEREST, OUTREACH, PUBLICITY

New Games

New Games is the title of a foundation that encourages participatory playing which involves as much creativity and community as can be squeezed into each activity. Starting out in the early '70s, this movement began as a means of promoting understanding among persons.

Soon there was the classic recreation book, **New Games**, by the New Games Foundation (found in most book stores), followed by training programs in how to play the games. These training enterprises have covered the globe and brought together amazing combinations

of persons of every age and background.

Actually, many of the games are very old while others get invented as groups make changes of their own to accommodate particular interests. Looking for usable old games and making new ones is the whole idea.

Resources
1. **The New Games Book**, edited by Andrew Fluegelman, Doubleday.
2. New Games Foundation (newsletter and materials) P.O. Box 7901, San Francisco, CA 94120.

See also NO-LOSER RECREATION

New Year's Eve

Holiday seasons have both a secular and religious character in our culture. No one has a better understanding of celebration than the faith community. Yet, the church often collapses (from exhaustion?) after Christmas.

This is too bad because the New Year's passage point has values for just about everyone. There is supposed to be a time of firecrackers, kissing and happiness when the new year comes. Unfortunately, it is a time of sadness for many folks. Perhaps the old see another year gone with dreams unfulfilled. The young either go to a party or stay behind and watch television. Most commercial New Year's Eve parties are boring.

Some churches have a tradition of New Year's Eve celebrations. Most are a mixture of worship and party. It is a good occasion for the gathering of teens and young adults who have returned from college or other out-of-town activities. One year, Jim and his folks had a scavenger hunt and bonfire celebration. They gave each carload of youth a list of items which had to be collected. Each object related to fire building (newspapers, twigs, rocks, pieces of wood, limbs and logs). The cars had to return to the church after each group of items was collected. The group built a fire and roasted hot dogs and marshmallows. Jim read scripture passages which contained images of fire. He featured Ecclesiastes 3:1-11 as a focus on the New Year's Eve setting. Different group members shared moments from the past year where they missed opportunities for faithfulness.

Another youth group used a railroad car as the setting for a New Year's Eve celebration. They rented the car and traveled to a point and back during the event. They built their worship around the image of movement. At one point, they all stationed themselves at windows and looked for certain things as symbols of what is missed in life. For example: "Find a light and seek the house or car from which it comes. Who are the people around it? If you dropped in, what message would you bring them?"

At one point in the journey, the youth advisor, Nancy, read the Hawthorne short story, "The Celestial Railroad" (a reverse image of **Pilgrim's Progress**). They discussed how they may have been riding this past year on a wrong path. At the transfer point, the young people gave out donuts to those boarding the rail. They then talked on the way back about how some people refused their gifts.

This special holiday can provide the opportunity for growth among your folk.

See also CHRISTMAS, EASTER, FALL CELEBRATIONS

No-loser Recreation

Perhaps you've been here: The conference speaker or Bible leader has just concluded a moving presentation on what marvelous things can happen to our world when persons love one another. You reflect on those thoughts as you hurry off to another activity in which the participants are divided into teams and urged to be so aggressive and competitive toward the other teams that hostility ensues. You leave that event thinking of opposing team members as things to destroy.

Maybe you have been here too: You are a new member of the group, and that was never so evident to yourself as when the weekly volleyball game began and old friends always set up the ball for each other. Unfortunately, the ball always seemed to touch ground near your position and people began to make comments about it. You never returned.

The No-Loser Concept

We learn from everything we do. Moreover, studies show that the best learning situation is for us to take part in the action. This fact makes recreation a super way to learn.

Recreation is theology in motion. It teaches, illustrates and emphasizes what the group, the leader, and the sponsoring organization have faith in and how that faith should be lived out.

Recreation within the Christian community can be a vibrant, contemporary way of visualizing and experiencing Christ's teachings. The way each participant is treated can emphasize what Christ did and said about the persons with whom he came in contact.

Persons planning church recreation might do well to first look at what Christ told his disciples about winning and losing. In Luke 9:23-24 we read: And he said to all, "If any man would come after me, let him deny himself and take up his cross daily and follow me. For whoever would save his life will lose it, and whoever loses his life for my sake, he will save it."

Slightly later in the same passage, Christ spoke about greatness. From Luke 9:46-48: And an argument arose among them as to which of them was the greatest. But when Jesus perceived the

Recreation within the Christian community can be a vibrant, contemporary way of visualizing and experiencing Christ's teachings.

thought in their hearts, he took a child and put him by his side, and said to them, "Whoever receives this child in my name receives me, and whoever receives me receives him who sent me; for he who is least among you all is the one who is great." In these words, Christ tells us that our actions should build up other persons, not convince everyone that we are the greatest.

It is very important to note that these teachings do not encourage us to see ourselves as losers. Quite the opposite, our greatness can be found in helping other persons to also see themselves as winners. Everyone gains.

Recreation need not be give-away activities in which the stronger or more experienced participant purposefully loses, for that would take away from both persons needlessly. Instead, the energies of both persons should be concentrated on helping both of them to grow by acknowledging what each has to offer. Both win.

But What About Competition?

This question often is couched in such phrases as, "The rest of the world is so competitive that our games should be . . ." or, "Competition teaches people how to become normal persons." According to this logic, if a person realized his or her garden were the only one in the neighborhood, he should dig it up! This logic would also suggest that nothing should ever be different from or better than the average world around it.

Recreation without cutthroat competition can teach us a lot about the way the rest of the world could become. Defeating another person or group is no more necessary in play as it is in any other part of life. The abundant life that Christ brings to the world is to be shared, not fought over.

If we can keep before us the idea of sharing and giving life, then activities that accomplish this through pitting one team or individual against another may be appropriate. Call it testing out our skills with one another or call it competition, but the goal is to build up all the participants and not to demolish or to diminish anyone.

When the stress is placed on mutual support and development, the need for points and score tabulation often becomes of such little importance, that activities are chosen that do not use them or at least do not revolve totally around them. This may even lead to changes in the way the game is played in order that all the potential participants can experience enjoyment and fulfillment during the event and afterwards.

Some persons may react to such ideas by saying, "You shouldn't change the rules; the players ought to learn that life has to be played by the rules." However, isn't the only real rule of life to love your neighbor as you love yourself? Many of the rules we hold so dear are at odds with that rule. Perhaps being encouraged in our play to make wise changes in the rules to benefit everyone would encourage us in other pursuits to mold our laws to affirm all persons.

Can Everyone Always Win?

The Christian has already won, ultimately, forever. No absence of points, poorly hit ball or wrong answer can ever take away that total victory. That truth should affect the way we work as well as the way we play. Perhaps those who do not know this victory can begin to learn something about it by the way they see us act.

One shudders to think what many of the teams with their "defeat the other team at all costs" attitude in church softball and basketball leagues teach about the church to the outside observer.

Even if open hostility and destructive, vindictive competition were a way of life in the everyday marketplace (which they are not), it would be all the more reason for the church to illustrate by its activities that a new life of victory brings new values.

None of us likes to lose. In the Peanuts cartoon, Charlie Brown stated what we all feel when he said, "Winning may not be everything, but losing isn't anything." And there are enough people all around us who feel like total, unredeemable losers that the church could well look for ways to enable persons to discover that they are winners.

An important part of no-loser recreation is that no activity should be played at any person's expense. Never should the group's attention be turned to an individual, or even a small group of individuals, who are the brunt of the joke. When this is allowed to happen, even with hilarious results, it jeopardizes the self-esteem of persons. On the surface the individuals may indicate that they enjoyed being shown to be foolish or awkward, but a very different, life-long response may be taking place within them.

Also to be avoided are games that involve destruction of property. There is no reason why our play should result in the demolition of any part of a room, camp, neighborhood or building. Our play then indicates that we consider ourselves more important than other persons who might wish to use the objects and buildings we harm in fun.

For a number of reasons it is highly questionable to ever use food in recreational events. When we do, the message is that the value of food as a sustaining gift from God is diminished. In addition, the use of a small bite of food during play can often result in strangulation and sickness, and for this reason alone most experienced recreation leaders avoid the use of anything that must be consumed during play.

The individual can learn from the leader, who intentionally took on a servant role for the good of individuals in the group, something of what Christ meant by "whoever loses his life for my sake, he will save it." And the individual can learn from the warm welcome and sustaining friendship of the group something of what was meant by "whoever receives this child in my name, receives me."

Resources
1. **The Cooperative Sports and Games Book**, by Terry Orlick, Pantheon Press.
2. **Learning Through Noncompetitive Activities and Play**, by Bill and Delores Michaelis, Learning Handbooks.
3. **Joy and Sadness in Children's Sports**, Human Kinetics Publishers.

See also RECREATION

Officers

Most youth groups want to have youth officers guide the progress of their group, and many youth want to be officers. The actual need for officers will vary from group to group. Such factors as size of group, leadership potential, variety and intensity of probable activities, relationship with other groups (representatives to this or that other body), subgroups that need a voice (7th grade representative or similar person in a large group containing many grade levels, southside representative in a group covering a large geographical territory) and anticipated functions will play a role.

Unless a group has a standing set of bylaws, the number and duties of the officers can be changed as the group chooses. It is possible to change officers regularly (three months, six months, whatever) and delete offices that are no longer deemed helpful. For instance, if your group has a large number of highly qualified persons, it might be advantageous to have co-officers in a number of positions and change them often. The same could be true if you have a number of persons who need to develop leadership skills.

Leadership changes should not be made unilaterally. The group should discuss potential changes and prepare for new elections so the group retains ownership and is more likely to follow the new leadership.

The officers plus the adult leaders may be designated as the council or planning committee, which is charged with oversight or the program, including long-range goal setting and weekly meeting planning. However, it could be that the entire group would prefer to do the goal setting and let the officers and planning committee work out the details.

Many groups wish to function with a small number of ongoing officers (chairperson/moderator/president, co-chairpersons, secretary, treasurer) and do most of the other work through task forces (program planning for a set period of time, project oversight, recreation, worship). It is usually wise to appoint persons as representative to other groups for a longer period of time (at least six months) so that some continuity can be developed in order that the person can adequately learn the mechanics involved and truly represent the group.

Officers embody the highest attributes of the group and should be selected as those who will lead the group forward. The election process should not be seen as a popularity contest, punishment, appeasement or nepotism.

See also CLIQUES, COMMITMENT, YOUTH COUNCIL

The Open Door

Bud and Lenore Frimoth are the producers of an award-winning radio show, "The Open Door." This show has also spawned a newsletter with the same name. The show is built around teenagers' writings and thoughts. Music is used as the context for the presentation of these moving stories. The fine thing about this show is that you can get it placed on your local radio station. The ministry is totally supported by gifts from church groups. Drop them a note for more information. This show will complement your youth ministry perfectly. (Write P.O. Box 12506, Portland, OR 97212.)

See also RADIO

Outreach

One of the characteristics of the earliest church was outreach. The early Christians gathered in a small group, worshipped, fellowshipped and studied. They then had amazing power to go into the world and touch the lives of others. This ability to stretch the circle of love to embrace others is one of the miracles of the faith. The church has been trying to do this in many different ways ever since. Many different labels have been affixed to the basic reflex to what God has first done for us. Mission, service, evangelism, outreach and work projects have been some of the titles for this theological impulse.

The youth group is caught in a difficult position because it is composed of members who have not been recognized as contributing much to the society. In fact, our culture has retarded the development of responsibility among the young; the day when the farm needed

Youth need the chance to serve as much as others need their service.

everyone to contribute has long since passed for most youth. Present economic factors tend to keep young people from getting into the job market and learning the responsibility such jobs would develop. Servanthood is in our spiritual genes. Therefore, youth need to look at this aspect of our faith seriously. They need the chance to serve as much as others need their service.

The thrust of touching the lives of others with the fruit of the faith can be experienced in many ways. One of the valuable ways of enabling youth to reach out to others is peer ministry. This is the task of intentionally taking on the problems and concerns of other youth.

It is wise to form a group of young people who have a special interest in practicing their faith in the tough situations of daily life. Find a skilled person to lead a series of training sessions on listening (check with your local mental health department). Agree to meet each week at a special time. Each person is charged with the responsibility of seeking a person who is hurting. Through the act of befriending another youth, the youth group member is able to provide a ministry of presence. The young person doing peer ministry returns to the group each week for support and prayer. In many cases, this kind of care will help the person who had relatively simple coping problems. But in other cases, it will be clear that the person being served needs further help. The peer minister can be the linkage point to get that person to the help he or she needs.

You don't have to be the expert who provides all the training and perspective. It is your task to enable all the needed factors to be assembled in order for this ministry to take place.

A youth group in Georgia built the outreach dimension of their youth ministry into their regular programming. Every member is required to spend two hours a week in outreach work. The youth advisor organizes and monitors the many different opportunities available to the students. Some work as volunteers in the local hospital, others are aides at a school for handicapped students and a few spend time in an information booth at the local shopping mall.

Outreach embraces both the witness and serving sides of the Christian life. Young people have a great capacity for exercising these gifts of faith. It is our task as youth workers to enable them to have these opportunities for outreach.

See also EVANGELISM, PEER COUNSELING, SERVICE, TAMING

Panic

Let's describe some of the ways it can strike:

• You frequently wake up at night with visions of young people jumping on top of you. They appear so much wiser, more coordinated, more up-to-date than you.

• You are driving in your car and all at once you remember numerous details of a youth event you had forgotten to plan.

• You are watching TV and hear news of a wreck involving teenagers. All at once you consider that everything you have done with your youth group is too shallow and too trivial in light of life and death issues.

• You keep having a recurring fear of being in the middle of a youth meeting when all of the youth say they are bored and leave for good.

• You are halfway along on a youth trip, 800 miles from home, and you realize that all of the money has been used up.

This list could go on and on. Each time panic strikes, you feel responsible for whatever has gone wrong.

It may seem to be poor consolation but you are in the majority of youth workers —the really conscientious ones. Thank heaven for all of you because you understand the enormity of the responsibility. You are concerned. The opposite of panic is self-satisfaction to the point of unconcern.

At the same time, it is important not to allow panic—those sudden flashes of inadequacy—to overwhelm you. When you get zapped by those terrible feelings, determine what caused the feelings and see what you can do to improve the situation. If the feelings are brought on by overwork or too much responsibility, take steps to get extra help. Often we panic when we feel alone in the situation or when we realize that no one else seems to care. In these cases, additional help can minister to us while we minister to the group.

The most devastating brand of panic is when we feel incompetent, useless,

unworthy. Remember during these valleys that we are always in a team ministry with God, in whose image we were made and in whose strength we serve. There is really no task or circumstance in youth ministry that God cannot easily handle. The more we rely on that constant source of direction, the more easily it can be channeled through us. If we really believe God can care for us in our death, we ought always to assume that love extends to all our needs in life.

We also need to remember that other persons panic too. Youth, parents, pastors, everyone has those same feelings of hopelessness that sometimes causes them to act in rather irrational ways. As others have often ministered to us, so can we to these in our midst.

Panicking over things in the past is useless, and does not serve us well in dealing with the future. We are left with the present moment, and with God's help, we can look it squarely in the face and proceed.

See also AAUGH, BURN-OUT, DOUBTS, FAILURE, SUICIDE

Parachute

One large, floppy parachute transforms any lawn into a field of zany fun.

No, it's not for jumping out of the window in the youth meeting room when things get rough! It's for helping your group to jump into a lot of fun. Any size group can have great spontaneous excitement by devising new uses for parachutes.

The size and intrigue of a parachute lures onlookers to join the crowd in flapping the monstrous piece of fabric. The movement of air and the rippling sound of the material quickly puts a smile on the faces of the group around the circle. And then someone in the group produces an air-filled ball (the inexpensive drug store type), tosses it in the middle of the chute and starts a modified version of volleyball by trying to propel the ball over the opposite side.

After a group has developed some ability with the chute (and a large amount of concern for each other), individuals can lie in the middle and have the incredible supportive feeling of being gently lifted and lowered. This can only be done with a strong chute that has roping across the middle and a number of well-placed virile persons to guide the gradual elevation. Remember that the volunteer in the middle is in a very vulnerable position and could be severely hurt if not for the constant care of the group.

One of the most spectacular tricks is to lift the chute high into the air, especially if you have a brightly colored one that the sunlight can shine through. Have your group grab on to places all around the edges. (Gather a little extra material in the palm of your hands.) Pull the chute taut about waist high. Take two steps in and two steps back. Then four steps in and four steps back and then six steps in and six out. At this point the parachute should be ballooning up in the center.

You can take this a bit further by getting it up to maximum height, probably with eight steps in and eight out. Then have everyone quickly turn around, put their edge of the chute to the ground and sit on it facing the center. This creates an igloo for a meeting, storytelling, a party or just plain keeping warm.

If your young people are interested in growing in numbers, they may find great success by playing with the parachute in a place where other youth will notice the fun the group is having.

Resources

Chutes are available at almost any army surplus store, air force base or recreation supply house. They are also available through Worldwide Games, Box 450, Delaware, OH 43015.

See also BUBBLE, BUS, EARTHBALL, WEATHER BALLOON

Parents

At times, parents of the members in the youth group can be your greatest support; at other times, they can be your worst enemies. There is nothing like the feeling of hearing parents tell how meaningful the group is for their children. And there is hardly anything like the feeling of hearing parents complain when a trip, a study or project interferes with their plans.

The very changeable nature of parental expectations of the youth program can present some of the worst problems you will encounter. Most of us have run into the parent who is very excited about church camp's high standards, but the same parent will encourage the breaking of several rules during a visit. And many of us have experienced parents who refuse to help with the youth program, saying that others are so much more qualified, but who believe the worst about the youth leader whenever a problem arises.

Certainly, we can convince ourselves that parents' actions are just human nature. People are funny, we say. But down deep we can feel trapped and hurt by these contradictory attitudes. It may cause us to question our own motivation and sense of direction. "I thought I was carrying out the type of program everyone wanted. But if some of these parents say I'm too strict. . .maybe I'm doing something really wrong."

Begin dealing with the problem by acknowledging the conflicts. Try to determine where your mixed signals are coming from. Above all, don't get bitter. Instead, distinguish if the advice or complaint was justified or just an emotional knee-jerk reaction. After all, the parents were not involved in your planning sessions and their children may be giving them a distorted story. Being outsiders to a program almost always distorts the view.

Remember that you are the youth leader. You act out of best interests for each person and the total youth program. Take the parents' suggestions, even the incongruous ones, as helpful resources. But you are not bound by anything but your loyalty to your calling as a servant.

The same is true with the flowery compliments. Again, these are helpful evaluations to record. The compliments may not hold up in other situations, but for the present, they are insightful readings.

Parents can often be most helpful as chaperones, cooks, drivers and other assistants when the relationship between themselves and the youth in the group is mutually supportive. Obviously, some youth resent their parents' intrusion, suspecting that they are there to inspect and snoop into their activities. Other youth appreciate the parental support.

You will find it helpful to keep the parents informed concerning the group's activities, goals and plans. Many leaders gather the parents occasionally to relay what occurs and let the parents know special ways they can be of help. Suggestions can be passed along as the program progresses rather than permitting conditions to mount that would encourage outbursts of suspicion and frustration.

Parents need to know that as a trusted leader of the youth, you may have occasions when confidences have to be maintained. Most parents will respect this since they will realize this is the only way that youth can feel free enough to come to the advisor with crucial problems. Parents should realize that you are not a substitute parent. Instead, you are a significant adult whose function supports the parent as well as the youth. When this dual relationship becomes apparent, parents will appreciate more than ever the crucial ministry you have undertaken.

Let us not forget those golden parents who will always be there to help. Sometimes they do not feel it best to work directly with the group, but they do know how to help you when you call for support or extra legs if things get desperate. They may not say a lot, and you may forget just how supportive they can be.

It's good to know that parents are on your side.

Resources

1. **Building Positive Parent-Teen Relationships**, by H. Norman Wright and Rex Johnson.

2. **Almost Grown: A Christian Guide for Parents of Teenagers**, James Oraker and Char Meredith.

3. **Between Parents and Teenager**, by Haim Ginott, Avon Books.

See also PARENT EFFECTIVENESS TRAINING, PARENTING

Parenting

"I wish you were my parents!" A time will come when someone states or implies this kind of compliment. This is a meaningful admission. Your position is special and important, but you are not the parent. Your role can never take the parent's place. It's easy to get confused. If things are working well with your youth ministry, the young people will yearn for a permanent relationship with you. But, even though vital kinds of things can happen in your programming, the young people go back to a full week of influence from a continuous relationship with parents. Whether or not the family influence is bad, you cannot balance the situation by being an hour-a-week antidote.

A complete youth ministry program includes a parent training and support dimension. You have a responsibility to those parents who just can't understand their developing son or daughter. "I love the kid. I just can't stand his outrageous behavior." "If she would just stop playing that crazy music!" Most parents feel some sort of responsibility for their children. But many find their attempts to show their love short-circuited. They just can't link their parental feelings with the adult-teen relationship.

Many churches have developed programs for training adults to communicate. Your community may have Parent Effectiveness Training resources. This is a nationally organized approach based on the work of psychologist Thomas Gordon. Even though it is a secular program, many churches have found it very helpful.

You and your teens could develop your own parent training course. Perhaps several adults and teens from your church could attend one of the parenting courses offered by another organization, return home and design your own course. Utilize the entertainment (sports, music), issues (taxes, military draft) and faith (virgin birth, sexual ethics) concerns of both adults and youth. Perhaps part of the session could be spent with adults and teens working in separate groups. They might discuss the concerns of the other age group. Then the multi-session course could feature a gathered time when each group shares what it has learned about the other group. Both groups could practice listening skills. (For instance, in heated discussions, you can slow down the process by asking the person to restate his point before you respond.) It is amazing how we often talk past one another without responding to what another is communicating.

You might build in a worship experience at the conclusion of each session to affirm the connection between the ages. Once you have designed and conducted this course with different adults and teens leading it, you might want to make this parenting training an outreach ministry of your youth group. Imagine how many community groups would welcome this contribution of your youth!

See also BURN-OUT, POWER, YOUTH, YOUTH MINISTER

Parent Effectiveness Training

One of the most practical communication laboratory experiences ever made available to parents on a local level is affectionately known as PET. Churches, schools and other community agencies have contracted with the PET program so that trained, certified leaders can lead the classroom instruction. Normally, classes have between 10 and 30 participants and meet one evening a week for several hours over an eight-week period. Tuition is realistic.

Several learning methods are used, including lectures, demonstrations, tape recording of conflicts, role plays and other exercises. Class members are encouraged to try out the learnings, report back to the group and make suggestions to each other about better ways that the situations could have been handled.

The textbook for the course is **Parent Effectiveness Training** by Dr. Thomas Gordon, founder of the course. It encourages persons to describe their own feelings and to express to other persons what they would prefer to have happen. Verbal negotiations are encouraged in resolving conflicts rather than unproductive bickering. Mutual respect is to be maintained in every exchange.

Resources
1. **Parent Effectiveness Training: The No-Lose Program for Raising Responsible Children**, by Thomas Gordon, New American Library.
2. You can get in touch with the PET people by writing to Effectiveness Training, Inc., 531 Stevens Ave., Solana Beach, CA 92705.

See also CERTIFICATION, PARENTING

Parties

Party is the code word for ultimate pleasure among many young adults. It is the freedom to enjoy oneself in a magical context. People have suggested that Americans work harder at having fun than any culture in the world. Yet, the quest for a party doesn't bring the promises people seek. Many young adults fuel their parties with booze and drugs. At least, both the young and old feel they must use stimulants to assure happiness.

The youth ministry realm inherits

Your youth group contains the key ingredients for memorable, life-changing parties.

some of these aspirations. Youth seek a good time. Most churches have a difficult time when they are compared with those graduation events or post football game bashes. Yet, it just may be the religious community which understands what celebration really means. It is the sense of celebration which has sustained the community of faith for the past 4,000 years. Perhaps youth ministry should look back at its roots for an understanding of *party* when they design these kinds of events for youth.

What contributes to a successful party? There seems to be several factors which can be found in every satisfying party:

1. There is a host or hosts who nurtures a sense of hospitality.

2. All the focusing activities (games, etc.) are designed for all the guests.

3. The size of the event is scaled for sharing and good interaction.

4. The setting lends itself to good interaction.

5. The food is enjoyable to participants and presented in a way that shows dignity.

The chemistry which transforms a party into a special celebration goes beyond these factors. The sense of hospitality is the real ingredient for the successful party. It is best if your young people can provide this hosting quality.

Many adults like to go for numbers when planning youth social events. However, what can be accomplished in terms of relationships in a crowd of 200 young people? Youth ministry is built around the theological concern for quality. It is the depth of our parties which make them special.

Environments are also an important factor in scaling your celebration to a human dimension. The church basement can be transformed into a setting for conversation and activities. Break up the large space by using resources around you. For instance, a call to the outdoor advertising folk can get you huge sheets of unused billboards. These pictures are put on wallpaper-like sheets and come in large sections. You will be amazed how a few of these tacked to Sunday school room dividers will change the setting. (See entry on *Bubble*.)

You can also choose special places to hold your party. One youth group rented a railroad car! As part of this traveling party, they had state police officers stop the train and "arrest" the young people because they were Christians. They then talked about being punished for their faith. A learning opportunity became part of the fun.

The party is a very important part of your ministry. You can throw a bash that can't be matched by anyone in the community!

See also DANCING, DRINKING, REFRESHMENTS

Passage Rites

"You look beautiful, honey. Have a good time on your first date."

"Here are the car keys."

There are moments when we mark the realization that a change has taken place in our lives. These hinge points are very important to the growing, developing young person and adult. The church has been particularly important at utilizing these moments of transformation as special encounters with God.

There are those who look at the history of salvation and see that God gives these moments for the purpose of calling each person to renew and restate his or her faith. The Old Testament is such a blessing for those of us working in youth ministry. Whenever God calls his people to faithfulness as a point of passage, the Old Testament records that the people celebrated what happened. A rock or stone was set up to mark what came to pass. For instance, Joshua called the people to make the passage of a covenant between God and his people. The people took the step to be faithful. He called for a stone to be placed that they might remember what had happened that day.

The New Testament also calls us to realize that key passage points in our lives are marked in special ways. Often these moments are remembered in relationship with the body of Jesus. The table becomes the passage rite for Jesus and for us. As often as we meet at a table, we are to remember the passage of the new community and our part in it through him.

The church of the past 100 years has moved away from expressing this basic emotional and spiritual need. Yet, the secular world has very willingly picked up on it. Symbols, clubs, songs and trinkets are offered to help consumers make passage rites. It is marketing for a profit. Yet, it draws upon a real need. For instance, the funeral in America has filled in with secular gestures for the inability of the faith community to celebrate this most basic passage point.

Youth need to symbolically celebrate the many passages more than anyone else. To prove they are no longer children, some young people smoke cigarettes or use tough language.

Joyce, a creative youth minister, is aware of the need and validity of such passage rites. When a young person receives his or her driver's license, there is a special portion of the Sunday morning service which celebrates this important passage rite of maturation for the young person. The person is called forth. In a short service, the youth kneels while several significant adults lay their hands on his or her head. A prayer of thanksgiving is offered in which God is praised for raising this person to this moment of responsibility. Then the youth advisor gives a short charge calling for the young person to remember that wherever he or she goes the prayers and affirmation of these people go along. A small key chain is given to the person. "May it always remind you that we love you and support you. This love will protect you no matter what temptation or danger you might face."

See also CARS, CONFIRMATION

Pastor

In most churches a pastor who cares about youth is the cornerstone of a meaningful youth program. This does not mean that the pastor serves as youth advisor on a weekly basis or even that the pastor attends many of the youth events (though it is usually mutually beneficial when possible). Having a pro-youth pastor does mean that he or she is an advocate for youth in various committees and other arenas, a ready counselor to youth and their leaders, a spiritual leader who can communicate well with you and a source of support during the good and the bad times.

Most pastors do not want to run the youth program, though most want to be

available to those who do. Make use of this resource as one who wants to be in contact with your team.

Your pastor is an excellent source of information on subjects. For instance, he or she is aware of the current mood and spirit of the congregation (especially nice to know if you're planning to involve the congregation in some future activity or need permission for an upcoming event), has a historical perspective on past leadership strategy and is an available resource.

Youth and their leaders need constant contact with all of the church staff. The church secretary and janitor are very much involved in the youth program, whether we realize it or not, and a good working relationship must be maintained. An interesting exercise is to ask the church leaders their expectations of the youth ministry and what the youth leaders should accomplish.

There are times when the youth leaders sense that the pastor is not really concerned about what takes place in the various youth functions. Assuming for the moment that the non-interest is a correct assessment of the situation, there could be several reasons for the pastor's distance. The pastor may have once encountered youth leaders who did not want interference, even to the point of being threatened by the presence of the pastor. Perhaps the pastor is purposefully holding back and is planning to offer more help once you have gotten your leadership strategy underway. Or the pastor could feel inadequate for youth ministry, in which case the two of you could be of great help in learning together.

Most of the time you will find your pastor to be one of the most concerned persons in the congregation for wanting the youth program to develop well and serving the needs of all of the persons involved, including yourself.

Helping youth to have a meaningful relationship with their pastor is not always easy. Some youth are afraid of their pastor, feel that the pastor is too busy to know, understand or care about them, and incapable of showing friendship. Yet, most youth want a positive relationship with their pastor.

One of the best results of having a Youth Sunday is the teamwork that occurs between pastor and youth as the plans for the service are developed. Youth get a chance to understand the function of the pastor related to worship and to become an instrumental part of the pastor's planning process.

Going on trips together often works well. There is nothing like watching what happens when the pastor joins the group in a work project or total involvement experience.

A youth meeting at the pastor's home is beneficial if the pastor will not erect a reserved paternalistic stance that forces the youth further out of touch.

Scouts working on their God and Country Award get a rare opportunity to visit with the pastor on an individual basis over a long period of time. These periods of shared humanity are golden for the youth.

An extremely valuable gift the pastor can give the youth is to introduce them to ways in which they can be ministers of the church and make a unique contribution. A congregation needs what youth can add, and the pastor's insights may be the key in your church for making that possible.

See also COMMUNICATION, MENTOR, YOUTH SUNDAY

Peer Counseling

Years ago when counselors were first added to the staff of large high schools, it was assumed their duties would be to help students plan courses in preparation for graduation and occasionally to help students who were having a difficult time adjusting. Little did anyone realize how this service would mushroom into a minor league psychiatric/counseling center.

The load became so demanding for some counselors, they had to look around for help. To the amazement of many, some of the best help came from the students themselves.

Special training programs have been developed to help these students in such areas as listening skills, sensitivity to understanding needs, knowing when to turn elsewhere for help and other useful preparation. The adult counselor carefully oversees the work of these students and only permits the help to be given when the individual has the required skills.

Local churches and other youth service agencies have begun to utilize the unlimited potential of peer counseling. Again, the teens are trained to handle a wide variety of situations. Many churches add several training sessions on how to deal with the religious and theological searching that they may encounter.

The major problem with this program

Youth all over the nation are receiving special training to help them better care for their peers.

is obvious: It is easy to create a monster. A youth may feel capable of handling any counseling problem, and in fact, may go around town convincing persons they have problems he or she can solve. This danger should be recognized and guarded against as youth are trained and screened.

Because of this concern, the term *counseling* may be too strong, since it conjures images of qualified, highly trained and experienced persons. Therefore, many groups have chosen to call this program *peer caring*, emphasizing that the youth is performing a ministry for a peer. The distinction is helpful to the youth involved in the service as well as those for whom it needs to be interpreted.

Resources

1. Palo Alto Peer Counseling Program, 25 Churchill Avenue, Palo Alto, CA 94306.
2. Barbara Varenhorst, trainer, 350 Grove Drive, Portola Valley, CA 94025.
3. **Extend: Youth Reaching Youth**, by Fletcher, Noreem-Hebeison, Johnson, Underwager, Augsburg Publishing House.

See also ADVISING, FRIENDS

Peer Pressure

Most surveys indicate that the two strongest influences upon youth are parental and peer pressure. There is some disagreement as to which of those two is the more powerful, but there is some indication that peer pressure is increasing as families become more separated.

Criteria for clothing and hair styles, words to use, hobbies, dates, even scholastic achievement are often established and disciplined by the peer group. Persons are not to be seen with other persons not approved by the peers.

The pressure can become stifling, repressive and dehumanizing. It takes a strong individual to assert his or her own standards against those of the crowd. It takes a person who feels confident enough in his or her own worth and belief system to stake that against probable estrangement and ridicule.

One of the most valuable gifts a youth group experience can give to an individual is the affirmation to be proud of personal convictions. As teens engage in youth group programs that challenge their beliefs, they often see their ener-

Most young people feel great pressure to walk, talk and look like everyone else.

gies making a difference. As the youth learn to construct meaningful worship services, a deep sense of inner reliance and stability becomes available for those times when they must take a stand and follow through in threatening situations.

For instance, Bob was leading a session on the subject of peer pressure when he abruptly said, "Let me give you a problem and see what you think is the correct answer. A man bought a horse for $60. He spent $10 to get it fitted with shoes and decided to sell the horse four months later for $80. Eleven months later he missed the horse and bought it back for $70. Okay, those who feel he is $10 to the good stand over here; those who feel he is out $10 stand here, and those who think he is even gather over there. Discuss your reasons together and go to members of the other groups and try to convince them you are right so they can join your group."

Ironically, even though the size of the groups started out about the same, soon one group was double its original size and growing, not because of the facts they presented but simply because of intimidation by group size and pressure. In a few minutes the group debriefed what had happened. Volunteers explained how they felt they could not resist the pressure.

Calvin was a seventh grade teacher, who noticed through a classroom window that one of his students was just entering the building. He quickly told those in the room about an experiment he wanted to conduct. He suggested that occasionally during the morning that various class members mention to the latecomer that he did not seem to be looking too well. Was he feeling okay? Within an hour the student reported to the teacher that he did not feel well and he needed to see the school nurse. Before the process could go any further the teacher helped the class to see how powerful their influence could be, even to cause physical stress and discomfort.

All of us can remember times when we wished to follow one direction but the crowd convinced us otherwise simply by making small demands and assumptions that went unchallenged.

Once your youth recognize the power of the group, they will need to discover a variety of alternatives for allowing them to follow their own best intentions. Of course, nothing can mold a person whose faith is applied to each decision of life. An important contribution of the youth group life is to realize that the Christian faith relates to everything we do.

See also BELONGING, CLIQUES, COMMUNITY, FRIENDS, SELF-IMAGE

Planning Council

Most youth groups have found it helpful to establish some kind of council to make executive decisions and to bring recommendations to the total group. Often composed of officers and adult leaders, this council can act on behalf of the group and represent its best interests.

Every council needs to know what it's supposed to accomplish as well as the limit for its authority. In other words, what do you absolutely need the council to do, and at what point does the council overstep its boundaries? How precisely the duties need to be defined is usually a matter to be decided by the council itself.

The size, function and special needs of the group will suggest how large and highly structured the council should be. Many groups can get along well with councils composed of four or five persons with loosely designated responsibilities, while other groups produce booklets of job descriptions for each person on the council and operational procedures (terms of service, election guidelines, rules of order for meetings).

If the number of persons on the council is large (10 or more), an executive council may be needed to occasionally meet on urgent or critical matters. For example, the council may appoint the president (or moderator or chairperson) plus another youth and one or two adults to act when it is not practical or preferable to get everyone together. Again, the margins of this group's authority should be spelled out.

In churches with several youth activities (youth fellowship, choir, ball teams, drama group, etc.), there is usually a need for a church-wide youth council to oversee the ministry being conducted by these various groups.

See also OFFICERS, TASK FORCE, YOUTH COUNCIL

Portable Ministry

The church basement seems to have won the permanent franchise for the youth group. In many cases, such a setting is quite overwhelming. Six high school youth sitting in a huge basement can be very discouraging. It is interesting that many of the successful parachurch youth movements make sure that they meet in homes. In fact, some of these leaders feel that the more crowded the meeting, the better the results. They deliberately work to create a tight-fitting setting. This also seems to be the case at the birthday of the historical

church (Acts 2:1-4).

It might be challenging to consider a "portable" ministry. Perhaps your group is limited in size. You might also realize that one of the important roles of your youth ministry is to introduce your folks to the worldly context for the person of faith. For example, a church in a small southwestern Pennsylvania town determined that a portable ministry was best for their youth. Of the six young people in the group most had never been out of the former mining town. The youth advisor knew that they would have to move away for higher education and to develop their careers. How could the church prepare them for this journey?

The youth group invited a guest from outside the community who trained them to communicate as a group. The advisor then instituted the "comfort corps": Each Saturday the group hopped into a van and took a magical mystery tour to a

Helping youth encounter a number of different life situations helps them learn that their biggest resource is faith.

different location. Even though the destination was a secret, their task was quite clear. The young people were to provide comfort and care among strangers. They were learning that their biggest resource was their faith.

The first week they went to a downtown park in a large city. They were asked to sit next to a stranger and note how the person acted, without initiating conversation. What was going on in this person's mind? Was there something sad or pleasing in this stranger's life? The group gathered to debrief the experiences. The sponsor asked each person to "present" the stranger or strangers he or she had encountered. The youth assumed the posture and manner of the new acquaintance.

The next week saw the youth going to a variety of places. Their involvement with strangers became more intense and helpful. They went to an airport and found people who needed help. Two of the teens came upon a woman who had spent the night at the terminal. Her father had died and she was not able to catch a plane home because of the fog. They encouraged her to share her story. She felt guilty because she had once fought with him, and he died without a reconciliation. At the end of the conversation she affirmed the youth, "Thank God, you were here. I have not been able to talk with anyone about this. I feel much better."

On another occasion, they went to the waiting room of a hospital before visiting hours. The chaplain had told the youth advisor that many patients discussed their problems with visitors during those too few visiting hours. If the visitors were prepared to listen rather than entertain, they could aid the patients. The young people listened as these visitors freely talked with them.

The church noted real growth in the confidence and insights of the youth as people of faith. They also found that the group gained five more youth. Word had spread about this exciting portable ministry.

Many youth groups have realized the value of moving their classroom to their state capitol, to Washington, D.C. or to the United Nations headquarters in New York City. They write ahead to schedule personal time with their representatives and to find out what important decisions are being considered during their time at these seats of power. Not only does this kind of portable ministry provide an impressive experience into the workings of governmental process, but it gives the youth valuable clues as to significant ways they can influence this power.

See also BUS, EVANGELISM, MALL, OUTREACH, SERVICE, TAMING, TRIPS

Post High School Youth

You know the situation. A person graduates from high school but still has good friends in the group and would like to remain as a member.

Usually, this creates no problem. In fact, it can serve as a temporary support system until he or she is involved in young adult or college groups. It can also serve as a graphic illustration that the church is always concerned about its people and does not drop them over such superficial reasons as age.

The post high school person should serve as a reminder to the local church that meaningful programs for this age group are necessary. When such programs do exist every effort should be made to interest the person in the group's acitivity.

On those rare occasions when an older youth causes problems for the group, an honest, caring search for alternatives should be undertaken by two

Post high school youth often have trouble fitting in anywhere. Make it your responsibility to minister to them.

or three responsible persons in the church who are also concerned for this youth. If, after all other alternatives fail, it is decided that the older youth should leave the group, extreme love and compassion should be extended and a continuing support group should be developed to relate to the youth.

Transferring from one group to another is always rather traumatic, and this can usually be aided (not always) by legitimatizing the passage by acknowledging it in a letter, ceremony or welcoming activity in the new group. Being in a youth group can seem like a church within a church, and it may take a formal welcome from another group to convince the youth that there is a new home for them, a new group that wants them and a place where they will feel comfortable.

Unfortunately, post high school youth are one of the most neglected segments of youth ministry. Most don't feel com-

fortable in the old high school youth group and the adult couples club is unappealing. "How can I meet people my own age?" The 19-year-old woman worked in an office. She did not want to hang around bars or use a computer dating service. Margo was also uncomfortable with those swinging singles youth groups. She wanted the balance of her local church, but a context which appreciated her special needs and concerns.

Some people would tell her to fit into the current situation. Yet, this is not a helpful response for most young adults. We simply lose them. Many return in a few years with their family. Many never return! This is such a telling judgment on the local church's insensitivity!

You may not want to consider young adults as part of your area of responsibility. Your focus may just be junior and senior highs. However, the young adult is also your responsibility. That senior in your group will suddenly need something beyond the group. How do you continue your ministry with this person? Can you just drop him or her?

Some youth sponsors find that they can involve some of these young adults by giving them leadership responsibilities in youth ministry. If you are developing an active program, there are needs for additional staff. On the other hand, some older youth can be hampered in their maturation by remaining in the high school youth program. You will need to consider carefully all implications before permitting a post high school person to take leadership in your group.

You might also gather this staff of young adults for informal meetings. This can easily evolve into their own group.

Singles ministry is one of the hottest areas of growth for church work. Those churches who take it seriously find an unbelievable response. One church moved from a handful of people to over 1,500 in just three years! Their secret was to give the young adults a great deal of responsibility. The programming was very inclusive. Every concern of this special age group was open for exploration. A strong young adult ministry will provide an enormous source of resources for the program of the local church.

You can't desert your youth as they grow older. They are important to you because they provide the models for your younger teens. "Is there life after high school?" You want them to answer that question by seeing young adults who are vital and excited about their lives.

Resources

1. **Saturday Night, Sunday Morning: Singles in the Church**, by Nicholas Chrisoff, Harper and Row.

See also BELONGING, FRIENDS, PASSAGE RITES

Power

You may have all the clout in your local congregation. This really doesn't change the fact that you have to deal with the different powers that control youth ministry. It is very easy to view those people in your church who have power as being automatically resistant to your concerns. There is a certain aspect of this dynamic in youth ministry which can be used improperly.

The seminarian did his field work at a large church in downtown Chicago. It was his job to be the youth advisor. He was fairly successful. At least, the teens and Merv got along very well. The church was so insensitive that the seminarian spent two years as youth worker and never met the senior minister! His group gathered in the church's second basement. Far below ground level they formed a tight cell. The young man shared his frustration with the youth over the coolness he found in the church. This sense of rejection by the adults fused the relationship between teens and adult advisor. Yet it did not help the young people deal with growing up or creatively holding their own with that which they wanted to change in the church.

It is quite easy to win teens by choosing a common enemy. This model is often used by the clergy. They blame the denominational office or some church-related organization. You will have to work hard to break this model. Your task is to help young people realize that they are part of a spiritual community which transcends time, geography, nationality and political views. The inclusive view of the faith family is important for youth to understand that they belong.

If you come from a highly organized church structure, there are many ways it can serve your ministry and many ways your youth can serve it. It is a natural starting point for resourcing and training.

We don't need to find opponents among those who are one in Christ.

See also PLANNING COUNCIL, PRO-GRAM, YOUTH COUNCIL

Power Magazine

The only writers for Power Magazine are youth. This personal devotional guide has been a proven resource for many years. Co-sponsored by several demoninations, the magazine proves the claim that youth are capable of creating meaningful resources for themselves.

Included are poems, short stories, reflections and other statements which can powerfully move the reader to action.

The Power Magazine address is 4466 West Pine 15-F, St. Louis, MO 63108.

Prayer

Most young people have not had very good prayer models. Their prayer experience in the church is usually confined to pastoral prayers or the unison reading of written prayers. The other source of prayer experience is the home. In some homes, the children learn an approach to prayer which will follow them all their lives. But homes where there are few shared prayer experiences are desperate situations. Prayer is the lifeline of the Christian. Without tapping into the talking relationship with God, the believer is cut off from a great spiritual resource.

Since prayer is an important part of your ministry, it is necessary for you to work on your own prayer life. It is vital that you share with youth that which you yourself have experienced. It does not help to invite them into a world which means little to you. For many people, it is necessary to include two factors to strengthen prayer life: 1. Form a sense of discipline about prayer; 2. Develop your prayer practice in community with one or more other folks.

Prayer is a personal experience by which you seek out your talking relationship with God. In prayer you talk to God and God communicates with you. The witness of those who have drawn upon prayer in the past can be a great help. Yet, after all your study and effort, there is a quality to prayer which is dependent upon God's initiated love. It is God who reaches out to touch our outstretched hearts and minds.

Some youth advisors have organized special prayer times during Lent and Advent. The early morning breakfast is a good time for developing prayer strength. You may find that there are only a few youth who will want to explore this area of the Christian life. Form a small cell. As the teens grow,

others will be drawn to your prayer opportunities.

You can also model some of the many different forms of prayer during your regular youth programming. For instance, a youth advisor in Alabama used guided fantasy as a means of leading his youth in imaginative prayer.

For a few minutes he led them in prayer where they could participate fully. Instead of creating a written structure which most leaders of public prayer use, George created a context in which each person could contribute the content. He suggested that they close their eyes and take a prayer journey with him. As he led them on this prayer, he was careful to suggest sensual awareness without telling them how to feel, smell and see.

He began by telling them to imagine that they were getting up from the youth room and going to the door. "Feel the ground beneath your feet. Take a deep breath. Smell the spring odors."

He then had them walk mentally down the road. "You can see someone approach. This person looks familiar. It

is Jesus! He smiles at you, and puts his hand on your shoulder. You know that you have things inside which keep you from feeling comfortable with Jesus. You have to let out these things. In your imagination, tell Jesus the sin which cuts you off from him."

George takes time and lets the teens work on this area of confession in their imaginative prayer. "Jesus looks at you after he has heard your confession. Then he smiles and hugs you. You can feel his arms around you. You know that he understands and forgives. You turn and see the most beautiful water in the world. Look at the sun glistening on the water. Jesus asks you to enter and wash yourself. As you step into it, it feels perfect against your body. You step out and you feel refreshed and renewed."

George then has them return to the room. The youth often want to talk about what happened to them in this prayer. They find that Jesus tells them things that they have not been able to hear at other times.

One of the most meaningful experiences for many groups is when individuals go off by themselves (usually somewhere out-of-doors) to have their own devotional period. This meditation time is generally a period of total silence in which persons can select their own Bible reading and engage in prayer as they choose. The period might be aided by written suggestions based on a theme that was selected for the day.

Significant events will occur when people feel the power of prayer in their lives. At the death of a group member, the death of a parent or friend of a group member, the birth of a child to a group leader, when a member has to leave the group for a long period of time—all of these can be times in which prayer will have extra meaning to the group.

Some groups set a time each week when they pray for the group. They mention the name of a particular group member and ask special concern for him or her.

Prayer is a rich and wonderful aspect of our faith. Don't be afraid to meet young people in it.

Resources

1. **An Autobiography of Prayer**, by Albert Day, Upper Room.
2. **Help Lord! A Guide to Public and Private Prayer**, by D.P. McGeachy, John Knox Press.
3. **Lord, Could You Make It a Little Better**, by Robert Raines, Word Books.
4. **Workbook on Living Prayer**, by Marie Dunnam, Upper Room.
5. **Tune In**, by Herman Ahrens, Jr., Pilgrim Press.

See also BIBLE, COMMUNITY, HOLY SPIRIT, JESUS

Premarital Counseling

Most couples are counseled by a pastor before marriage. Every pastor uses a different approach to this important opportunity to form a relationship with the couple. However, some people claim that two people cannot really hear or see anything about relationships until after their marriage.

The youth advisor can play an important role with teens before they consider marriage. For instance, Jim is a counselor who has developed an interesting process by which teens can rehearse the roles they may consider in marriage. He gives the youth 20 blank 3x5 cards each. He encourages his young people to fill them out according to what roles they assume their future husband or wife will play in a marriage. The roles can include household duties and work roles. They can also include feelings and emotional concerns. He then asks the young people to rank the importance of these items by putting the cards in order on the floor. Jim then leads a discussion on the roles of males and females in a marriage or dating relationship. The teens are encouraged to share their cards and the ranking of the roles. He sometimes uses the blackboard to write them down. He groups the roles according to areas of disagreement.

If your group members are mature, you might have them form in clumps of four or five and develop the outline of a marriage contract in which the roles are spelled out. This can lead to more discussion about the patterns they have seen in their families and community.

This is preventive ministry. It is vital that we walk with our youth as they face the significant passage points in their lives. What better place can teens explore what it means to be a man or a woman!

Jim's process can be a fine way to get youth and adults talking together. Imagine the conversation in homes when your youth return from such a weekend of discussion.

See also ADVISING, ROMANCE, SEXUALITY

Priorities

One important task is to guide young people through the process of listing and selecting youth group priorities.

Anyone involved in planning soon realizes the value of selecting priorities, those undisputably most important themes or goals. Whenever the best choice of direction has been made, it is easier to prepare for action than when the efforts have to be scattered in many directions.

Youth leaders can help the progress of a group immeasurably by guiding the process of selecting youth group priorities. Budgeting, program planning and scheduling can do their part to see that the priority is developed to its intended level of participation.

Setting priorities can be an exciting

and rewarding procedure. Often leadership in your church or people in the employment of your denomination can help you develop a priority-setting system. One method is to have the group list on newsprint or chalkboard what future action (programs, projects, activities) they consider to be the most important. Then each person is asked to rate these on a card from first to last preference. Tabulating the results will give a preferential scoring. Or you might appoint short-term task forces to take a particular area of the group's concern (faith, fellowship, outreach) and bring in some priority possibilities for each area to encourage the group's discussion and vote. Or every individual might be asked to project his or her greatest dreams for the group, develop these into specific goals, and submit them for the group's choice.

What do you do, however, when you have more than one priority? Which priority has priority? For instance, the denomination and/or the national youth organization can have a particular priority, the regional youth organization can have another and an interchurch youth organization in town may set another. If this happens the group must set up a procedure for evaluating each one of these priorities and the reasoning (need, urgency, uniqueness) behind the selection to estimate how all of this relates to the major interest the local church group has for this same period.

When final selection is made, spread the word. Let people know why you made the selection, and what other groups are involved. Set measurable immediate and long-range objectives so that news can be distributed as work is accomplished.

Easily recognizable themes and symbols can greatly aid the effort.

See also BALANCE, GOAL SETTING PROGRAM, STARTING UP

Program

"What do you want to do?" This is probably the most familiar and the most unfair question that an advisor asks of the youth group. It is unfair because teens can suggest only that which they have experienced. In most settings, they have had very little opportunity to taste the wide range of program possibilities. Throwing the burden of programming on youth in this situation is really a very confining act. The adult leader limits them by drawing upon their weaknesses.

One advisor noticed that many youth groups were sponsoring a weekend program which was a new kind of coffeehouse. Instead of imposing the idea upon her youth fellowship, Judy suggested that several carloads of teens visit three of the clubs. "Talk to the kids who are sponsoring the event. Find out everything you can about it."

On the way home, the teens in each car talked about what they had experienced. The different groups met at a fast food restaurant. "What things did you like most about the evening?" Everyone had something to say. A short time later this youth group developed their own club. It was different from those they had visited.

Adult advisors often feel most comfortable in reproducing that which they have experienced. It is wise to give all adult leaders experience in new teaching and program methods before presenting the youth group with new ideas.

Howard is part of a youth advisors team that includes six couples. They don't divide the responsibilities; they all work on the meetings. In fact, Tom claims that it is their life together in prayer, study and sharing that gives power to their ministry. "If you don't have something to share, there is not much that kids will get." They often try

One leader asked her kids to write down one thing that bothered them the most. The responses provided the base for a lively discussion.

new Bible study methods on each other before using them with the youth. They have seen a satisfying response by growth in depth and numbers of their group. Tom says this leadership team has sparked many other dimensions to the church's life. "We really grew together when one of our team died from cancer. It was the time we really had to reach inside for spiritual strength. The kids could feel the faith which sustained us during this terrible time."

In another situation, Ann and the youth group are sitting in a planning session. She knows that authentic youth ministry can exist only if there is a continuous flow of ideas from the lives of youth. This gathering must determine programs for the next six Sunday evenings. Some youth advisors are tempted in these moments of reality to push through a list of preconceived ideas or place all the burden on the teens: "What do you want to do?" Either position seems unfair.

"I come up with the ideas and make the kids think that they thought of them." This attitude doesn't seem honest. Ann bypassed these temptations.

"Let's take a break in these practical matters. I am going to pass out some cards. I want you to write the one thing which bothers you the most."

After a couple minutes of writing with music playing in the background, she asks them to write something on the other side. "What are you looking forward to the most?" After they have done this, she collects the cards and shuffles them. They are passed out again. "Let's look at the side with the happy face. What kinds of programs are suggested by these ideas?" After they have discussed these, they turn the cards over and do the same thing. She had found that this process can be repeated by using magazines. "Find a picture which expresses your greatest worry." It is always amazing how the programs surface once everyone has come in touch with individual life rhythms.

As the youth advisor and youth form a sense of communion about their ministry together, a program design will emerge. No one can come up with a winning program each week. On the other hand, this is not a service club with the weekly-entertaining-program syndrome.

Planning programs as a group helps to develop a wholistic sense of your life together. Acts 2:46-47 reports that the early church moved from the outdoor service to small groups in which they worshipped, studied, had fellowship and then went out to perform miracles. Solid youth programming should take under consideration all those aspects of the Christian life.

Resources

1. **Youth Worker's Success Manual**, by Shirley Pollock, Abingdon Press.
2. **Free to Choose, Youth Program Resources from the Black Experience**, by Mary Adebonojo, Judson Press.

See also BIBLE KNOWLEDGE, GOAL SETTING, GROUP BUILDING

Publicity

The ancient Christians weren't hesitant about spreading the news about their faith. They hit the streets and utilized every communication system the Roman Empire could provide. But for some reason, modern church groups are probably the most hesitant folk around to publicize their events. A local church may have a notice of its meeting times printed in the local paper. Yet these vanity notices are rarely newsworthy and often treated just the way they deserve to be handled by a publication which is designed to entertain and excite the reader.

Pastor David does a marvelous job of turning the internal excitement of a vital program inside out. He utilizes different print forms that range from imprinted calendar, to stick-on telephone numbers to personalized youth group pencils. He has also found that mail is particularly important to young people, who like to receive their own correspondence. David follows a few simple principles:

1. Have something to say or communicate. He spends time with the youth planners in developing a theme. For example, the planning group picked up the image and focus of the "Rainbow Connection." This became a rich theme. The biblical, mythical and popular dimensions overlapped.

2. David urges his folks to brainstorm the wildest possibilities in terms of pro-

grams, pictures and music. They designed several events around the "Rainbow Connection" theme.

3. He used the talent of folks in the church and community. The youth quickly found a helpful artist and printer.

4. He refuses to discourage any idea in drawing upon his young people's creative gifts.

David also publishes a yearly directory for the youth group members. They are able to call and communicate with each other easily. Being listed in the directory is a way of saying that you belong to this group.

Another youth advisor lives about 20 miles away from his church community during the week. This means that he usually sees the young people on weekends only. As he travels on his sales job during the week, he writes notes to the students. These handwritten notes pick up a comment dropped during the meeting or emphasizes some other special aspect of the relationship. His notes are effective epistles of promotion and publicity for the coming programs.

Many youth groups have received superb publicity in the newspapers about their mission or service projects. For instance, the newspapers love to run pictures of youth caring for an egg in order to study parenting. Or things like money-making walks for world hunger organizations bring Christian service to the attention of the larger community. Can we present the news of our life together as being "good" or vital news for the world?

Many youth groups fail to reach their full potential by not letting all possible group members hear about the planned activities. What a difference it makes when a fireball youth takes over and puts flashy posters and notices all over the buildings, writes notes to all the active and inactive members, submits catchy announcements for the bulletin and comes up with increasingly clever ways of telling the group and the rest of the church that a lot is going on during every event.

Funny thing, super publicity has a way of producing super programs. When a large group filled with anticipation turns up for a project, program or retreat, the enthusiasm can turn a normally dull event into something spectacular.

Publicity is more than just drawing a crowd. Adults want to know what was learned or completed during a function. Their support will usually increase as they understand what important things are happening. Youth who never attend youth group events may thaw their resistance when they read a well-written account of who came and what they did.

Publicity should always include people's names. People relate to people, not events. Not only do most people like to see their names in print (it is an acknowledgement of their presence, perhaps even an appreciation of their support), but others like to see who took part in the event.

See also COMMUNICATION, HUMOR, YOUTH NEWS

Public Schools

Many youth advisors and sponsors are frustrated in their attempts at planning because of commitment demands by the public and private schools in the community. In some communities almost all of the teen's non-school commitments comes from the school system. Marching band, soccer, debating and even skiing is provided by the schools. The major activities in town spawn all kinds of social activities.

Perhaps you live in a town where the churches are recognized as deserving time slots for their life and work with teens. Yet, that situation seems to be disappearing everywhere.

It is hard to fight an expansive school system. Administrators may hint that they can do a better job at developing free time activities than the churches. They may also cite the needs of young people who are outside the influence of the faith community. These are some difficult challenges. We have failed in most of those areas. However, we possess the reason for doing the job better than just about anyone else. The question is: "Are we really interested?"

If you and your folk are putting strong programming together, collect a group of pastors and youth advisors. Approach the school board with the request to coordinate activities. Suggest that a master community calendar be organized. Perhaps one evening a week could be recognized as belonging to the church for youth work. You might also have discussions with the athletic leagues about Sunday games. We may not be living in Calvin's Geneva, when no games or activity could take place on Sunday. However, Sunday morning games for youth destroy most local church programming.

The public schools also offer another realm of interaction. State laws differ, but many youth folk are finding situations under which church leaders can actually work in the schools! At first, this may seem impossible with the church-state separation. However, many schools have optional modules or study times for their students. Elective learning experiences are offered during this time.

In suburban Pittsburgh, one local youth worker has been teaching a course on drugs. It is one of the most popular in the elective section. Another worker has been teaching a series on values clarification. Both people report that the reception has been wonderful from students and school administrators. It is a meaningful experience for students to see a linkage between school and church.

There are also folks from your congregation working in the school system. Get with them and probe ways of nurturing a better involvement of the church in the school world. What kind of support do they need from you? What are problems which should be faced? What can you contribute to the school system?

See also AVAILABILITY, OUTREACH

Puppets

Puppets are one of the most rewarding, inexpensive ministries available. A group can practice by making stick puppets, progress to an unlimited number of hand puppet possibilities, and eventually advance to string puppets.

The sky is the limit for involvement. Staging, lighting, costuming, scripting, sculpturing (carving, paint-

Puppets give youth a chance to say what they want through another voice and a loveable body.

ing, rearranging, etc.) and acting can make use of every bit of talent in the group.

A bit of scrap lumber or plastic pipe can quickly make a stage, and extra fabric can add the curtains and bottom skirts. Photography lamps can supply the lighting, and a cassette player (perhaps with an external speaker placed in front of the stage) can provide the sound effects, special voices and supporting background music.

Puppetry offers more than just a chance to present some entertainment or even a meaningful drama for all ages. It gives the youth a chance to say what they want through another voice and another body. At a time when many youth feel embarrassed about their own body and voice, they can become whatever they want as a puppet, ask any questions or make any statements they wish. If the puppet character fails to get a laugh or do an act perfectly, that's okay, because it is not the youth in the spotlight. However, if things go well, the originator of the character gets all the credit.

Resources

1. **Bring on the Puppets**, by Helen Ferguson, Morehouse-Barlow.
2. **Be a Puppeteer**, by Estelle Worrell, McGraw Hill.
3. **Using Puppetry in the Church**, by Everett Robertson, Broadman Press.
4. Organization: Puppeteers of America, Cricklewood Path, Pasadena, CA 91107. Membership includes a subscription to the quarterly Puppetry Journal.
5. Organization: Fellowship of Christian Puppeteers, 16 Albro Ave., Troy, NY 12180. Membership includes newsletter subscription.
6. **Making Puppets Come Alive**, by Larry Engler and Carol Fijan, Tapplinger Publishing Co.
7. **Puppet Scripts for Use at Church**, by Everett Robertson, Broadman Press.
8. **Teaching Bible Stories More Effectively With Puppets**, by Roland Sylwester, Concordia.
9. **Let's Try Puppetry**, Graded Press, United Methodist Publishing House, 201 8th Avenue S., Nashville, TN 37202.

See also CHOIRS, DRAMA, MIME

Questions

Who? What? Where? When? How?
Questions are both the youth group's
best friend and worst enemy.

You have probably experienced cold
silence as your discussion questions
sailed out over the group and died. No
one says a word. The space between
your query and the youth seems to last
for an eternity.

Of course, the opposite experience is
no more reassuring. Remember when
that junior high student stopped you
cold with an unbelievably difficult
question? You were just getting comfortable with the silence when another
student answered it!

Posing questions is an art that is
developed by practice. For instance, the
radio host was quite uncomfortable with
the rock star. The host was happy that
the interview would be taped. He could
always edit it to take out any bad spots.
His knock on the door of the hotel room
was met with the half-clad star, who
waved the disc jockey into the cluttered
room.

The interviewer was prepared. He
had typed out 20 carefully worded
questions.

"Do you think that the American educational system is helpful to the students?"

"It depends."

There are two full minutes of silence.
The radio host tries once again. "Is
there any hope in the American political
system?"

"No."

Another minute of strained hush fills
the air. The nervous interviewer rattles
his papers. Three more questions draw
the same one- and two-word replies.
Finally, in desperation, the man with the
microphone draws upon his feelings to
create a bridge of dialogue between the
legendary star and himself. "Frank, I

have two children and you have three.
How do we raise them to be sensitive
people in this crazy world?"

The star looks at the interviewer
carefully. His expression changes and
he launches into a passionate account of
how he tries to raise children of goodwill
and creativity. The interview starts to
work.

When you are forced to ask lots of
questions, you quickly learn that the
purpose of your queries is very
important. Many youth leaders often
play verbal charades with their
students. Their carefully worded questions are designed to get the answers
they want. Many students will refuse to
play those mental games in which they
are put down for not knowing the exact
worded answers sought by the teacher.

In college we used to laugh at the kind
of questions Socrates asked. The
Socrates and slave dialogues were seen
as leading the blind through tortuous
alleys which only the master knew. The
slaves solved the problem without
knowing anything about the answer or
the question.

It is tempting to work with youth in
this manner. Perhaps the leaders fear
that open-ended questions will lead to
areas and issues where they don't have
the "right" answers. We wonder why
youth don't play along with our simple
question and answer games. Let us not
forget that many teachers have played
that game with them for years.

In fact, you may initially find a lot of
resistance from your young people when
you begin to ask questions only they can
answer. They will not know what you
expect. Your answers will not be
apparent. However, some of the best
discussion will unfold when you take
this path.

For example, Ken was teaching an
ethics class in high school. One day he
was 15 minutes late. He stormed into the
class and slammed his briefcase on the

desk. "You won't believe it! Some dumb cop stopped me and gave me a ticket for speeding! Was that fair?"

A student immediately responded to Ken's rhetorical question. "You were wrong! You could have killed someone." Ken immediately defended himself: no children were present and his car wasn't going that fast. The discussion took off in many different ethical directions. Afterwards Ken noted that he would take a ticket every day if his classes would be this lively.

When the leader is willing for the discussion to go in directions desired by the group, the results can be exciting and beneficial. And it is possible at the same time to prevent the discussion from chasing useless rabbit trails that may involve only a clamor of voices and no exchange of helpful insights.

Well phrased questions can be the key to bring this about. Usually, it is preferable to avoid questions that can be answered by a simple "yes" or "no" since very little personal response is encouraged. Moreover, relying rather heavily on "yes" and "no" type questions can be restrictive on the group to the point of stifling their participation when so little is requested from them or, even worse, permitted of them. Picture yourself in a courtroom when the opposing lawyer keeps demanding of you, "Just tell us, yes or no, do you agree?" when you may desperately want to tell the extenuating circumstances and the significant logic.

There are unlimited approaches that can be used to encourage a more lengthy answer, such as:

How do you feel about. . .
What would you like to see happen. . .
What indicators are available to. . .
In what ways might a person. . .
What is the greatest. . .
Let's each share our opinion about. . .

Some of the best discussions will unfold when you ask questions that don't have obviously correct answers.

Describe the feeling when. . .
What do you say to persons when/ who. . .
Share what you think will happen next in the story. . .

Your opening question for a discussion is crucial. Some leaders like to pose a controversial or contemplative question to open the discussion through a dramatic surge of response. Other leaders prefer to lead into the subject more gradually with a non-threatening question that affirms each person in the group and lets them answer as an expert ("Each of you has noticed that old house on the corner; what do you think should be done with it?" or "If you had to put it in a phrase, how would you tell someone what makes our church so friendly?")

A question is an open-ended invitation. Don't be upset if not every question is answered. Sometimes no one chooses to respond and that in no way lessens your leadership capabilities. And don't be upset over long periods of silence; let the group have time to think in quiet. Some persons may not come up with what they feel is an adequate answer for days. (You don't have to wait that long!) Some answers may be offered at the beginning of a session as a carry-over, and this adds its own stimulation for the topic of the day.

See also CIRCULAR RESPONSE, DEBATES, DISCUSSION, SIMULATION GAMES

Radio

What do young people spend three and one-half hours each day consuming? What do most people have in excess of the number of rooms in their house? Which mass medium most narrowly defines the age and values of its audience? What follows us when we are good and we are bad? What community can we take to bed, jogging or to the bathroom?

Radio is the answer to all these questions. It is the most popular electric medium in the world. Radio offers one of the most highly specialized communication forms in our culture. While adults think only of television in terms of media influence, among teens radio is far more influential and utilized than the tube. The active teen would rather be involved in life than passively watching it on TV. Radio can accompany the

Radio is the most used medium in the youth world.

youth in all of his or her activities. The late Marshall McLuhan, the media guru of the '70s, compared the radio medium with a tribal drum. In most homes, the teen need only turn up the volume on his or her radio to clear the room of those who do not move to the beat of this kind of communication.

Radio is an important means of getting in touch with youth cultures. If you love a person, you must take his or her trivia seriously. (Trivia is the stuff and nonsense of life in which we invest our values and meanings.) This doesn't mean that the adult has to like the trivia of another. However, if you are to understand the personhood of the youth, you must make the journey into the land of the transistor.

One group in Colorado took this adventure a step further and produced their own radio program! After learning the basics of interviewing (see *Interviewing*) they went to the streets to gather comments around several questions. They transferred the interviews from the audio cassette to a reel-to-reel tape recorder by using connecting plugs. Using a razor blade and an edit block, they spliced together about 15 different responses to the question, "What is rich?"

They then submitted five finished 60-second spots to the local radio station. The program director was delighted to use high quality, locally produced material. He played the finished material during commercial clusters. The final spot on getting rich was quite interesting, by the way. The young people spliced in the expected comments about houses, cars, etc. The last statement made the minute sparkle: "Being rich has nothing to do with money. If you have faith in God, a family that loves you and your health, you are rich."

See also GROUP MEDIA, THE OPEN DOOR

Rebellion

The battle-worn, inner-city pastor shook his head. He had just spent three hours with a group of suburban church teens who were quite open in their hostility toward the neighborhood's black, poor people. "The kids who grew up in the '50s didn't know any better. But these kids have seen how the world really is through the news and television shows. They are pretending that reality isn't, well, real. They know that they eat well while more people go hungry every day. I feel so sorry for our youth. How can they maintain their integrity?"

As this gentleman suggests, we face a decade when young people need prodding to bring their faith and the state of the world into conflict and resolution. This is more than getting young people to rebel for the sake of rebellion. The foundation of faith demands a radical appraisal of every aspect of life.

The process of questioning is an uncomfortable stance for many people. Most adults would rather have young people absorb everything the older generation suggests without any challenge. Yet, the Christian faith is not caught without the process of receiving it as one's own commitment.

We are called to a ministry of transformation rather than conformity. There is nothing so damaging to a youth's spiritual hunger as an adult's claim that, "You will change in your concerns for others when you grow up."

There is a native quality of teens which embraces a sense of rebellion. This is stifled at almost every point in their educational and social training.

If youth in the church can find adults who will walk with them and encourage them to test the way things are, then the positive values of the faith will be strengthened.

Ted was working with young teens in

a church school class as they studied Christian discipleship. He decided that they should have a chance to be disciples in service to others. They found a lady with seven children in a housing project of their neighborhood. She had tried to get food stamps and failed. She was unable to produce records of her expenses. Using simple cameras and a cassette tape recorder, they created a simple media show of her situation. They made an appointment with the local director of the program. It was hard for them to get a serious hearing. However, they confronted the director and he finally let them make their presentation. He was impressed and the woman was given food stamps! They then talked about this constructive challenge to the authorities. The teens felt so good that their challenge to the system had resulted in a person getting food for her children.

Extremism in rebellion results from a person being isolated in his or her questions about the way things are. When a church community supports faith values, a person can stand against evil with courage and hope. Many people of conscience will feel isolation during this time of selfishness. You can provide a model situation in which young people can battle against suffering and evil without being victimized by despair.

See also ADVOCATE, RISKING

Records

One of the most influential parts of most young people's lives is the message that is delivered directly to the brain from the latest hit record or album. Thomas Edison never dreamed that his little recording machine would do much more than take dictation.

Today records comprise most of the broadcast time on radio and are the most popular media for contemporary youth. Records played on home stereo units account for an additional several hours of daily listening. The average youth listener will hear a particular popular record (one that makes it to the top-40 position or above on the best-selling charts) over 300 times. That short little module of musical information will be heard over a 6-month to 3-year period, first as a potential hit, then as a top hit, and later as a golden oldie. Occuring every hour or so throughout the broadcast day (additionally on the personal turntable), the record will fulfill all the perfect learning criteria outlined in any psychology textbook for retention, duration and reinforcement.

Almost nothing else in life is delivered that often for that amount of time with that type of encouragement. Almost anything could be taught under those conditions.

Records are often personal state-

The average youth listener will hear a top 40 record over 300 times—a perfect learning situation.

ments from the recording artist. The songs are an expression of the lifestyle and mental orientation of the writer and singer (often the same person). Many teens consider recording artists close friends, and the voices of these friends are often heard more regularly and with more volume than any other person. When earphones are used, the friends speak more directly into the brain than does any other human being.

Youth are no different from anyone else, they don't like to hear their friends talked about. Also, they don't want to talk too much about these friendships else they might seem cold and institutionalized by putting them under a clinical analysis. Therefore, youth understandably do not want to talk about the records or recording artists who mean the most to them unless they know that the climate will be supportive. When all of this has been assured, youth will pour out unlimited feelings of what their favorite music means to them.

This opening-up process can be enormously helpful. Not only can the youth tell what the music means to them, but also they can deal with any subtle manipulation that might have come through the music. Often such realization involves help from trusted friends—the live, human kind and not the ones on plastic discs.

The youth group can be a uniquely crucial group for helping the youth to objectively critique the extremely powerful media. When beauty is discovered it can be shared, highlighted and made even more spectacular by seeing it in the lives of other persons. When other influences are found, they can be recognized and criticized.

One very critical action that the church can take in relationship to records is to help the individual and the group highlight that which has great worth. This judgment process can be most helpful to youth in doing the same

act for themselves. And it can create some of the most moving experiences of worship that can be imagined because it unites the best of the contemporary world with God-given inner love and joy.

See also CULTURE, MEDIA AWARENESS, MUSIC

Recreation

Recreation can be "wreck-creation" or "re-creation." It can be a chaotic embattlement of egos striving for selfish gain, or it can be a therapeutic interchange that results in growth for individuals and groups.

Most of us have experienced times when recreation was refreshing, life giving and helped us to become a more integrated part of the group. We felt that all of the other participants valued our contributions to the shared activity even when what we did was not perfect. We were recognized and appreciated for being who we were. We belonged.

And unfortunately, most of us have also experienced recreation when we felt uncomfortable, either for ourselves or for other persons. Perhaps we did not know how to catch or run or serve well enough. Perhaps we were too intimidated to try. We were embarrassed. We felt we didn't belong.

Some of the same feelings flood over youth when recreation is offered. Will I be able to shoot the ball, ride the horse, swim, or draw well enough so that the group will approve of my efforts? Will I be embarrassed in the relays or tricked by the leader? If I make a mistake or get hurt will I be able to maintain my composure?

Every recreation period offers that possibility of destruction or rebirth. That is why persons who excel in one area often like to steer the direction of activity toward that area. The simple

Recreation should involve people in a fun-filled time of laughter and relaxing enjoyment.

act of throwing out a football to a group actually sets up some of the group (and those who might be drawn to the group) as favored participants and others are less favored. Throwing out a golf ball, ping pong ball, or mental quiz often changes the favoritism.

Most of us as leaders long for recreation periods in which relaxing but challenging play can help the participants to shake off whatever fatigue or boredom they might have and invest themselves in a complimen-

tary, fun-filled time of laughter and enjoyment. Such enrichment can uplift the entire event as well as the lives of the individuals and the group for a long period of time.

Such events don't just happen. The choice of the activity that is best for the occasion and the group will need to be made carefully in light of known interests and limitations of the group, as well as the overall purpose of the event. What activities can best rejuvenate the life of every person?

The answers are never simple. Gathering a reliable library of recreation books and a file of ideas can be invaluable when a proven activity is needed in a hurry. Developing a sensitivity to group process and the splendor of spontaneity can work wonders when games need to be created for the occasion. Attending recreation workshops and observing groups at play (especially during the time when instructions are given) provides a wealth of possibilities and flexible alternatives.

It is important to realize that we teach much to others about who we are by the way we play. A group will display its faith by the way it engages in recreation. Therefore, when newcomers attend an activity of the group, they can be taught about how the group and the God it worships regard their worth as an individual by the way the group reaches out to them and welcomes them. If the group is engaged in some game that may require explanation and group members volunteer to assist the newcomer, that act communicates volumes about love and acceptance—an extremely powerful sermon lived out. The way the leader introduces the activities and delivers the instructions also communicates how the leader regards the value of the group and each individual.

Resources
1. **Guide for Recreation Leaders**, by Glenn Bannerman and Robert Fakkema, John Knox Press.
2. **The New Games Book**, New Games Foundation, Dolphin/Doubleday.
3. **Recreation in the Out-of-Doors**, John Knox Press.
4. **The Good Times Game Book**, compiled by Doris Rikkers, Baker Book House.
5. **Games for People of All Ages**, compiled by Mary Hohenstein, Bethany.
6. **Party Planning and Games**, John Knox Press.

See also EARTHBALL, HANDICAPPED FOLKS, NEW GAMES, NO-LOSER RECREATION, REFRESHMENTS

Recruitment

Most youth advisors face a challenge in recruiting other adults. "Would you chaperone the hayride on Saturday?" "We need help for the fall retreat. Could you and your wife come along?" It is so hard to ask these questions of adults outside the youth ministry commitment. Yet, the use of significant adults in your youth ministry is imperative. You can't pull it off alone.

The usual attitude in seeking help is what we call "the body count approach." We give the impression that we just want another police officer for an event. No wonder people are hesitant to respond to our invitation.

The task becomes easier and the results more effective when we approach recruitment from a different philosophical perspective. If we believe that adults and young people in creative relationships have a great deal to share, then the task of matching them becomes mutually rewarding. We can then look for skills and sensitivities beyond the caretaking role.

A small church in New Mexico lost one of its older members, who had been faithful to the congregation for many years. One of the lady's biggest worries was her non-believing husband. He was a retired carpenter and very much against the church. The church's celebration of her death deeply moved her husband. He felt the love of these people, but could not accept God's love.

A sensitive youth advisor noted during a visit that the man had extensive equipment in his work shed. He turned out to be an extremely talented wood worker. The advisor asked if he would help her in a forthcoming retreat. What could he do with wood which would involve the teens? He accepted the challenge.

The old man led the young people into the wooded area near the camp where they selected pieces of limbs and other fallen wood which appealed to them. They returned to the man's work shed to create religious symbols by using simple woodworking techniques. By the time of the closing worship service, the team of young people and this old man had created an amazing collection of wood pieces. During a time of dedication, each person received a wooden symbol of the faith to remember the commitment of the hour.

The retreat brought about an amazing transformation in the old man. He gave so much to the retreat. The young people immediately loved him. After that weekend he opened his shed to the young people in the neighborhood and taught them how to work with their hands. The toughs whom the church could not reach were drawn to him. He became a member of the church family through becoming involved with the youth group.

Dale is very intentional about the use of skilled adults in his youth ministry. He has carefully scouted the talents and skills of folks in his church. One of his key discoveries is that you don't directly ask people about their talents. They will often respond to that question from a vocational perspective. "I'm an accountant." Dale found that in the leisure or hobby time people often have developed incredible skills. For instance, he met a talented filmmaker who spent his time away from his sales job creating super 8 films. He had built complete sets for a series of space films. Dale found five or six teens from the youth group interested in film. The skilled adult and the youth worked on the project together and shared the results with the group at a Sunday evening meeting.

The relationships between the adults and the youth are first class. And volunteers always agree to be used in this way again.

See also ADULT ADVISORS, COMMITMENT, JOB DESCRIPTION

Recycle Theology

Creativity is a naughty word for many people. Many think it has been captured by folks who play flutes and do ballet steps. This is a shame because the gift of creativity belongs to everyone. You don't have to be an artist or musician to claim this special mentality. Creativity is the ability to find wholeness in the midst of fragmentation. The painter doesn't invent the colors. He or she mixes existing hues into new and complete patterns. The musician doesn't invent notes. He or she arranges and interprets the existing sounds in fresh, new ways.

Too many adult and young people shy away from the gifts of creativity. "I am not very creative." The youth worker shakes his head and thinks little of himself. Yet, if you are in Jesus Christ, you are a new creation; the old fragmentation has passed away. You can make or create new possibilities out of every situation.

Dennis and Marilyn Benson are pioneers in what they call recycle theology. This is the process of finding new teaching/communication uses for existing resources. This means that the best youth programming can be developed out of who you are, where you are from, and who you are with. If you can't teach with a leaf and find new meanings with your youth, you can't communicate with a videotape machine.

Books, tapes, magazines and other resource materials may be helpful. However, there are so many opportunities for creative ministry already at hand! We simply have to draw upon the gift of the Spirit which permits us to see that which others do not see.

For example, the leader made a couple introductory remarks before the group of 150 young people and adults. He then passed out pieces of wood he had picked up in the school wood shop. "I want you to become a child again. Fully experience the piece of wood that you have. Let it speak to you and lead you to find new things. First, I want you to smell it. That's right. Can you catch the special odor? What does it remind you of? Go back in your experience. Now look at it carefully. Bring it close to your eyes. Note all the special little marks on it. What kind of stories can you imagine that they might tell? Do you see the rings of growth? Now listen to your piece of wood (laughter).

"No, seriously. Rub it across your ear. See, you can hear it. What does it say to you? Use your taste buds. Put the piece of wood to your lips. Does its taste remind you of another time and place? What memories come to you? Now touch it with special care and awareness. If you close your eyes and just let your fingers do the walking, what kinds of feelings do you have emotionally as you touch the wood?"

The speaker then asks the gathering to break into small units of four or five. They share the feelings they had and the random thoughts which flashed back to them as triggered by the wood. After ten minutes, the guest broke into the buzz of the room and asked them to go around their small circles and share the ways by which they could use a piece of wood in a Bible study with their youth groups. "You don't have to worry about how you will do it or how the teens will respond. Just share the bits and pieces on how you might use the wood in an actual study."

After ten minutes the group shared ideas which came out of their recycling. The response was amazing! People built on the ideas of others. The pieces of wood became the seeds for many fine programs.

Jesus often drew upon the common experiences and objects around him to teach. He took bread and broke it with his disciples in order that we might recycle his life again and again. Recycle theology is a very special opportunity for you and your folks.

Resources

1. **Recycle Catalogue and Recycle Catalogue II**, P.O. Box 12811, Pittsburgh, PA 15421.
2. **RECYCLE Newsletter**, P.O. Box 12811, Pittsburgh, PA 15421.

See also CIRCUS, CREATIVITY, GROUP MEDIA

Refreshments

"Bring on the bug juice!"

Well, that is often what comes to mind when it is time to have refreshments. Cookies and Kool Aid fill out many Sunday evenings. Yet, are these the best foods for "refreshment"?

Many groups are now exploring ways by which this portion of their life together can be richer. Isn't nourishment both a spiritual and physical need? There are those who firmly believe that sugar-laden snacks are actually obstacles to strong group experiences. They believe that behavior patterns are altered by this kind of intake. It is true that teachers have observed less hyperactive responses among younger children when they depart from heavy sugar-filled snacks.

One youth leader gathered a collection of cookie recipes which excluded refined white sugar. Once the group members started baking them, everyone was very happy with these nutritious treats.

A group in Michigan has discovered a favorite refreshment. During the fall and winter season they serve baked potatoes for their snack! The potatoes are washed and placed in the church kitchen oven for cooking during the meeting. Someone brings cheese and other things (cut up hard-boiled eggs, meat slices, diced peppers, etc.) to be added to the snack. The youth can even smell the treat cooking during the program!

Other groups have focused on using vegetables and even salads as their refreshments. The salad bar has now become a popular part of the menu for the fast food restaurant. This food format permits each person to assemble his or her favorite combination.

Another approach to refreshments centers on tailoring the food to the evening's program. This sounds hard. However, some of the best programs have emerged from this kind of thoughtfulness. A discussion on hunger obviously lends itself to having a restricted diet in the refreshment time. A visitor

Many leaders are discovering a correlation between the refreshments they serve and the behavior patterns of their youth.

from another part of the world could give direction to a special snack.

Refreshment time is more than a break from the content of the evening. When the community of faith eats together, there is a special significance to the moment. Jesus reminds us, "As often as you eat and drink. . . ." How do we gather intentionally in this moment of sharing? What is the most meaningful way of returning thanks? Bill has started the tradition with his group of giving thanks in a special way. They stand in a circle. One member takes a piece of the food and breaks it. He or she invites the others, "Won't you break bread with me?" Each person breaks off a piece. Bill is interested in establishing a biblical prayer manner which the youth can use in public which does not seem alien. He says that it is quite moving to see folks from the group at a fast food restaurant breaking off a piece of hamburger bun before eating. These are the same youth who would never bow their head with folded hands in a public place.

How can the ritual of eating or snacking become a reflection of the sacrament of the Table? How can that throwaway time on Sunday evening become an expression of the values and concerns of the faith?

Resources
1. **Diet for a Small Planet**, by Francis Moore Lappe, Ballantine.
2. **Planning Food Experiences**, by Craig Cramer, Discipleship Resources.
3. **Youth Group Activities**, by Craig Cramer, Discipleship Resources.
4. **More With Less Cookbook**, by Doris Janzen Longacre, Herald Press.
5. **The Whole Thing: An Alternative Snackfood Cookbook**, edited by Catherine Mumaw and Marilyn Voran, Herald Press.

See also RECREATION, ROWDIES, SLEEPING

Relating

When you have been chosen as the youth advisor or sponsor you have a few things going for you. At least, youth know who you are and why you are there. However, there will be many times in your youth ministry when you will have no context or point of reference for the nameless teens surrounding you. It will be like open field running. The one-on-one or 50-on-one situation is frightening for everyone involved. The youth are fearful of the stranger in their midst. You will also feel uncomfortable in the all-teen setting.

If you let things happen around you without taking any initiative, the atmosphere will remain frosty. In fact, it might become quite hostile. In some all-teen settings, the visiting adult might be viewed as a narc (narcotic agent) or undercover police officer.

Fifty or more high school students were hanging out at the school's sports stadium. It was the midday gathering place for those who could sneak out of school between classes. This was student turf. Knots of youth talked, smoked and snuggled. The air was filled with the smelly odor of those funny looking cigarettes.

Suddenly the lone figure of a middle-aged man came jogging into the sports complex. He moved slowly and surely toward the track oval directly bordering the crowd of teens. There was an uneasy stir as they felt this new presence. As he passed about three feet from the edge of the throng, someone yelled, "Go pops!" A ripple of laughter could be heard. The hostile climate was being seeded. The French philosopher, Jean Paul Sartre, has called this the "drainpipe" syndrome. We are comfortably wrapped in our privacy when suddenly we realize that someone else is watching us. This awareness sucks away some of

The way you relate to young people is a model of how they will relate to others.

our being. Youth find hostility a natural way to stop the drain. ("Just turn up the music I like and all the adults in range will leave the room.")

As the jogger completed the quarter-mile for the first time, he upset the tense atmosphere building in the crowd. "Hi! What a super day!" He smiled as he looked into the eyes of several students who were facing him. They didn't respond. The next time around he dropped another comment. This time he kidded himself when one of the students asked, "What do you call that stride?"

"Desperation!"

They all laughed.

After 10 laps, one of the students yelled out, "How long do you run?"

He nodded appreciation when the jogger gasped, "Six or seven miles."

The crowd relaxed. They had included the stranger in their circle. He was now part of the scenery. As the teens would drift away, they would shout comments to the lone figure on the track. "Hang in there!" "You're looking good, man!"

The adult has the responsibility to create the cradle in which infant relationships with teens can be nurtured. So often cold, hard faces of a teen will magically be transformed into smiles and friendliness when the adult will look him or her in the eyes and smile. So often we want to be befriended by the teens. They do have a responsibility to be hospitable. However, the burden of breaking through the hostility and fear most often remains on you.

A Christian theologian reminds us that the task of the faith is to transform hostility into hospitality. This is an awesome task. Yet, this is one of the special gifts youth advisors bring to tense situations. It will be the model of your ability to relate in tight situations which will give them the capacity to do likewise in their ministry.

This kind of open field relating has been one of the most impressive gifts of some peace groups. During the height of social disorder in the '60s, a small band of people dedicated themselves to being peacemakers. At some of the street encounters, they would place their bodies between the police and the angry demonstrators. By touching and gently talking, they would often calm explosive situations.

Dick tells of one wild anti-war demonstration in Washington which was on the edge of getting out of order. The huge march was composed of people from every place on the peace spectrum. At one point, the National Guard came over to the peace groups. "I hear on the radio that a radical group is coming to this corner. They are shouting and claiming that they will go right to the White House gate. If they don't turn and follow the others, I will have my men stop them forcefully."

Dick quickly gathered five other people. At that moment, the hostile marchers came around the corner. They carried huge flags and were angrily shouting. The small group stepped in beside the people leading the protestors. They put their arms around their shoulders. With smiles and all the warmth they could muster, they talked to them. "We are glad that you are here. What a fine day." "Peace has a chance!" "It is so good to have brothers and sisters together." As they talked and comforted these intense folks, they guided them away from the gates and down the parade path.

Imagine the challenge of leading your youth into this kind of relationship! There is a great brittleness to youth society when viewed up close. Small knots of people broken off from each other compose most gatherings. School dances have boys and girls standing apart in uneasy tension—just the way it was in your high school days. It is in the context of the uncomfortable setting that the youth adult can be peacemakers.

See also ACCESS, ADVISING, ADVOCATE, HOSTILITY

Resources

We are living in time of church work when there are more resources for our work than at any other time. The shelves sag with films, audio and video cassettes, magazines, books, games, multi-media kits, newsletters and countless experts to be hired or visited in workshops. You may even live in an area served by a resource center. These multi-faceted sourcing cafeterias are treasure-houses for youth ministry. Many resource centers have a much wider selection of material than most libraries. Don't be discouraged if your denomination does not have such a center. There may be an interdenominationally sponsored one in your area. Check with other churches in your community.

The value of these depositories is that the staffing is usually extraordinary. The media or resource center staff is interested in the nature of your group and what your goals are. They want to help you use material in ways which will accomplish your objectives.

Even if you do not have this source in your area, you can enter into a cooperative resourcing stance. Work with other youth advisors in buying and sharing materials. There is no reason why you have to own all that you use. By working together with three or four youth advisors in nearby churches you have more materials to use. Some groups have even worked together to form a film purchasing co-op. You will be surprised how your options will open once you begin sharing resources.

Utilization is the key to the effective employment of resource materials. We have seen the finest film, the best simulation game or the best speaker result in a terrible program because of improper usage. Again, working with other advisors can help you brainstorm how to use materials effectively.

No book or technique is the answer to all your programming problems. You may love the possibilities of puppets or clowning. There is a place for each approach. However, don't run a good idea into the ground. Pack your "survival kit" with every technique you can make your own. When the right time arrives, you can reach into that closet and use that creative idea, whether it's using Contact paper to make slides or conducting a program on competition-free games.

It is a wonderful time to be in youth ministry!

Resources
1. **Complete Universe of Youth Ministry**, by Christian Board of Publication, Box 179, St. Louis, MO 63166.
2. **Kaleidoscope**, by the Presbyterian Church, U.S., 341 Ponce de Leon Avenue, Atlanta, GA 30365.
3. **Resource Directory for Youth Workers**, published by Youth Specialties, 1224 Greenfield Drive, El Cajon, CA 92021.

See also BIBLE, CARS, EQUIPMENT, ICE BREAKERS, MATERIALS

Resource Person

This is an overworked job title for which there is a catchall term for leadership that has been invited to help with an event.

It might be expected that such a person would be in charge of the resources or would have been invited to bring special resources. Occasionally, this is part of the invitation. But normally, the resource they are expected to bring to an event is their experience and expertise. Further, they are usually invited to speak or demonstrate their knowledge and insights in special time slots, though it is expected that they will be available for long periods during the event to share their "resource" whenever individuals or groups request it.

See also CONSULTATION

Respect

Rodney Dangerfield doesn't have it. You can't buy it. You can't demand it. Respect is something which is given by youth to significant adults. Every adult wants that special quality relationship. Yet, respect is a gift which is hard to define or seek.

We have all seen those teacher or police films in which an adult enters a group of ruthless youth and wins them over. You may feel such a showdown tension when you face a new group. The adult in the film does not have much experience or special qualities which attract young people. Yet, by the second reel the kids will do anything to support this strange adult. We often overlook the process documented in these films. It is easy to assume that the star's personality or a well-written script did the trick. Nevertheless, a careful look at the adults in these stories usually reveals a demonstration of several desirable qualities: honesty, understanding, courage, loyalty and faithfulness in standing with the youth.

There is a lofty nobility in such a list. One beautiful thing about youth is that adults of every possible style and size can receive the gift of respect. Teens love adults who can communicate the Christian life to young people. This means that anything you can do to break down the walls between the adult and young person will create the climate for respect to grow.

Many adults lament a lack of respect from young people while at the same time they have no respect for their teens. We must respect in order to know the respect of others. A few years ago we attended a conference of counselors and psychologists in New York. The panel discussion featured several people who were experts in dealing with troubled youth. As the conversation unfolded, we became quite uncomfortable. The experts talked about their charges from an emotional and personal distance. It seemed that cleverness had displaced their respect for these teens. The exercise of analyzing the relationship of respect between youth and adult can kill the natural flow of this foundation of the Christian life together.

See also ACCESS, ADVOCATE, LOVE

Retreat

The retreat is a vital time of spiritual growth for most teens. Probably more growth takes place on these overnight events than at any other time in youth ministry. Even though every area of the country has access to adequate retreat facilities, secluded settings and an infinite number of activities doesn't ensure success.

The quality of this kind of outing depends on the amount of planning you put into the event before it begins. Many well-intentioned adults have planned for months and found that the retreat dies because they have not included teens in the planning process. Young people must make a genuine emotional investment in the event to make it successful. As you plan, help create an environment in which dreaming is nurtured. Sweep into the center of the discussion every contribution or idea. Don't worry about how everything will fit together.

It is easy to strip away possibilities when you have too many options. However, it is deadly when a discouraging setting destroys ideas until there is nothing with which to work. Play with a suggested theme by dreaming how it could be totally experienced. Stay away from format restrictions which break everything down into categories ("free time," "speaker," "eating"). For instance, some folks were looking at the theme of relationships. They came up with some interesting possibilities for their retreat:

"Don't be half-safe." Music sweeps into the quiet, stark room. It is dark. Slides flash off one wall and then another. Radio commercials fill the room from the tape track.

Twenty-five young people sit on the floor. They are sitting within individual circles drawn with chalk on the floor. They sit apart, facing different directions. They are experiencing the first part of a four-part retreat theme, "Being Alone." The next day they move through the experiential dimensions of "Being with a Special Other," "Being with Strange Others," and "Being with God."

Another segment of the high school retreat is gaming. Each person is given a new name, role and viewpoint. A situation has been established: A local

Surveys indicate that more spiritual growth takes place on retreats than any other youth ministry function.

school has an honor code. No one is supposed to give or to receive help. Each person is asked to sign a pledge that he or she will report any cheating. During the final exams for seniors, someone cheats. The teacher discovers it and fails the whole class. A chasm develops between several factions: teacher, administrators, parents and students.

The students are divided into the four groups. They are to plan a strategy for the public meeting where a final decision will be made. When the mock meeting begins, the confrontation is heated. The suburban students who apathetically have accepted their way of life and condemned the restlessness of others suddenly explode. There are signs, singing and a number of other reactions to what certain factions consider injustice. The game has given them freedom to enter another person's shoes.

Remember that you can change time

frames, eating and just about everything else. Once you have centered on a theme and found an exciting format for exploring the content by using the context, think of promotion and other details. Now you can assign all kinds of jobs. Who will develop the promotion approach and materials? Who will arrange transportation and food details with the camp site you have chosen and reserved?

Once the group has gathered at the camp, it is important to form a covenant in which the rules for your life together have been established. It is important that these be created by the group. The results of a broken covenant should also be established. The adults shouldn't be the police force. The covenant community can handle the enforcement.

Kit developed an interesting retreat design with his junior highs. They lived near a cave area. The retreat was an overnight cave experience. Imagine the catacomb theme that could be created around this setting!

There is also a retreat model which focuses on equipping youth to do ministry upon returning from the retreat. Groups have retreated to learn how to conduct peer ministry, radio programs and other specialized ministry. Retreats are incredible opportunities for youth ministry.

Resources
1. **Retreat Handbook: A-Way to Meaning**, by Virgil and Lynn Nelson, Judson Press.

See also BIBLE KNOWLEDGE, CONDUCT, EARTHBALL, GROUP MEDIA, NO-LOSER RECREATION, PUBLICITY, SIMULATION GAMES, SLEEP

Risking

"Don't be half-safe."

"Don't live with the discomfort of a headache."

These claims fill our lives. Ads tell us again and again that we should seek comfort and ease. Unfortunately, such a philosophy has oozed into our theology and lifestyle. We are encouraged to teach and lead in a church setting guided by methods and styles which are most comfortable for us.

Even the behavioral sciences have promoted a psychology of comfort. It is true that needless suffering is disabling. However, the biblical witness to faithfulness keeps placing the disciple in an uncomfortable and stretching position. Just when all seemed well, Jesus pushed his followers into risky stances. He still pushes his contemporary disciples.

Youth ministry is particularly noted for placing adult leaders in new and risky positions. Your cultural conditioning will resist trying something which may not turn out right. Most of our secular business, school and community experiences will be of little help when it comes to risking in youth ministry.

When you follow the new wineskin approach to youth ministry, you will find that as you overcome your own fear, several other layers of resistance will face you. The high school students will be initially resistant to your encouragement to do clowning, experiential Bible study or street interviewing. They have been tracked and conditioned by the secular school system which rarely offers rewards for entertaining risky ideas, actions or values. Most adults in control of youth training institutions are providing "charade" learning opportunities—they want students to parrot back the safe information given them previously. Those who respond properly are rewarded with the best marks and awards. So your folks resist by acting out the question, "Why should I trust you by sharing myself with you, when I am punished for doing the same thing in school?"

After the young people understand the risky nature of your life together, you will find that parents become upset. "Why is the youth group always late in getting out? I had to wait in the parking lot for 20 minutes." Parents may even become suspicious of the bond between the advisor and youth who have come to risk for the sake of their faith. "I don't like the way he keeps calling the youth advisor's wife." "Why does a woman her age pay so much attention to a teenager?"

You may even find little enthusiasm from other adults who work in the church. The risking person is threatening to others. Those who teach youth, say, on Sunday mornings, will quickly sense that something different is happening to their students. They will feel judged when the youth say that the current program "is the best thing we've ever had."

The risking never gets easier. The leap of faith is always a risk. However, once you feel the thrill of this kind of ministry you will never want to move away from it.

The leader of the youth event at a private school had shared slides depicting the moments of wonder in his life. He then asked the two hundred students in the high school to share in a special experience of awe and wonder. He slipped off the stage. In just a few seconds the room was filled with music from "Star Wars". The rear projection screen flashed pictures from the science fiction film. With a loud shout, the speaker appeared at the rear of the auditorium dressed in the flowing robes of Ben, the priest of The Force. He moved through the audience waving his lasersword (plastic tube with flashlight attached.) When he reached the platform, he told the story of the film as slides were flashed on the screen. Then he reminded the audience that what they were viewing happened in the past. He invited the high school students to create a "Star World," a new world that exists without fighting and war. After clustering the youth into units of 10 or 12, he asked them to imagine they were going to another planet to create the way the new world will rule itself, distribute food and deal with disagreement.

The only thing the groups had to go on were these directions: God so loved the cosmos that his only son was given for you. Over there is a huge pile of 'space waste.' You are to use the paper, pieces of plastic, old tennis shoes, body paint, etc., to alter yourself. In 40 minutes we will gather again and each planet will have a chance to present a message from its society. You'll have one minute to share by acting out something that your imagination and awe have created."

There was an aching period of time as the leader wandered to each group. Would these young people from a different culture respond to this risky experience? They were wearing uniforms and were under the influence of the British cognitive learning system.

The leader stopped at one room. The dozen teens were throwing an eraser around the room. They didn't seem to be working on anything! "You have just 10 more minutes." Should the leader step in and rescue these young people from the risk of being embarrassed by not having anything? He decided to let them face this situation on their own.

At the gathering of the planets, the sharing moments were fantastic! The group of youth who were playing with the eraser had their presentation completed. They carried in a student who had beem completed wrapped in strips of paper. Two green brushes were tied to his head as antennae. One of the group members reported that their planet had overcome hatred. Each person had a band of paper around his or her wrist. "We have a way of dealing with the person who is overwhelmed by hatred and bound up with his evil force." The student took water and sprinkled it on the wrapped person. The paper broke away and the once-wrapped person encircled the "hater" with a giant hug.

The young people placed in a risky

context of love and expectation will almost always exceed your hopes. Even when they fail, the risk is worth it.

Resources

1. **Believing the Impossible Before Breakfast**, by Ernest Lee Stoffel, John Knox Press.
2. **Why Am I Afraid to Love?**, by John Powell, Argus Communications.
3. **Why Am I Afraid to Tell You Who I Am**, by John Powell, Argus Communications.

See also ACCESS, AVAILABILITY, CRITICISM, SUPPORT SYSTEM

Role Playing

Often our discussions are academic word plays that do not let us get inside the feelings and mental framework of the persons who are involved in the subject matter we are discussing. Role play is one way to project the class into the situation and let them enact the struggles and make some of the decisions. It is a contrived simulation involving class members as participants in a dramatic enactment of the way they might respond.

There are several ways to create the role play situation. The group can decide what characters are needed to make the simulation come alive, and then act out events that led to the scene. The more details that can be gathered will give the scene and the characters substance and dimension. As the characters are developed, various group members may volunteer to become that person and act out the scene as they might.

The scene is set, the background is given and the characters respond to each other the way that they feel the actual person would. After the scene has unfolded to its logical fulfillment, it can be cut off so that discussion can make use of what took place.

An intriguing way to begin this debriefing experience is to ask characters to describe their feelings toward themselves, the situation, and the other characters. If persons have acted out the character of someone very different from themselves, it is often quite revealing for them to discover the logic that they had not thought possible before. For instance, a person portraying someone from a different economic class is often amazed at the dissatisfaction they feel when they become the other person.

Another way to develop the scene is to create it prior to the meeting, even to the point of developing the characters in crucial detail and setting up the background so that the scene will provide maximum development of the roles. Characterization can be written out on cards and given to volunteers as they enter the room. Tell the group that a role play will take place, that you have given several volunteers specific characterization to act out as the simulation takes place. This time the group will not know in-depth details of the characters. Nor will the volunteer actors know the motives behind the actions.

The possibilities for role play situations are endless. The most usual examples are those that place persons from different backgrounds (racial, income, cultural, etc.) into a situation in which breaking out of the molds of the past may have to occur. For example, one person might represent a very poor Mexican who has slipped across the border into Texas and appears late one night in a grocery store attempting to steal some fruit when the owner of the store appears with a friend from the church. (Note that references to the participants' sex have been omitted since the group might want to try the role play more than once by changing the sex of the persons to see if it affects the role play.) With the situation set, the leader could add details about the setting to give some extra dynamics, such as: the grocer has had five break-ins lately and was hurt badly the last time; the immigrant could be getting food for a sick child; the church member could be an immigrant official or the son or daughter of an immigrant.

Usually, role plays demand that the participants make character judgments and ethical negotiations which may lead to understanding the ways we make decisions.

Another example: One person might be assigned to portray a school principal; another, the parent; another, the child. The parent has been called to the school because of the child's last three absences (which the parent did not know about). The child has missed school because he or she has been helping an older friend (whom the parent does not like) to get set up in a business that will probably be the friend's sole means of support. The situation begins as the parent walks into the office. After the role play has established some direction, call for a time out and introduce new facts which might drastically alter the responses. Add information concerning the friend: The friend has just gotten away from drugs and this is the first sign of positive entrance into society.

See also DEBATES, DISCUSSION, LISTENING, SIMULATION GAMES

Rowdies

"What do you do with the person who always keeps the group in an uproar?"

"I have two tenth graders who always pick on the seventh graders and try to pull a little prank each week."

"I couldn't begin to tell you how many times Jeff has set off firecrackers behind the cabins, put salt in the sugar and disrupted programs with comments just loud enough for half the group to hear."

To begin to deal with such problems, it is important to do a little detective work to locate the cause of the person's need to disrupt. A person who consistently causes calamities and confusion usually feels the same way internally, and his or her actions may be the only way they know to tell you. Loneliness, bitterness, envy, boredom and fear can be translated into various attempts at gaining attention, regardless of the method.

For Jack, it was a desire to have the attractive youth leader notice him. For Melba, it was a lashing out at the group when she felt her parents were deserting her. For Jim it was an unconscious rebuking of the youth council, since he felt he was unfairly omitted during the council's election. For Tim and Jayne, tickling was the only way they knew to touch members of the opposite sex.

An often overlooked cause of hyperactivity in the past is now coming to light as we are beginning to understand the direct relationship of the foods we eat with our outlook and activity levels. One

Rowdy youth group members are both the church's horror and its glory.

youth group was able to significantly lower the number of disruptive occurrences by eliminating all sweets from the evening's supper and snacks. Many camps are now gearing their menus to foods that contain high nutrition but low levels of stimulants, even to the point of replacing the candy in the camp store with fruits.

How do you help rowdies? The same way you help anyone—love them! Love them until you begin to understand them. Then love them some more until they know you have begun to understand them.

Only as a last resort should any person be separated from the group. Preferably, discover ways to unite them with the group in productive ways, though in this process you and the group may need to unite them with other missing links in their lives: family, school, neighborhood, themselves.

Sometimes, but not always, you can unite them with the group by giving the rowdy persons a significant responsibility which makes the group dependent on them. Many a youth has found mean-

ing and developed self-esteem by having a major role in a church drama or singing group, setting up electrical equipment (this one worked for us when we were rowdies), serving on a regional council or being a camp counselor can benefit everyone involved. The important thing is to let them know that they matter to other people.

It is also possible to discover ways to help disruptive kids by analyzing the methods they use in their disruption. Some persons who interrupt programs with a distracting personal commentary are actually exhibiting impressive abilities for humor. We could easily make use of their articulate phrasing for creating publicity, inventing clever ways of attracting new members or writing funny letters to those who are sick or lonely. The firecracker/spitball/practical joking rowdy is almost always a natural with technical skills that can be applied to workcamp projects, backstage productions and craft instruction.

Our group will always remember Dan. He was the one who came to camp one year and carefully left pop bottles around the campground in conspicuous places right after the announcement that bottles found not in the bottle rack would mean that the camp store would be closed for the week. The penalty was enacted and within minutes Dan had opened up four suitcases of overpriced candy and soft drinks to reap a financial bonanza. Yes, we'll always remember Dan because a wise adult leader asked him to become group treasurer—we've been solvent ever since.

See also BELONGING, CONDUCT, HOSTILITY, REFRESHMENTS, RELATING

Rules

Every collection of people has rules for ordering their lives together. Unfortunately, most people usually don't consciously recognize what these rules are. Or one person may post his or her understanding of the boundaries for the group without the consensus of others.

In the local church youth group, there is often an absentee method of rule determination. "The elders don't want us to use that room." "The priest doesn't like smoking in the church hall." "The pastor doesn't want anyone to use their cars while we are on the retreat."

These rules may be important or right. However, it is very hard for a youth group to have much ownership to this kind of declaration. There is a covenant quality of youth ministry which needs to be exercised in the group's life together. In the biblical context God and his people had a vital binding at the moment of accepting the relationship. The commandments or ordering of this relationship were undertaken by both sides of the covenant.

At the beginning of each season, it is wise to take some time to form the nature of the covenant. You will be

amazed at how sensitive your youth will be about making the rules for their life together. Be nondirective. Help the group define the nature of who they are as a group. Whose are they? What are the perimeters of their time together? Are there building and fire codes? What about the neighborhood? Will others be disturbed by certain kinds of behavior? Will others in the larger church community be offended or hurt by certain kinds of activities? How can the ordering of our lives as a youth group be more complete and exciting by the way we make our covenant to each other? What happens when someone breaks our code of care?

The youth advisor doesn't have to be the law enforcement agent for the rules the group develops. If someone breaks the law which the group has created, he or she must accept the results promised by the law. Perhaps the person who breaks the rules for your weekend retreat can appeal to the whole group for final judgment. This may sound like a ponderous process. However, please note that the process of unfolding our lives as parts of the body of Christ is the substance of our time together. Content becomes context.

Most young people develop rules much more demanding than those imposed by adults. And when the youth make the rules, they are much more easily enforced, interpreted and supported.

The value of the rule is to serve the group, not the reverse. Often the group will recognize the wisdom of changing its rules or their enforcement for the benefit of the total group, which is the utmost consideration and must not be overlooked in strict rule keeping. There will always be that overlap of law and grace; but therein lies the greatest potential.

See also CONDUCT, ROWDIES

Rumor

One of the ageless delights of people is gossip. Every culture seems to warn people of the dangers in such a practice of spreading half-truths and misinformation. The Bible warns about it, mothers forbid it and friends struggle to abstain from practicing it. Yet, rumor infests most communities. Youth groups often thrive on this disease. There is something irresistible about a juicy bit of news which destroys, belittles or scandalizes another person.

The rumor becomes a vehicle for hatred and destruction in the hands of some youth. You are in a key position to model what idle conversation can and shouldn't be.

You might even think of programming to work on this facet of youth society. Ask five young people to leave your meeting and wait in the hall. Put a slide on the screen. Be sure that you have chosen a picture which shows the interaction between people of different races and ages. An action scene will be most helpful. Ask one person to enter the room. Let him or her look at the screen for a minute. Then have the person turn away from the screen. Only the first person gets to see the slide. The next teen is brought in and not permitted to see the screen. Have the first person describe the picture. Repeat the process until all the young people outside the room have returned. Discuss how the picture changed in the description process. How did preconceived ideas get placed in the description?

One youth group ran a "rumor line" phone service during a community busing crisis. The youth at the church volunteered to serve on the phones. Anyone could call and hear what was actually happening at any given time. This source of solid information overcame the power of rumors and helped to bring peace during a time of transition.

The rumor. The Bible warns against it, mothers forbid it, friends struggle with it and youth groups thrive on it.

Runaways

"Those crazy kids. Why do they leave home and run to the big cities? Don't they know they'll be killed?"

That is a typical adult comment as he turns from the newspaper or TV to demonstrate superior intelligence to those youth being reported as just found by the Los Angeles or New York police.

However, the stories on the other end of the reports may reveal that intelligence or judgment had little to do with running away. The youth had run away from where they found life to be intolerable. The fact that they wound up as prostitutes, drug addicts or burglars may not have come as a surprise at all.

Many youth leave home because they feel they are causing the problems, and they depart to relieve their family of the burden. They have so little self-esteem that they feel their family deserves a better break than for them to stay around and drain the budget and emotional reserves. They may feel that a divorce between their parents is imminent and they are causing it, so it is better for them to get out of the way. Then everyone will be happy.

Another reason for the act of running away is the lack of support many youth feel at home. As the youth gets older, his or her energy, freedoms and attractive qualities are resented by parents who feel tied to unliked jobs and debts. In cruel attempts at leveling the scales, the parents stay away from home for long periods of time and the youth becomes the housekeeper, cook and the full-time babysitter for younger siblings. Even more tragic are the many instances in which youth are the targets of incest, harsh punishment, torture and other forms of daily abuse.

To the youth, anything appears to be better than staying around home. So they head for a locality they have heard about from a friend or have seen on TV or in the movies. The west coast and the deep south seem like warm, secure places for someone who feels frozen out at home.

Runaways come from all kinds of homes, some of which appear in your church. Some potential runaways are in church youth groups, and the kinds of ministries that lift up the individual to understand that he or she is loved and sustained by the creator of the universe can help to change homes and to change individuals. The conditions as we know them in our homes do not have to remain static when the Holy Spirit is able to work through us. It could be a life and death issue with members of your group for them to comprehend the power of God that is available to them.

Counselors of runaways say a little loving concern by someone in the home might help youth to realize the family's problems are not solely due to them, and that their leaving will not result in marital stability. A positive youth group experience might have helped them to talk about these feelings and search for alternatives.

Resources
1. **National Directory of Runaway Programs**, National Youth Work Alliance, 1346 Connecticut Avenue, N.W., Washington, D.C. 20036.
2. **Adolescent Life Stress: As a Predictor of Alcohol Abuse and/or Runaway Behavior**, by Therese van Houten and Gary Golenbiewski, National Youth Work Alliance, 1346 Connecticut Avenue, N.W., Washington, DC 20036.

See also ACCESS, BELONGING, RISKING

Scouting

Scouting has always been a significant part of many youth ministries. It is one of the few programs in existence that helps persons to make that terrifying leap from the security of elementary school into middle school or junior high. It is true that a person enters scouting as a child and leaves as a youth, man or woman.

Scouting is a program filled with steps of affirmation for the participant, and though it operates from a solid, personal support base, it continually nudges the individual to try limited personal risks, assertion and achievement.

Seldom is there any rivalry between scouting and other segments in youth ministry since the fellowship program, church school class and musical program clearly have different pur-

poses. The scouting program is one of the best examples of what a church can do to provide groups for specific interests and needs at different points in a person's life.

Churches in a community could link together to make every facet of the scouting program available. One church may be able to sponsor a Cub Scout troop. Another might sponsor a Campfire troop and a Boy Scout troop. Another, a Girl Scout troop; and another, an Explorer troop.

One of the most satisfying relationships between church and scouting is the God and Country Award program. This deep relationship enables a young person to learn and grow as a person of faith with a church leader mentor.

From time to time, leaders of the church's other youth ministry programs should meet with the scouting leaders to ensure that their common objectives and scheduling progress well. This also helps with the transition when an individual wishes to attend more than one program.

Resources

1. **Boy Scout Handbook**, Boy Scouts of America, P.O. Box 61030, Dallas-Fort Worth Airport, TX 75261.

2. **Girl Scout Handbook**, Girl Scouts of America, 830 Third Avenue, New York, NY.

See also ADVENTURE CAMPING, CITIZENSHIP

Search Institute

Founded as a research center by Merton Strommen, Lutheran minister and research specialist, this extremely valuable agency was first called the Research Survey Service. For many years its primary function was to administer the survey service which gave local churches a profile of interests and traits of their youth group as well as an in-depth profile of each youth.

A number of additional projects were undertaken, including a research survey telling what factors discourage or allow changes in a congregation, a survey giving the factors that prepare persons for a full-time church vocation, and a far-reaching survey of the particular needs and interests of early teens.

Perhaps the best known project was the compilation of data indicating the satellites of personality traits of youth in mainline Protestant denominations, the data for which resulted in the best selling book, **The Five Cries of Youth**.

The Search Institute is located at 122 West Franklin Ave., Minneapolis, MN 55404.

See also CONSULTATION, WORKSHOPS

Self-image

People who deal with drug abusers and runaways say that the critical issue is whether the youth has a positive self-image. So many youth have concluded that they are totally useless to the world, a drain on society and not worth caring for. People who feel that no one cares if they live or die will often ignore the body's normal warning about health or comfort. They often seek out masochistic punishment since they feel they are doing society a favor in carrying out its wishes.

We don't have to look far to see where these messages are obtained. Advertising has a powerful ability to tell viewers or listeners that they are hopeless without a certain product. A double zinger for a youth is that after using the product, the results may not approximate what happened to the person in the ad. The youth concludes that the difference is her or his fault.

Sports are usually built on a system of

The youth group has the potential to become the support base that lets people realize their own immense value.

elimination in which all players and teams except the champion is eliminated during each season. And the champion finally gets sent off to a higher level of competition to be eliminated.

In their frantic plans for obtaining the most comfort-filled home for their family, parents often fail to let the children share in and contribute to family plans. Many parents unwittingly demonstrate to the child that though they can provide all this, the kids can do nothing.

Society tells youth that they have to jump hurdles to be accepted. Yet it keeps changing the hurdles of education, job experience or initiative. In the end many youth feel that society has succeeded in shutting them out. Even the church often (indirectly perhaps) tells young people that their ideas about worship, local community needs, building decorations, and program plans are off base, and the youth feel isolated from the faith community.

Rarely does anyone give youth spontaneous affirmation for self-fulfilling efforts.

There are a number of activities that a group might consider for building the self-image of its members. One method is an admiration exchange. Have persons pair off and work through a number of exercises together that develop trust. Trust walks are a natural and regardless of the number of times one has tried it, the experience is always different because the partners and situations vary. (A trust walk is when one person gently and carefully leads another, whose eyes are closed, around the general area of the meeting place for a nominal length of time. The pairs usually switch roles after a set time.)

Another activity is to mirror the other person by moving one's hands and body the way the other person does. Again, after a time, the roles are reversed. Another is to fall back into the arms of the partner (from a safe distance).

After the trust has been mutually shared, the two persons can share their complimentary feelings about the other person, saying things such as: "I really like the way you. . ." or "You are good at. . ." or "I feel very close to you when . . . ." It is so rare in our society when we let ourselves tell another person of our appreciation for them. Perhaps if we did this more often, fewer persons would conclude they are losers.

The youth group has the potential for becoming a support base that lets the individual realize her or his own immense value. Through service and work projects, the youth can realize that they do have something of worth to give. The lives of those who receive the benefits are much richer for the person having come their way. Through experiencing a caring fellowship they can recount times when their support of others increased their spirits and lightened their load. Through periods of worship the individual can begin to comprehend that the Creator of the universe cares about them and wants to minister to the world through them. Speaking of self-image!

Resources
1. **I Count, You Count**, by George Calden, Argus Communications.
2. **I Am Loveable and Capable**, by Sidney Simon, Argus Communications.
3. **Do You Sometimes Feel Like a Nobody**, by Tim Stafford, Zondervan.

See also IDENTITY, SERVICE

Serendipity

The dictionary defines this term as being "the gift of finding valuable moments in unexpected places." The term should mean much more to those working within the church. Lyman Coleman is a genius of faith who has webbed together the insights of behavioral science with biblical and theological truth. *Serendipity* is the title of his approach and the label for many of the books he has produced. Many youth workers know him from the amazing series of workshops he conducted across North America during the '70s. These important and helpful events enabled leaders to experience small group sessions which encouraged them to draw upon their own stories, faith and resources.

He has designed so many helpful exercises and study approaches that one is overwhelmed by the quality and quantity of his material. It is all created to utilize resources and faith.

Many of his techniques have slipped into all good Christian education materials. If you find an item which asks participants to draw a life map and then share the key points on it, you are probably reading a thing written by someone influenced by Lyman. If you have not experienced this kind of educational model, use one of his books and try it with yourself and a few others. It will open the door to many exciting new options as you grow in community.

You can get in touch with Lyman at Serendipity, Box 1012, Littleton, CO 80160.

Serious Subjects

"Why can't the youth ever get around to dealing with some serious subjects for a change? I'm tired of watching them play games every Sunday evening."

Often the "play" is serious business to the participants, but is not evident to non-participants. The expressions may not be serious, but the interactions are. There is nothing that says a group has to sit around a table to deal with serious items, though a basketball court may not allow all persons to participate in the discussion who would like to. It may be possible for your group to carry the topics into a more involved discussion following the game.

See also COMMUNI-TY, GROUP BUILDING, ICE BREAKERS

A trusting relationship and secure atmosphere are keys in getting youth to talk openly about serious subjects.

A group may hesitate to open up because they do not know how. Many hero models in recent years have been oblivious to concern for personal or social dilemmas. Youth have rarely been taught by example to work with others toward mutually beneficial solutions to problems. Name the number of occasions recently when a TV plot included a group of persons working together in a discussion on a matter of concern. The norm is the hero who bears all the burdens, keeps personal feelings bottled up and lashes out to destroy the restrictive forces. (Incidentally the youth realizes that it may not be possible for him or her to be the hero or heroine. The result is to become even more subdued.)

Young people carry so much baggage today that they don't want to risk opening the first latch for fear everything will burst out. You might mention subjects such as the draft, scarcities of resources and sexuality only to get blind stares. But when the trust level is more secure and the persons are made to feel that what they say is okay, mountains of questions and raw emotions may come tumbling forth.

Let's face it, if you were a teenager and were frightened about war or college or being respected and you knew that the evening schedule allowed 30 minutes for recreation, 20 minutes to eat and 20 minutes for program, would you be willing to open up your painful, naked soul and submit it to this easy answer session and Band-Aid clinic?

Youth become serious only when we take them seriously. This involves time because caring involves trust, which comes in no instant packages. Some of the serious concerns will demand special events, retreats, camps, lock-ins and periods of prolonged personal contact. And it may mean that we need to be more honest about the 20-minute sessions we have, sharing your hopes for those times and exploring how they can be the most useful.

See also BIBLE KNOWLEDGE, DISCUSSION, QUESTIONS

Service

We learn to love by loving, and we develop a better understanding of Christ by serving as he did. He came not to be served but to serve.

Many young people are just beginning to comprehend the many ways that those who care for them have served them through the years as well as the vast incomprehendable love that God pours out on each of them daily.

We love because God first loved us with a love that enables us to respond. Our response is poured out in service to others, for as we do this in his name, we serve him.

Thus, our worship is a service. Our hope is a service. (To be afraid or filled with worry is to deny God's role in our lives—he is not afraid.)

Service is a state of thankful response. Service is also action, not to earn God's love but to proclaim and invest it in the lives of others.

Youth need to experience the cleansing energy that flows through a person's life as what God has given them is passed on to those in need. Young people need to sense the passion which enflames a person's being as they identify with their common brothers and sisters around the world and care for the hurts and pains.

Once the youth know what true service feels like, they will never be the same.

Different groups will sense different needs they can meet. Many think in terms of performing hard work as service while others will think in terms of performing strenuous manual labor as

Self-esteem abounds when youth give to others without expecting anything in return.

service while others will think in terms of helping persons with physical, mental, emotional or spiritual needs.

Somehow, when we discover a need that we feel called upon to answer, the extra strength and energy we did not know we had suddenly comes forth and is put to use. And as we make changes in our lives to help others, the results are often far more lasting and useful than we ever thought possible.

When we have given our lives away in love, we look back and realize how much more we've received than we have given. We have found ourselves by losing ourselves.

Resources
1. **Handbook on Service**, compiled by Dale Dieleman, Baker Book House.

Sex

It doesn't help to remind church folk that sex isn't a dirty word. The faith family has generally put sexuality within a context of judgment and fear. The adult experiences of worship, study, fellowship and outreach function without any acknowledgement of the existence of sexuality. This may work well for a generation of folks who have received their orientation in the ethics of sex in a different time. However, we live in a cultural context teeming with self-conscious sexuality. Every situation comedy and TV commercial seems to utilize sexual images. The values expressed by this erotic environment are often exploitative and devoid of love.

Pastors and adults preach many sermons concerning the low morals of youth. However, the entire faith community must take some responsibility for not providing a positive presentation of sexuality. Authentic youth ministry must journey with youth through all

the byways of maturation. Sexuality is one of the most important areas of growth.

If you choose to include this aspect of your programming, you are headed for a complex situation. There will be criticism if you don't handle this challenge carefully. Jesse has faced this opportunity for many years with a balanced program which brings praise from every quarter. The course runs for nine weeks each fall. Jesse chooses a married couple to teach the course with him. Parents go through the course themselves before their teens take it. "It is important that the teens and parents both know what the other knows. This means that they can talk about the course more easily."

The course focuses on the relationship of love, which is the basis of sexuality for a person of faith. The husband and wife discuss aspects of their relationship. They even let the students share some of their stress points. A doctor who is a member of the church leads a session for the men and one for the women on the physical aspects of sex. Jesse has found that most teens have a very poor grasp of how their bodies work. Familiarity with nudity and sexual language doesn't assure teens of sound information.

The course concludes with the couple rededicating their marriage vows. The youth are witnesses and the service includes everyone.

It would be wise to gather a committee of teens and adults as you design this experience. There are new materials to aid you. Feel free to create the course that best fits your folk.

This type of course is also difficult because the adult advisor must first probe his or her own sexuality. Many adults have not worked out their concept of sex within their faith experience. The questions and concerns of youth can be quite frightening. How do you answer

An authentic youth ministry must journey with youth through the area of sexuality.

7-8th grade girls, 9-10th grade boys, 9-10th grade girls, 11-12th grade boys, 11-12th grade girls, college. Preliminary discussion in each group is led by significant adults who agree to help with the entire six-week course. Everyone is asked to write questions on pieces of paper to be answered the following week. (Everyone is encouraged to write something so that no one will be self-conscious.) Glossaries of medical terms were distributed.

Session 2: In the evening, separate films of different maturity levels are run for all 7-8th graders, 9-10th graders, 11-12th graders, college students. Then a doctor joins each of the seven groups. The questions from the previous week are dealt with and additional questions can be asked if desired. Questions again are written.

Session 3: Doctors again meet with the seven groups. The other adults help to conclude this week's session and direct thoughts to additional sexuality issues.

Session 4: In the afternoon, parents are told how the program is going, the general types of questions the young people have asked, and shown additional materials to be used in concluding sessions. The parents are invited to the next session. In the evening, the different age groups meet. Separate films for different maturity levels are shown and the discussion centers on social aspects of growing up.

Session 5: The parents and youth meet together to discuss mutual concerns of parent-child conflicts, communication, expectations.

Session 6: The 7-8th grade deals with dating, 9-10th grade deals with going steady and engagements; 11-12th meets with the pastor and talks about marriage and the wedding vows; college group deals with parenting.

The course if offered biennially, and persons are required to register for the entire six weeks. It is assumed that

questions when you are not sure how you feel?

One group in Virginia worked out the following human sexuality study for its youth:

Session 1: In the afternoon parents attend an orientation meeting where all the materials are displayed, questions are answered. In the evening, youth and parents are invited to the opening session in which the pastor explains that sex is a gift of God. Youth are divided into the following groups for this and the next two sessions: 7-8th grade boys,

youth and parents will discuss the study during the period using the textbooks and the glossary that are assigned to each group. Youth from the community attended faithfully.

Resources

1. **Love and Sex in Plain Language**, by Eric Johnson, Bantam Books.
2. **A Guide for Christian Sex Education of Youth**, by Thomas Brown.
3. **Everything a Teenager Wants to Know About Sex. . .and Should**, by Harry Preston and Jeanette Margolin, Books for Better Living.
4. **Growing Up With Sex**, by Richard Hettlinger, Seabury.
5. **Teenage Pregnancy: A Report, A Study Action Guide**, by Bill Stackhouse, United Church Board of Homeland Ministries, 132 West 31st St., New York, NY 10001.
6. **Adolescent Sexuality in Contemporary America**, by Robert Sorenson, World Publications.

See also BODY, LOVE, PREMARITAL COUNSELING, SEXUALITY

Sexism

This term is often misunderstood. The exclusion of females from full personhood in the Christian community is inexcusable. Any attitude which dehumanizes any person in God's creation is sinful.

It is amazing to discover the anti-feminism feelings among many young males in Christian youth groups. From a developmental perspective we know the insecurity young males feel in the threatening quest for maturation. Yet, things must be different within the fellowship of Christ. God's kin support and affirm both the uniqueness and equality of *all* its members.

Those groups which are anti-female are also those which most likely have a difficult time dealing with handicapped people, minority groups and old people. The prejudice of the young can be very frightening. They are most often reflecting the values of their parents and peers. Yet, such an attitude among faith

youth undercuts the action of the Holy Spirit.

You have an active role in raising the consciousness of your youth. Barriers to love and acceptance are stumbling blocks to authentic faith. Sexist language and jokes are indicators of values. Your witness concerning sexism, ageism (prejudice against the young or the old) and racism is incredibly influential. The teens will know what is important to you.

You also have the responsibility of helping young women and other victims of prejudice to gain a sense of self-worth. Again, your perspective will communicate a lot. If you value each person in your care as creations of God, they will know that they are special persons capable of special faithfulness.

Resources
1. **Changing Roles of Men and Women**, by Edmund Dahlstrom.
2. **Masculinity and Feminity**, by Henry George.
3. **Humanness: An Exploration Into the Mythologies about Men and Women**, by Ella Lasky.

See also CULTURE, DATING, EMOTIONS, LOVE, PRE-MARITAL COUNSELING, SEXUALITY

Sexuality

Sexuality refers to everything in our concept of what it means to be masculine or feminine. Our own concepts of sexuality constantly change as do those of society. That constant change makes the whole issue of sexuality one that deeply troubles youth, who would prefer everything related to this area remain constant.

Every new clothing and hair style adds the threat of redefinition. Blatant macho exhibition, feminist demands, beauty queen contests, homosexual displays—all such extremes, as well as the broad middle ground, force the youth to hurriedly decide where they feel they fit in.

Decisions about how to display their sexuality is also disconcerting. Usually, films and magazines urge youth to assert themselves sexually while parents and traditional culture urge restraint. The youth may feel caught in a no-win compromise.

Premarital sex is an even more pressurized issue with imposing arguments on both sides and few helpful resources offered by the church. The way the church hesitates to say anything speaks volumes to the youth. Surely youth are at a time when they know enough to comprehend that sex relations are the ultimate symbol of commitment of one person with another and to enter it lightly or tentatively is to have less trust for themselves and the other person throughout the rest of their lives.

Even though many youth may be hesitant to request a formal study of sexuality, this is one subject where the church can provide assistance. After all, the church is God's people and God is the sexuality expert of all time.

Resources
1. **Givers, Takers and Other Kinds of Lovers**, by Josh McDowell and Paul Lewis, Tyndale House.
2. **The Good News About Sex**, by David Knight, St. Anthony Messenger Press.
3. **Human Sexuality, A Preliminary Study**, United Church of Christ.
4. **Teenage Sexuality, A Crisis and An Opportunity for the Church**, by Steve Clapp, C-4 Resources, P.O. Box 27, Sidell, IL 61876.

See also BODY, CULTURE, SEX

Simulation Games

A Native American saying explains that we can never really understand another person until we have walked a mile in their shoes. Of course, we can never do that; that's the point. No one truly knows the world the way another person does because we have never been in their exact situation.

However, our understanding can be aided greatly if we can approximate or simulate the type of conditions that surround other persons' lives. Judges of trial cases often encourage reenactment of the situation that led to a crime or accident in order to understand the reasons (and the reasoning) behind the actions.

Simulation games have been constructed for participants to better understand how they will react in a given set of circumstances. The games establish a context for the action (a community emergency, a corporate decision, an exchange of goods and services between nations, etc.) and each participant is given a role from which to act. Latitude for decision-making changes with each game. Often, the way the games are played will cause conditions to change, affecting the decisions, and pressures to mount for the decision makers.

These experiences give us a chance to view the world as a person of another sex, race, nationality, income bracket, level of responsibility, etc. Not only can we better appreciate the reasoning process of other persons, but we can better operate from our own perspective by knowing something of how others feel.

Such games can be bought, borrowed (usually from a regional resource center) or built from scratch. In most instances, a few modifications need to be made to best suit the group's needs.

Time is an important consideration in using simulation games. They cannot be rushed. Some of them require two or three hours to complete, and the potential for the group is definitely diminished by not scheduling adequate time to complete the game. Time must be permitted to become a major participant in the game, sometimes demanding the players to make quick decisions and other times delaying reactions so that various forces can seize an opportunity to move.

Be sure to debrief the participants. Schedule an unrushed period of time in which each person can offer personal reflections on what was happening to them. And do not jump into any applications of the learnings until the group has absorbed these insights and compared them.

Few people are the same after they have walked in another person's shoes, even by simulations.

Resources

1. **Simulation Games for Religious Education**, Richard Reichert, John Knox Press.
2. **Learning Through Games**, by Philip Gillispie, Paulist Press.
3. **Using Biblical Simulations**, Volumes 1 and 2, by Miller, Snyder and Neff.
4. **Gaming: The Fine Art of Creating Simulation/Learning Games For Religious Education**, by Dennis Benson, P.O. Box 12811, Pittsburgh, PA 15421.
5. **Baldicer**, a group game by Georgeann Wilcoxson, John Knox Press.
6. **Island**, a group game by Colin Proudman, Friendship Press.
7. **Ghetto**, a group game by Western Publishing Company.
8. Source of games: EMI, Box 4272-g, Madison, WI 53711.

See also DRAMA, ROLE PLAYS

Singing

Group singing helps build unity and helps generate a sense of worship.

Ironically, today's culture has turned singing into a spectator activity rather than a participatory one. Listening to someone else perform a song is much more emphasized than singing for your own pleasure. Youth may have hundreds of albums in their record collection but less than a handful of songs they can actually sing.

Further, very few popular songs today are singable. Try turning off a radio midway through a currently popular record and see how many in your group can complete the song. Being unable to sing along discourages the average youth from lifting his or her voice and thereby stifles deep personal expression.

How immensely valuable it is for directors of youth choirs to compliment an individual's vocal offering. The praise affirms a person's whole being.

This is further enhanced when someone graciously contributes a few microphones and spotlights which impressively underscore the value of the human voice.

Singing in a fellowship group or church school class is still not as easy as it once was, but when a group has been to a large conference and joined hundreds of other youth in some enjoyable singing, it is easier to get some of that going in the bus on the way home or during a special program at church (caroling or commissioning service, for instance).

A campfire is a natural setting for singing. Blended with the sounds of nature, the songs of the youth can finally be freed for worship. The semidarkness helps to lend autonomy to the vocal statements.

There is evidence that darkness does encourage singing. This could be one reason why singalong slides which project the lyrics onto large screens are increasing in use and excitement. The singalong slides are also fun, inexpensive, legal, eliminators of paper duplication and capable of supplying all the information (announcements, scripture and prayers as well as song lyrics) needed by a congregation for worship or any other program.

Even though singing some contemporary music is more difficult than earlier folk music or traditional styles, it is worth discovering contemporary songs that convey a meaningful message compatible with the faith expression of the group. Such music illustrates very graphically that the Christian faith is not trapped in some civilization centuries ago but is very much alive today in the midst of our culture.

Once a group has learned the joy of singing, you will want to locate a good songbook that has a lot of the favorites and some new songs to learn. Some people prefer songbooks without the notes so that those who are not musically trained will not be intimidated and will sing to the best of their ability. A melody line is helpful to others.

A temptation is to find some songs you like and make your own songbook or song sheet without asking permission of the persons who own the songs, the writers and publishers. Without asking, such reprinting is stealing, regardless of any number of rationalizations that might be found. Permission is usually available fairly rapidly at a reasonable fee.

Resources

1. **Songs**, by Songs and Creations, P.O. Box 559, San Anselmo, CA 94960. (This company publishes one of the best all-around informal songbooks for group singing, with words and guitar chords for over 500 sacred and popular songs.)

2. **The Good Times Songbook**, by Abingdon Press, Nashville, TN 37202.

3. **Afterglow**, by Singspiration Music and Recordings, 1415 Lake Dr., S.E., Grand Rapids, MI 49506.

4. **Gather Round**, by Resource Publications, P.O. Box 444, Saratoga, CA 95070.

See also CHOIR, MUSIC

Sleep

This is probably the most perplexing, controversial and discussed issue in youth ministry. Some adults will even refuse to work with youth because of their fear of sleepless nights on every youth trip.

At the risk of overgeneralizing, the amount of sleep that takes place on a youth trip has more to do with the philosophy of the adult leadership than the universal insomnia of youth. Some adults set late night bedtime hours in order to win youth admiration while other adults will set early bedtime hours in order that the adults can get together later.

And there are others who bring along a dozen old movies to run all night for those "who just can't get to sleep." Or there are people like George who schedules activities right up to 2 a.m. and start the next day late. The only problem is that some youth who go to bed at midnight cause problems the next morning while everyone else wants to sleep.

Another approach is to reverse the days and nights for a weekend retreat with a schedule such as: Friday, 6 p.m. —breakfast; Midnight—lunch; Saturday, 7 a.m.—supper, 6 a.m. to 2 p.m.— sleep; 3 p.m.—breakfast, and so on. The usual retreat schedule can be maintained in this unique arrangement. It is best to encourage participants to take a nap before attending.

A youth group overnight event is not the same as a family vacation. Large group gatherings are not flexible, especially when they are using institutional facilities, depending upon staff assistance, using cooks or trying to maintain even the barest of schedules. Many youth will complain that they are accustomed to staying up late since they have no set bedtime at home. But when they become a part of a group activity, they and the adults need to conform to whatever is best for the group.

Sleeping hours should be determined on the basis of the needs (physical and mental) of the group, especially the youth participants, and on the demands of programming and facility availability. Generally, youth of ages 12-14 need approximately 8-9 hours in order to function efficiently the next day, and youth of ages 15-18 need at least 7 hours. And adults working with youth need substantially more than they allot for themselves. After two or three nights, adults tend to take out their fatigued and strained emotions on their group or they slip away for some needed rest. Neither need be necessary.

The quickest way to destroy a planned sleeping schedule is to not be firm about it. The pre-determined sleep time should be followed so far as is practical. The schedule should be developed and agreed upon prior to the trip so that any objections can take place before leaving. Obviously, an unavoidable program delay, facility difficulty or unique event will force new sleeping hours. Such flexibility in light of known significant variables will be accepted without destroying the overall intent. The exception must not become the rule, however.

The most effective sleeping schedules are those that quiet the entire facility, usually at 11:00 p.m. for junior highs and 12:00 p.m. for senior highs for 7-8 full hours. One of the easier ways to encourage abiding by the sleeping time is to plan the schedule so that the activities have a regression of pace as bedtime approaches.

See also RETREATS, WORK PROJECTS

Slides

According to many multi-media specialists the easiest, most accessible, and most effective audio-visual medium is the 35mm slide. Programs can be assembled and changed at the producer's discretion. The variety of possibilities are endless:

Photography—New or old slides can tell a story. Sometimes the effect is aided by the proximity of two slides being projected at the same time, sometimes the addition of sound effects, narration or music helps the slides to come alive, and at other times it is the rapid succession of different images that stirs an audience. Photography slides let you share the emotions and instances in the lives of real persons caught by the photography. There is

A simple way of adding life to your meetings is by putting together a creative slide program.

nothing like seeing yourself on the screen, either in a picture made a decade ago or an hour ago.

Contact Slides—An easy method for making slides without a camera is to use clear Contact paper cut to the size of a slide frame. The back is peeled off and the sticky side is placed over a chosen illustration which has been printed on clay-based paper. (You can tell by wetting your finger, rubbing it over the paper and seeing if some of the paper comes off on your finger.) All of the air bubbles must be worked out by pressing your thumb or stiff object over the Contact paper until the image can be seen very clearly. The section of the paper with the illustration or picture is cut from the magazine and dropped into clear, warm water. In a couple of minutes, the paper falls away (peeling it along may be needed), and the ink remains in the Contact glue. The transparency can then be mounted and a slide has been created.

Singalong Slides—For years contemporary music presented not only a threat to churches because of its unfamiliar phrases, and often outspoken references, but also because it was profoundly difficult for organists, choirs, and congregations to learn quickly. The result was that the most devoted fans of the music—the young—were disappointed with the amateurish representation of some of their favorite selections.

Things improved greatly when Garrett Short of Riverside, California, discovered that he could project lyrics on several screens while playing the record of a favorite, singable pop song over the PA system, and everyone could sing together. He used Ortho film to photograph art contributed by members of his congregation, and his son, John, added color to the slides to create a spectacular worship environment.

The copyright law makes unauthorized printed duplication of lyrics illegal (as in the familiar song sheets) while at the same time it permits the owner of a copy of a song "to display that copy publicly, either directly or by the projection of no more than one image at a time, to viewers present at the place where the copy is located" (S109 of Public Law 94-553). Illegal song sheets allow a member of the congregation to physically take home a copy of the song and thereby not need to purchase a copy. But the projection of the material allows the person to be introduced to the song but not have ownership of a copy. The "no more than one image at a time" clause permits short quotes at a time, else the projector with all the lyrics could be left on and anyone could copy the entire song.

The singalong slide-making procedure can be a fun experience for groups and can involve numerous persons, particularly those with technical and photography skills. Artists, typists, even attentive lyric listeners, are also definitely needed. Often the process can be done on two successive Sunday evenings and serve as a combination mixer, program (lyric analysis), creative activity and Bible study.

Here are a few general tips for use with any of the previous three methods. Use at least two screens and two projectors for projection since even a brief pause for changing slides on just one screen makes group singing difficult. The sound source should be sufficiently strong to be heard so that when the group really gets involved, the accompaniment, especially the tempo, will not be lost. Place only a few phrases of lyrics on each slide, preferably in a way to represent pauses, loudness and feeling. Graphics should be added for use during instrumental portions of the song. Complete credits (song title, author, singer, record label and number, copyright date and publisher) should be printed on the first slide.

In addition to music, slides can also be made of liturgies, scripture, prayers, illustrations, announcements or whatever.

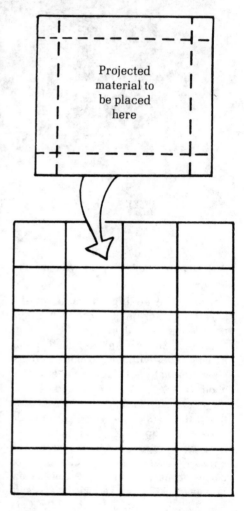

Projected material to be placed here

Offset Slides—This is a way to make slides without having to own a camera, buy film or develop it. You can utilize as much or as little artistic talent as is available. The process involves having an offset printer (usually located in every community) make a negative of your material. You can then color the negative and mount it as slides.

First, you will need a roll of butcher

paper (or any other totally white paper—newsprint is not white enough). Draw a dark black line (magic marker) 16 inches across the top of where you are going to place your material. Then draw two 21-inch lines down from both ends of your first line. Connect at the bottom–you have a vertical rectangle 16x21 inches. Across the first line make markings at each 4-inch length and draw lines all the way to the bottom. On both sides, starting at the top, make markings at each 3½-inch length and draw lines across to the other side. At this point you should have twenty-four boxes, each 4x3½ inches. Each of these will eventually be a single slide. (See diagram at left.)

Now you will need to set margins on each of the 24 slides in order to know what will later appear on a screen and what will fit inside the slide mount. The margins on each of those 24 squares should be one-half inch on top and bottom. You can indicate this on your drawing by using a light blue (non-reproducing) pencil and actually drawing these margin lines across and down each line of slides. Or, you can make a pattern of these on another piece of paper with a dark pen to put under your drawing (which is faster in the long run because you can use that pattern over and over).

Inside the margins of each slide put any kind of print, type, or art work you may choose, using a rather dark impression. You can fold the paper and put it into a typewriter. You can cut out art, preferably line drawings and high contrast graphics, and paste it within the margins. You can even paste corrections over mistakes. Make each frame as full as you wish.

When completed, take the entire sheet to your neighborhood offset printer. Tell that person that you want a negative made of the material. (Normally, the negative is the middle

process prior to burning a metal plate that will be used in the printing.) Explain that you will need it to be *reduced on a setting of 38 percent*. Actually, this means that the reduction will really be almost two-thirds, so that you will wind up with a negative approximately one-third the size of the paper drawing you brought in. Or to say it another way, you will want the negative to be 38 percent the size of the original.

We have tested the price of this at various places in the nation, ranging from $2 per sheet in one community, where the printer was a member of one of the churches, to $8 in another city, where I'm sure the clerk was reading the wrong scale. Normally, we have found that the price is four dollars per sheet almost everywhere, and that's not bad for 24 perfect slides with no other photography costs. And normally, the time involved is less than an hour. We have conducted workshops in which all the art work of an entire week could be made into negatives during a lunch hour one day.

Speaking of costs, watch this next item. The coloring you will need in order to transform these stark negatives into radiant color positives for projection can be found at your neighborhood grocery at 69 cents per set of four containers of food coloring. Better pick up a small box of toothpicks and cotton. You now have enough supplies for several years!

Twist a tiny amount of cotton onto the end of a toothpick. A Q-tip of cotton contains too much cotton. Put a few drops of food coloring, full strength or diluted, on the cotton and begin coloring the lines of the soon-to-be slides. The coloring works just like water colors and needs to be blotted occasionally before circles of residue form and two different colors mix. Most persons will use all of blue, let it dry, then use orange, etc. The more layers of coloring you apply, the darker will be the picture.

Felt-tip marking pens also work well for coloring the negatives.

A light table (opaque surface with light inside) is delightful to use for this, but if one is not readily available, a slide sorter tilted to one side works well.

Either side of the film can be colored. You will probably notice that some printers will blot out all little dots of extraneous matter that might appear on the film. The ink they use may run with your coloring, so it is usually a good idea to put the coloring on the side of the film opposite the black ink.

When you are ready to mount the slides, cut out each small square along the first bold lines that you drew. They can be mounted into cardboard mounts and lightly ironed together, or you can use any one of the variety of plastic mounts.

Most groups have a camera buff who could easily be the key to a process that involves a 35mm camera, a roll of Pantomic-X film (found at most photo supply stores), a few sheets of butcher paper, Magic Markers and a little time in a dark room, makeshift if necessary.

Lyrics are written with bold markers on the butcher paper in any size with a 2'x3' proportion. For instance, if the camera to be used is a rather simple one with no close-up lenses, you might prefer to put the print within an area 14 inches in height and 11 inches in length. You can discover the exact margins for your camera by looking through the viewfinder (probably about three feet from the paper) and checking out the scope that can be clearly captured. You may wish to make a pattern using bold lines for the margins within which the lyrics can be placed, and put this pattern under the butcher paper to serve as guide for where each section of the lyrics are being printed.

Load the camera with the Pantomic-X

(used because of its non-grainy texture).

In order to avoid using a flash or special lighting, the entire sheet of paper containing the lyrics can be placed on the side of a building outside and photographed using available light, preferably a shady space or the light of a cloudy day in order that the glare not be too harsh.

Once all the pictures have been taken, develop the film (based on the instructions with the film) or have it done by a commercial photo shop. If you have the film processed by a commercial shop, just order the developing, no prints. In fact, the film should be left in rolls, so that later you can add color, cut the slides apart, and mount.

At this stage, the film will look like an X-ray or a negative with all the letters transparent and the background grayish black. Magic markers can be used to give color, though they will give a slightly streaked effect; food coloring for the entire slide will add a solid tint throughout. More preferable, thin colored plastic sheets or color gels can be placed beside the film and put into the same slide mount. Various shapes and designs can be made with the colored plastic to give symbolism and variety.

Glass Slides—Admittedly, this is not the best name for a very exciting method of creating slides. It may give the impression that we are talking about the old-fashioned mounts that were made of glass. Instead, this is a process of photographing images through glass, with wording printed on the glass and the final slide being a combination of the words and images. Any camera that makes 35mm slides is acceptable, and either Kodachrome or Ektachrome film can be used.

The process came about when we discovered that audiences seem to appreciate actual pictures of objects and scenes mixed in with line drawings and graphics. In order to get words written across the scene, we came across the idea of holding up glass in front of the scene or object, with the words printed on the glass. After a little exploration, we realized that large sheets of storm windows, conveniently encased in an aluminum frame to make it more easily moved from place to place, could be held in front of large scenes, making a striking slide with amazing clarity.

The painting can be done with tempera paints available from any education supply store. The best size of strokes are made by a medium-sized brush. It is at this stage that your imagination can run wild. For instance, in making a slide of a children's song, finger paints could be used (it gives a neat hollow effect since the finger will usually touch the surface in the middle of each letter). Or a cake decorator can give unusual effects, in addition to adding a raised or textured feel to each letter (perhaps emphasized by a colored spotlight across the letters.).

A variety of glass can also be used. We've used outside windows, windows between offices (some have stimulating frosted patterns), car windows, storm windows of all shapes and sizes and mirrors.

If a close-up lens is available, glass can be placed over pictures in magazines and books with the words written on the glass. Obviously, the glass need not be as large as in the prior examples, even an 8"x10" piece of glass out of a picture on the wall can be used. As far as we can tell, the same copyright restrictions apply to pictures as to lyrics, and complete credits will need to be given somewhere in the presentations (sources, copyright date and publisher, and photographer, if known.).

The background can give meaning and symbolism to the words. If the mood of the lyric is joyous, a suitable background can be chosen. Abstract concepts can also be supported with appropriate representations, causing a dialogue between the viewer and the presentation. A song about rain could be written with words that have started to run with a drop or two of water applied to them; some mud puddles and wet leaves could be used as background. A hymn such as "Blest Be the Tie That Binds" could have scenes of the church members leaving the sanctuary

Though not necessary, various accessories could be helpful during this process. To further cut down on possible glare across the glass, the use of a polarizer on your camera is a little extra insurance. An automatic through-the-lens metering device will help to ensure that the right amount of light will be allowed to enter the camera.

Since these will be regular slides, development can be accomplished at any photo store or individuals can do their own.

See also MULTI MEDIA

Smoking

Our grandparents who talked about "coffin nails" and "death sticks" were right. Cigarettes are not healthy; we all know that now. It is true that the government subsidizes tobacco and famous people smoke. Yet, there are some attributes of smoking which raise some important theological points for those in youth ministry.

What are the appealing attributes of cigarettes? Peer pressure is one of the most often cited reasons behind smoking. It is a sign that you belong. Teens are sometimes dared to smoke by their friends. Since smoking is also a forbidden activity, there is a sense of breaking the taboos of the adult world. Those who smoke are often caught in a nicotine habit which cannot be easily

given up. Whether it is a chemical or emotional need, smokers have a hard time leaving it behind.

The probes about smoking raise vital issues concerning faith and life. How does the ordering of your life reflect your discipleship? This line of probing bears more workable positions on habits of this sort than the old lines used by the church in the past.

It is a difficult matter to walk with teens through a concern like smoking if you are also struggling with it. How do you ask a young person to reconsider his or her habit when you are addicted to it?

It was hard for Margaret to tell the story even after so many years. "When I was 16, my dad caught me smoking in the garage. He was furious. He called my younger sister and me into his study. He lectured to us for a long time about the evils of smoking.

"When we got a chance to respond, we told him that he had no right to lecture us when he smoked. There was a silence. My dad got up and walked around the room a couple of times."

Margaret had tears in her eyes as she finished the story. "Dad looked at us for a long time. Then he said, 'You are right. I have no right to ask something of you that I will not undertake myself. I love you girls so much and am so sure that smoking would be bad for you that I promise to stop smoking as of now.' My sister and I were so moved by what Dad said. We knew that he loved to smoke. He would do this for us!"

Some youth groups have a number of people who smoke. Since most city fire laws forbid smoking in certain public gatherings, it will be important to work through the rules with your group. But don't try to deal with it by just imposing the rules from outside.

Smoking around teens is a modeling factor which has impact. There are so many influences moving the young toward the use of tobacco. For instance, the lines at the registration building were long and slow moving. Everyone at the large university wanted to get his or her course schedule finalized. Teams of students moved up and down the lines passing out special packages of cigarettes. Each packet contained four cigarettes. When the student working for the tobacco company was asked about this gift package, he shared the philosophy behind the practice. "The company has found that a lot of students give up smoking when they start college. It is an easy time to drop the habit. Our research has shown us that if a person smokes four cigarettes, he or she will be back on the habit."

How do we provide the context in which youth can deal with this addiction? How does their faith enable them to live out an ethic which faces these kinds of problems?

See also COVENANTS, CULTURE, DRINKING, DRUGS, PEER PRESSURE

Speakers

Every creative youth ministry uses speakers. However, some folks use them as fillers when things are slow. It is very easy to find yourself organizing a service club set of programs, which focus only on speakers. Youth ministry is so much more than a week-by-week speakers parade.

If you should decide to invite a speaker, it is wise to spend some time in preparation so his or her skills can be utilized properly. Many speakers are determined to speak the whole evening.

It is very hard for a guest to restrict his or her contribution to a few minutes. This means that there is often very little

If used properly, guest speakers can add an exciting dimension to your ministry.

interaction between youth and these adult speakers.

Create a format which will assure the guest that he or she will have a chance to present a worthwhile contribution, but can also invite the youth to participate.

One good setting for a speaker is the "hot seat." This format was developed during the coffeehouse days. A person of responsibility (police chief, principal, etc.) is invited to the meeting. The teens carry on a press conference in which the guest would respond to student questions. Even though this is a demanding process, it is excellent for teaching young people to raise questions.

You will have to create the kind of meeting you want because many of the speakers will have some pet message they want to put across. It is hard to break into these programmed pitches with suggestions for alternative speeches. In other words, a speaker must be seen as a resource who is compatible with the direction of the total youth ministry. Youth ministry cannot afford to have speakers who manipulate the youth.

Some of the best resources are people who do not make the youth group circuit with their canned talks. There are neat people in the congregation and community who have a great deal to share. It is your task to put these worthy people in dialogue with the young people.

See also INTERVIEWING

Starting Up

Starting a new youth group can be immensely rewarding and challenging. It begins many weeks before the first group meeting, at a time when one person shares his or her dreams with another.

There is no perfect step-by-step plan for starting up a group, but here are a few natural stages:

Stage 1—Initial interest. At least two people discuss their dream for a group. They may tell others. Dreams have remarkable lives; they can appear in the strangest places within quite varied personalities.

Stage 2—Validity. The persons who have the dream get together to see how sincere their interest really is. They firm up their commitment. This would be an excellent time to look at scriptural passages concerning the early church (see Acts 4 and Ephesians 4) as it began its existence and mission.

Stage 3—Planning. Those persons who have the concern for a youth group should now meet with the pastor and other church leaders to tell of this interest and discern if anyone else is working toward forming a group. If so, additional planning is helpful to widen the view by evaluating the different possibilities.

Stage 4—Strategy. Soon these persons will want to go before an official church board to gain approval of the church to sponsor the group. It will be very significant for the group if the church will not only approve of the idea but pledge financial support, leadership and meeting space. In preparation for the presentation to the board, these persons might wish to visit other groups to see what is now taking place, read books on youth groups, talk with church leaders about what groups can do and be, and begin to survey the interest of all youth concerning the formation of a group. Some momentum at this point by the youth would be helpful. With this information, a proposal incorporating the best of what is known should be drawn up.

Stage 5—Approval of sponsor. The proposal should be presented to the board and firm pledge of support obtained.

Starting a youth group requires common sense, persistence and teamwork.

Stage 6—Preparation for first meeting. Don't hurry this step. Take time to spread the word to every possibly interested person (youth, parents, congregation, neighborhood, etc.) that the group will be starting soon. (Give yourself a few weeks.) In the meantime, do a lot of promotion and a lot of planning for the first two or three meetings of the new group. Avoid letting that first meeting become one of those "what do you want to do" duds. (You might want to discuss "what do we need" soon, but not now.) Plan to have an exciting, intriguing first few programs so that those who attend will be amazed by all that this new group can offer them. Send out invitations.

Stage 7—The first meeting. Unveil the new group with a fun-filled, individually affirming program with meaningful content concerning the Christian faith. Illustrate that a wide variety of activities and programs are possible and that each individual is definitely needed and there is an important place for them in the group. Name tags might help as well as games that encourage community and place no stress on participants. Heavily promote the next meeting and urge persons to bring more friends and to reach out to those who have no youth group.

Stage 8—The second meeting. Make this meeting an even more fun, more varied, more meaningful experience. Again, emphasize community with no stress on participants. (Forget those games that put persons on the spot to remember names or anything else that will make them uncomfortable.) Show some continuity and progression from the first meeting. Promote the next meeting and explain that persons will be needed soon to plan upcoming programs and activities.

Stage 9—The third meeting. Again, try for an improved experience suited to the needs of potential participants. Add some persons to the planning team (or elect officers, set up duties of leadership, ideas to give to planning team). Perhaps give out an interest finder for future programs and activities.

Stage 10—Think of the future. Do some long-range planning (sketchy at this point with details to be added as possible. Dream some more). Evaluate what is happening in the group. Have everyone, including adult leadership, tell what they like best and what they would like to improve.

Resources
1. **A New Start in Youth Ministry: A Manual for Youth Groups**, by Eldon Kaiser and Leo Symmank, Concordia.

See also *ADULTS, CULTURE, PLANNING COUNCIL, RISKING, THEOLOGY OF YOUTH MINISTRY, YOUTH COUNCIL, YOUTH MINISTRY*

Stories

"Tell me a story."
Children often make such requests of parents and adults. It is the story that catches the spirit and imagination of all people. Lewis L. Wilkins reminds us that we are a band of storytellers. He suggests that we must be able to tell seven: 1. Eve and Adam; 2. The Exodus event; 3. The church catholic, east and west, beginning with Good Friday and ending with Easter; 4. The protestant camp in the larger people of God; 5. Our particu-

lar denomination; 6. Our congregation; and 7. My personal story of faith. Lewis notes that the role of pastor or youth advisor is to build a warm and friendly campfire around which our people can tell their stories.

This thesis suggests that we are not just called to be clever technicians of the storytelling art. It is our task to invite our youth into the realm of our total story and to release them to share their own stories. This aspect of the story fits well with the use of interviewing. Youth can become the means of helping others to tell their stories.

The communication of our stories is not new. It is probably the oldest practice in the church. The church in North America once invited its people to bear testimony or witness to their story. There has been a subtle shift which has placed the storytelling role in the mouth of the preacher. You can help teens discover their role in this recital of faith.

Teens love to tell their immediate story. They often find that adults are not interested in hearing the installments of this unfolding saga. You as youth sponsor have time and energy to encourage such an exchange.

It has been pointed out that our Christian heritage has wrongly emphasized our Greek roots in which we are urged to deal with abstract concepts that have to be continually refined and redefined to remain logical. This change-oriented process can be traced back to the days of the great Greek thinkers who insisted upon defining every idea, object ("What is a table or a wall?" they asked) and a group of people. Instead, our Hebrew background is more similar to who we are as a pilgrim people, people who relate to others their story of what has happened to them and tell of their dreams and hopes.

Storytelling need not be a long, involved recapitulation of every individual's experiences. It might simply involve telling of a current state of existence: "I cry late at night. The world doesn't understand when a man cries." "I think my parents are immature. When I have troubles, I talk with my brothers. I wouldn't talk with my parents about anything. They are in another world." "If I could be anything, I would be a kite. Just moving back and forth in the breeze. So free in the sky."

Storytelling can be a personal testimony of where we have been and where we would like to go. As we relate these experiences, we need not tie down all the logical implications of each action but simply indicate our response of feeling and preference to these experiences.

Resources
1. **Stories You Can Tell**, by Bob Kuntz, Discipleship Resources, Box 840, Nashville, TN 37202.
2. **Telling Your Story**, New American Library.
3. National Storytelling Resource Center, P.O. Box 112, Jonesburg, TN 37659.

See also INTERVIEWING, WITNESSING

Success

The fear of failure freezes more people into inaction than just about any other threat to youth ministry. "How many did you have last night?" "How much money did the car wash bring in?" "How many teens from Sunday night came to our Sunday School?" "Wasn't that kid in trouble with the police from your group?"

The threat of failure is sprinkled over everything we do in youth ministry. Most of the fear comes from within the youth and adults involved in youth ministry. A whisper from others will bring shivers to those running solid programs.

We are often trapped for several reasons. In the first place, true feedback concerning our work is not available in most congregational settings. The pastor is usually victimized even more than you. He or she hears three or four negative comments about a sermon and fears that a major problem exists. In fact, many folks in local congregations can only get attention by complaining. Even if three or four people don't like something, what are the opinions of the other 200 people who experienced the criticized program or message? No one asks and no one knows.

Feedback also causes problems in many churches because the pastor doesn't have an opportunity to communicate with youth advisors. She or he hears the bad rumors and the overblown praise young people like to give to others. The pastor gets the worst of both extremes. On the one hand, she or he has to defend you against an

The way you define success will to a large degree determine the shape of your ministry.

unknown situation. On the other hand, praise of your work sounds like a slight criticism of her or his own work ("The youth advisor is just wonderful. It is good to find someone who finally cares about our youth."(Out of this situation can come feelings of criticism and jealousy.

The best way to succeed in such a situation is to be intentionally inclusive in your ministry. There are many reasons why the pastor will want you to be on your own with the youth. However, you must include the pastor in the continuity of youth ministry. A successful youth program enables the minister or priest to experience the gifts of youth as well as encourage the teens to appreciate the personhood of the clergy.

In the second place, most church leaders rarely establish any basis upon which success can be fairly judged. The question of numbers may not have a bearing on the value of the groups at all. We should help others in the church to evaluate youth ministry accurately. We could make sure that the congregation is aware of the goals that the youth group has set for itself and the ways of measuring whether they are being fulfilled. More youth advisors have resigned in despair because they have held one set of objectives while those who are critical to the program's success have had another. The sad aspect of these situations is that neither party realizes that it is a matter of different values rather than failure or success that is being debated.

The third aspect of the success-failure pinch is that we often think in the wrong set of terms as people of faith. Success is really a cultural value. The societal measurements often do not apply to the biblical concept of faithfulness. We are called to be faithful, not successful. It does feel good to experience "success" as the group gets bigger and better each week. However, those who followed Jesus from the earliest days did not stake their salvation on the worldly marks of success. They preached, healed, risked and died without much to assure them of success.

If the fear of failure creeps into your spirit, you will find it very hard to risk for your faith and your folks. In fact, you might reverse this comparison. If you are not reaching beyond your comfortable grasp for the sake of the youth, you may be too worried about the goddess of failure.

"Do you remember when you came out to Washington to do that retreat a few years ago? It was wild. You had us in groups of ten. We weren't allowed to say anything for four hours. It was a Garden of Eden game." The youth leader nodded his head. He certainly remembered that weekend. People running in every direction. He could still feel the pain of communication the young people experienced when they started to communicate with their voices. They felt that their great non-verbal communion was suddenly transformed into a Babel of tongues. The leader anguished as he remembered the two youths who slipped away from the camp and stayed out all night with some youth from town.

"Well, I just wanted to tell you how important that experience was for me. It was that event which made me realize that God could use me in the ministry. I was a college student. That wild weekend made me confront God in a different way. Thanks for being there."

Resources
1. **Helping Church Workers Succeed**, by D. B. Heusser, Judson Press.

See also AAUGH, BLUES, DESPAIR, EVALUATION, FAILURE, FEEDBACK, JOB DESCRIPTION

In all suicide situations, the best thing we have going for us is our willingness to let God work through us.

Suicide

The very thought of a young person taking his or her own life is incomprehensible for persons who are concerned about youth. "You have so much to live for" is often the response. "Why could any problem seem so large that a youth would not realize they could overcome it with a whole lifetime ahead?"

And yet, suicide is the number two cause of death for teenagers, just behind accidents, many of which could be suicides in disguise.

Taking one's life is obviously the ultimate form of escape from any problem. Suicide is one thing that youth can complete on their own when other efforts may have seemed to be blocked. For someone bored with his or her existence, suicide offers an experience no one has ever described. For a society fascinated with any form of trip, drug or otherwise, this is the blockbuster of all times.

Despair seems to be the main cause of youthful suicide. Every friend, every avenue of hope appears to have vanished, and the youth is unable to locate any resources within his or her own reserve to cope with life. Meaning is gone. Self-worth is unknown. There is nowhere to go. The future gets grossly worse with each breath. And often, the youth feels that he or she is totally to blame for the peril.

Most adults working with youth should come to grips with what they could or should do if a youth they know gives any indication of contemplating suicide. What words would be helpful? Should fear be expressed or repressed? On the bottom line, will whatever we try turn out to prevent or encourage the act?

Certainly, it is a good idea to seek advice about what to say or do should the need arise. Local counselors who have been face-to-face with the situation will probably be able to offer great help as would qualified authorities who have concentrated their attention on the real causes of suicide and what seems to offer the most authentic reassurance. A number of excellent books can be consulted at your public library.

However, in the final analysis, the person we will deal with will be unique, unlike any other person who has arrived at this same point. The reasons, the circumstances and the arguments will be unique. We will have to tailor all our resources to this unique situation.

If it is possible for us to get the individual to a skilled, sensitive counselor, this will probably be far better for all persons involved. In fact, if time allows we may need to search very carefully for the type of person or persons to whom to refer this individual.

But time is not always that plentiful, and we alone may be the one to whom an individual will turn for help. We alone may be the one giving testimony to the value that life has for us and potentially for them. And since we are the one to whom they turned, it may be that our perspective is the most helpful for them of anyone in the world.

The best thing we have going for our efforts will always be our willingness to let God work through us. God is the one who gave life to each of us, originally and every minute since, and God is the one who awaits us on the other side of death.

Resources
1. **Growing Up Dead**, by Brenda Rabkin, Abingdon.
2. "Suicide: Causes and Preventions," a filmstrip by Human Relations Media.
3. **Suicide Among Youth**, by Richard Seiden, National Institute of Mental Health.

See also ADVISING, COUNSELING, EMOTIONS, SELF IMAGE

Summer

"Goodbye, God, I'm out of school!" Such a statement is silly. Yet, most youth groups seem to follow its thinking.

The American church has developed its whole life around the secular school system. Everyone seems to sigh in relief as soon as warm weather comes and the kids are out of school. The thrust of its programming year sputters to a stop. It is ironic that this should be the case. Our programming cycle is really based on an agricultural model from the early days of the country. There was a time when every school child was needed to plant and harvest. While a few youth are still involved in this important task, such a rhythm no longer is justified in most of North America.

The economic environment suggests that youth will have a harder and harder time getting a job for the summer time. An enormous number of youth are at home with nothing to do on any given week any summer. Bored people, young and old, are led into their most uncomplimentary behavior.

Some folks are changing the dog day summer cycle. Pastor David escalates programming for youth during the summer! He hires college students to help and the program really takes off. Forty of the youth travel around the country for five or six weeks performing plays from their tent. They have worked all year preparing a first-class play ("Diary of Anne Frank," "The Lilies of the Field," etc.) and raising money for the journey. They have their own generators, tents and trucks.

While these folks are undertaking this itinerant youth ministry, there is also a five-day-a-week, summer-long, junior high ministry! The program runs for the full day and gives junior highers a chance to grow through learning sessions, trips and new challenges. The

high school group is also going full speed. There is a flexibility in this action to utilize the evenings. The college young people are also given a vigorous program during the summer. The response to this inversion of the typical youth ministry has been sensational!

The summer also provides an excellent time to plan cooperative programs with youth from other churches. Many small youth groups never think about the unlimited possibilities offered by combining activities with one or more other churches in the same community. Imagine a rotating youth program which draws upon the adult and youth resources of several churches!

Nature also offers an incredible context in which to grow and learn. Camping, retreats and other special moments provide an amazing opportunity for the person of faith.

Ed has an active summer youth program in Oklahoma. He varies the emphasis and format each year. One summer he led the group in a week-long experiential study of the communications industry in their community. During the morning the group of junior and senior highs toured the most popular radio station, TV station and morning newspaper. In the evening the group discussed the controls and flexibilities they had observed, and an outside resource person helped them to discover the way media affect our perceptions of ourselves and our world.

Summer ministry doesn't have to be a frustrating attempt at coordinating remnants of your former youth group. Summer ministry means creatively using small groups and combinations of different groups in ways that capitalize on summer youth free time.

See also CAMPING, CANOEING, RETREATS, VACATION BIBLE SCHOOL

Summer is a perfect time for creative, out-of-the-ordinary ministry.

Sunday School

Sunday school sessions provide perfect opportunities for creative programs, modular lessons and elective classes.

It goes by a number of titles. It was once known universally as Sunday school. Then when the church's education program began to expand to other days of the week, it seemed necessary to change the name to church school or school of the church.

For youth Sunday school has often meant sitting around a room listening to a lecture, in almost identical fashion as what they have experienced for over a decade despite the radically different and changing learning techniques in their school system and in modern media (the other two major places where they spend their time in learning exercises).

But these days are changing for some. Increasingly, those who guide the church schools are realizing that youth classes can be very exciting and creative opportunities for growth with just a few improvements that any size church could institute.

A Tennessee church has set up a modular system where youth can select various elective classes in addition to regular core programs. The fall and spring quarters feature core courses on the Bible, church history, and Christian living. The winter and summer quarters offer several options taught by specialists who often hold the classes in locations around town and involve the class members in skill developing projects. One class has worked with a video recorder and made for the church an excellent resource on symbolism found in the building. Another class met at the newspaper offices and learned ways to communicate to the other youth through an attractive newsletter.

Youth classes are also spreading out from Sunday morning. When leaders see that parts of the upcoming curriculum offer more materials or depth consideration than can be adequately utilized during a class session, a retreat is planned so that this can be the theme of the outing. Some of the best learning has come from creative ways to promote a redemption retreat or a Wesley weekend.

Some of the best things happen to the Sunday school when leaders start inviting the youth to help plan the class sessions. Such participation in the planning helps the students learn the significance of the material in a memorable way.

It has always been a temptation to take the youth out of their class to help teach children's classes. Youth even volunteer. It could be argued with good logic that this experience is most helpful for both the youth and the children who greatly admire the older persons. However, this short-changes the youth who need very much to be with their own age to confront issues and understandings that they are now able to comprehend. Such preparation is necessary for life now and in preparation for the adult years.

See also BIBLE, CURRICULUM, DIS-CUSSION, DRAMA, MATERIALS, MOD-ULE, PROGRAM, RESOURCES

Develop close friends and acquaintances who can support you during those overwhelming times.

Support System

It is quite natural for adults working with youth to realize suddenly that they are in over their heads; no one person alone can meet all the needs. When you consider the various needs of the youth, the need of the church for the youth, the inadequacies of any person meeting all those needs, it is cause for being overwhelmed. (The sum total of all the ministry's needs seems to hit like a load of bricks about 9 p.m. on a Sunday night!)

Youth ministry is one situation where it can be honestly stated that if a leader is not overwhelmed, he or she does not understand the enormous demands.

That admission is important. There is no way you can do this job alone. Don't try.

Before continuing any further in your

ministry, locate a support system for yourself. And don't count only on your family; that is not sufficient, as well as being unfair to yourself and them.

Identify a number of significant persons from a variety of involvements to whom you can turn when the responsibilities overwhelm you. Some may now work with youth or have at one time; others might never have even considered it. Some may be related to the church; others not. Don't look for people who will agree with you on any position. Instead, look for people whose objective insights can lead to clarification and stimulation, whose goal is not only affirmation for yourself but growth for everyone involved. There are times when we need friends who can care for us by putting us back in the battle with only a pat on the back.

How many support persons you need depends on you. They need to know how they can help you most. Tell them how important they are to you and to what you are doing.

At the same time, locate persons in the church, in youth ministry and others you know who will have additional resources when you need them. This may be a person or persons on the the staff of your church, serving as a regional or national youth leader, or someone else who has experience and insights in youth ministry and access to aids.

Your ultimate support will be God. Regular Bible study for yourself, prayer (mention specific needs, call out the names of the youth, ask for more significant directions), meditation, corporate worship and music refreshes and replenishes by allowing you to hear God. Never forget that God can accomplish all that needs to be done. This strength, wisdom and love can do everything through persons who allow it to flow through them.

See also BURN-OUT

Symbols

It is interesting to watch the folks who are marketing professional sports. This mass media enterprise is big business. Logos of the home teams appear on posters everywhere.

Symbols are outward signs of inner values. Yet, so many of the faith communities have failed to acknowledge the need to express these values in symbols.

This was not always true. Hundreds of symbols fill the history of the Christian church. Stars, crosses and many other significant objects related to the story of the faith have been transformed into symbols. Symbols are more meaningful than the assorted words that might be used to describe what they represent. One of the more fascinating studies for youth groups concentrates on the symbols of the faith, tracing their origins and dealing with their multitudes of meanings.

Many youth groups have taken the symbolic aspects of their life together very seriously. One suburban Chicago group designed a logo which incorporated the goals of their program: S (service) M (mission) E (education) and F (fellowship). An adult in the congregation helped them make their own stencil. They bought T-shirts and painted on the logos. Group members wear them when they travel together.

Symbols do not need to be printed. They can be any object that represents feelings and the understandings of individuals or groups.

A group of young adults was studying love. They began a six-week series by gathering around a thick piece of wood. It symbolized their study. Mold and dirt covered the rough bark. The students were asked to share how this rejected piece of wood symbolized love. After a number of responses, they went on with their discussion. At the end of the ses-

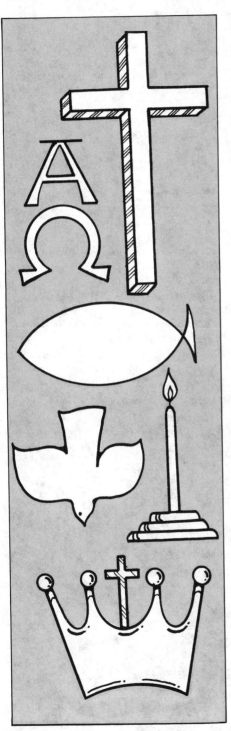

sion, they gathered in a circle again. Two members of the class were given the ugly stick and told, "Take this and let your love change it."

The next week the class gathered around the wood. It had been cleaned and altered by the two class members. This process was repeated each week. The love of the students discovered great beauty.

At the last session, the class was dismissed by cutting the wood into parts and giving each person a piece. "Let's share how this symbol reflects our needs and gifts as people who love."

Shared experiences become special. Symbols help Christians to remember the meaning of these special shared experiences.

Resources
1. **Seasons and Symbols**, by Robert Wetzler and Helen Huntington, Augsburg.
2. **Our Christian Symbols**, by Friedrich Rest, Pilgrim Press.

See also CONFIRMATION

T.A.

In many books, the two letters TA appear. These initials stand for Transactional Analysis. A number of writers have built upon work of the late Eric Berne (**Games People Play**) to provide convenient handles for understanding our behavior. Transactional Analysis assumes that we "run tapes" from several different levels of our past development sources as we interact with others. There are the child tape, the parent tape and the adult tape. It is easy to imagine what kinds of behavior each of these "tapes" represents. The problem in relationships often comes when two people interact from different tapes. This becomes a confused and unhelpful transaction between the two people.

Young people understand this concept very easily. They enjoy these simple handles for probing their relationships. There is probably someone in your community who is skilled in this field.

Imagine the fantastic retreat that could be built around the use of this technique! TA can release energy in the power of sharing as people within the bigger group. Laura Jane Eiger (**Finding Hidden Treasure: TA Groups in the Church**, Jalmar Press, 6501 Elvas Ave., Sacramento, CA 95819) has provided an excellent introduction to TA with an eight-session course.

This will be a super series of programs for your people. There is also extensive literature in this field. Your local public library will be a good place to start.

Resources
1. **Born to Love: Transactional Analysis in the Church**, by Muriel James, Addison-Wesley.

T.A.T.

The three letters were added to the alphabet of resources a few years back. Stewart M. Hoover, Carolyn K. Lindekugel, Ben Logan and Nelson Price developed a comprehensive course to equip people in their understanding of television. The materials have been packaged in several different ways. The basic course for leaders takes several days. Reading material, films, exercises and discussions prepare adults to teach others about the enormous impact of television on their faith and life.

There is also a shorter learning experience for the general public and youth groups. This course is taught by a trained and accredited T.A.T. leader. This course would be a super retreat program!

Abingdon Press has published the basic course as a workbook (**Television Awareness Training**, edited by Ben Logan). You could lead the retreat yourself by using this basic book. Add some

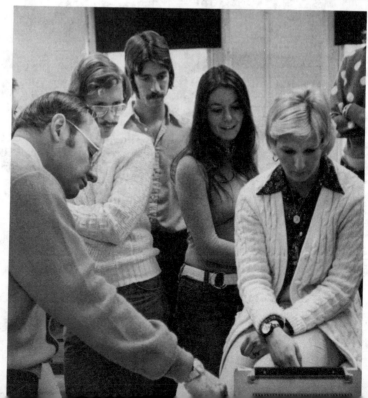

Well-written and creative courses enable youth groups to use TV for personal growth.

television sets and a couple of films and it would be a fine course. Media Action Research Center, Inc. (Suite 1370, 475 Riverside Drive, New York, NY 10115) can give more information about T.A.T. training and trainers.

A set of church school curriculum has also been developed by MARC (Media Action Research Center). Called "Growing With Television," this set of materials is available for each age level group. The study booklets created for youth deal with such issues as the consumerism mentality fostered by TV, the premise maintained in most programs that all problems can be solved rapidly with little harm to the hero, stereotyping, sexuality, the isolation that viewing encourages, violence permitted for the hero, and choosing programming.

Resources

1. **Image and Impact: How Man Comes Through in the Mass Media**, by William Fore, Friendship Press.
2. **Media Culture: TV, Radio, Records, Magazines, Newspapers, Movies**, by James Monaco.
3. **Man, Media and the Message**, by Merrill R. Abbey, Friendship Press.

Talents

The greatest resource for a local youth group is the young person. Your young folks have unbelievable gifts! However, they may be too shy to share the skills they have honed by lessons and practice. In most cases, they won't think of themselves as talented people. Most educational systems are not designed to surface or nurture latent gifts. There is little affirmation for the person in the process of becoming. Fortunately, the church youth group is the very cradle in which such development can take place.

Your hardest task in breaking through

the "impossibility" mentality will be your own self-image. You may be one of the many youth leaders who have not been affirmed or encouraged to risk the exposure of your budding gifts. You might confess this outlook with your teens. "Look, I don't have much experience as an artist or musician. I have never done much in the way of doing creative things. Yet, I am a new being in Christ and I am willing to rest upon this Good News to risk in new ways. Will you join me?"

You might try a simple process like the writing of poetry. Using the cinquain style, you and your youth group can write beautiful verses in a few minutes. The form goes as follows:

Line 1: Choose a word or words to serve as a title.
Line 2: Write two words that say something about the title word.
Line 3: Add three words depicting action about the title.
Line 4: Contribute four words describing an emotion about the title.
Line 5: Conclude with one word which captures the essence of the title word.

A teen wrote the following poem:

Snowflakes
Pure white
Falling uniquely still
Snowflakes luckily resting together
Free

There are many other expressive forms which will enable your folks to find a communication shape to the spiritual forces they feel in their lives. The quietest young person may be bubbling with feelings which only need an outlet in order to touch the lives of others.

Some groups have combined artistic forms to create many new opportunities. For instance, you may find that some of the most striking cinquain poems can be set to music by the musicians in your group. Imagine applying this creative expression to prayer! Your group could create its own musical prayers!

A youth group in Pittsburgh found that woodworking is an excellent creative expression. John and his young people use scrap wood to make crosses. They use blow torches to scar the wood. These small crosses are finished with a varnish and fitted with a small wood screw eye. They give these crosses to other youth. It has become a unifying ministry of the group.

An important feature of this thrust to youth ministry is that young people experience the model of a significant adult who risks to learn new ways to express the faith.

See also CREATIVITY, GROUP MEDIA

Taming

Taming is the experience of transforming alien environments, persons and ideas into friendly allies. *John Washburn*, creative teacher, poet and gamesman, is the enabler of this exciting concept. Drawing upon an idea found in **The Little Prince**, he has created an outlook very valuable to the local youth group. At one point in this interesting children's book, the prince faces a strange animal that tells the boy they cannot play together until it has been tamed. There can be no transaction of depth between the new and the familiar until a certain transformation has taken place.

John hosted a tour to New York City for a group of rural youth who had not experienced the city. There is always fear in the unknown, strange or alien. Fear is not usually seen as the source of transformation and hope!

John prepared mini-decks of cards. He gave each person a sheet which encouraged them to become "people tamers." Each small group was given a packet of instruction cards. They suggested such things as talking to a person in the elevator or going into a department store and asking people if they needed help finding something. The city and its people became the arena for transformation and discovery.

After several hours of people taming each group stopped for lunch and reflected on the experiences: How can you tell whether a person will be

friendly? Under what circumstances were people suspicious of your taming? What sort of things help the taming process? Would you like to build close relationships with the persons you met? Why? Why don't people tame more often?

This concept of taming is vital to the life of a faith-based youth group. There are a number of factors which make new and challenging aspects of living fearful to youth. Some youth leaders see their most important contribution to youth as that of giving them new, enlarging experiences. How can youth from the cultural and spiritual ghettos of suburbia, rural and urban areas be enabled to tame the complex of values and culture nationally and internationally?

See also CITIZENSHIP, FAITH, PORTABLE MINISTRY, SERVICE, WASHINGTON-U.N. SEMINAR

Task Force

If you've ever spent years on committees with frustratingly nebulous responsibilities, you may really enjoy being on a task force, quite a different animal from a committee. Task forces have a limited life span, a well-defined goal, a definite budget and a predetermined structure within which to work (who the group reports to, who relates to the ongoing work). In short, the purpose of a task force is to solve a specific problem.

Task forces can often break up log jams that committees encounter. An example: A church committee continues to wrestle with declining youth attendance at worship, and the problem is brought up often in lengthy fruitless discussion. One night Ellen suggested setting up a task force to interview the youth, both those who do not attend worship services and those who once attended. Six weeks later the task force reported that the youth dropped out because they never saw any of their own group up front in leadership and concluded the service was not meant for them. The result was a specific recommendation to the worship committee, some changes in the worship services and increased youth attendance within two months.

Task forces can utilize specialized talents without the persons feeling that it will be an endless infringement and burden.

Another joy of task forces is recruitment of members. Very busy persons who avoid serving on committees will often bring surprised smiles to those enlisting members by quickly accepting responsibilities on limited duty task forces.

Youth ministry can make excellent use of the task force concept since youth usually have very busy and changeable schedules and do not want to commit themselves for a long period of time. Youth like to visualize both the goal and the ways to achieve it as well as experience the joy of seeing the completion of a task. Some examples of youth task forces are: planning the next retreat or party or project, making arrangements for youth Sunday or work-day or room decoration, surveying other local church groups, drafting a proposal to the pastor or industry official or congress person, handling a campaign to get a new group name or symbol.

See also INTEREST, PLANNING COUNCIL, YOUTH COUNCIL

Team Teaching

You may have been teamed with another person to lead a youth group. This will probably be of great help to both of you, though an occasional doubt may cross your minds.

Leading a group by yourself may seem the simplest strategy that requires the least amount of effort. Working alone would appear to give you more freedom and flexibility. Most of us know freewheeling youth leaders who seem to enjoy doing whatever they want to at any time.

However, rarely is being a "lone ranger" leader as productive as other alternatives. Most of us need and profit by the input and continuous planning suggestions of other persons. It makes a difference to hear another leader's observations of our own leadership responsibility.

Tom and Lois worked out a good group leadership arrangement. They sometimes rotated the primary leadership responsibility by the month and sometimes they rotated it by daily program needs. Lois enjoyed helping with anything that related to history or biblical research while Tom preferred to be called on for music, group process (suggesting various group methods and arrangements) and constructing challenging questions. While they did not

In a team approach to youth ministry, the leaders benefit from each other's input.

limit themselves to just these favorite areas, Lois and Tom made as much use of their interests as possible. When one of them was up front, the other consciously observed all of the dynamics taking place in the room so that the two of them could compare notes later.

At vacation time it helped that Tom and Lois were not married to each other. When the Barkers had to be out of town or were sick, Lois took over. Sometimes she recruited her husband Graham to help.

Husband and wife teams often work extremely well. Since they know each other so well they can better utilize each other's abilities and thoughts.

Not only do husband and wife teams have a common project and goal, they also model to the youth communication skills and caring relationships. This modeling can be very valuable in a day in which there is so little of this for most youth to observe.

Of course, planning for these teams requires less travel and formal scheduling, but not always. One of the biggest difficulties husband and wife teams point out is the tendency not to plan since familiarity can lull both persons into complacent, second-rate leadership habits.

Regular planning for any team needs to be scheduled, prepared and thoroughly carried out. The lack of planning leads to more destroyed hopes, hurt feelings and missed opportunities than any other part of being a leader.

Team leadership also implies a very important point: We are never in any church leadership responsibility by ourselves. We are a part of the church and ought to regularly call upon other persons to serve on our team, if only for one session, to share the unique talents and insights they have. Remember, your team can function best when it realizes that God is its most important member.

See also SUNDAY SCHOOL, VACATION BIBLE SCHOOL, YOUTH MINISTRY

Television

For many young people, the television is their best friend. It helps them escape problems in coping with life. Television introduces viewers to thoughts, concepts, experiences and goals they had never known before. It gladly dishes out hero models, even anti-hero models. Like a good friend, it almost always is there when you turn it on and it helps you burn up time when there does not seem to be anything to do.

Though most youth do not realize it, TV is also one of their worst enemies. It consumes and pollutes their energy and creativity. It destroys their image of themselves and it magnifies the image of their opponents, everything from acne to

On any given night, half of America watches television.

rival love interests. Television idolizes characters who act flawlessly with no time spent in planning.

With the advent of the video disc, videotape cassette, large screens, multi-channels on cable and other TV accessories, the consumptive ability of TV for any person's time is unbelievable. Even though youth watch TV less and listen to radio more than their younger or older brothers and sisters, it is still an enormously powerful influence.

We will never know the extent of that influence, but we do know some of it. Consistent research shows that steady viewers of TV tend to stereotype persons with sexist and racial overtones, expect violence in everyday situations (causing them to be more suspicious of the negative to other persons), are bored more easily when life is less than spectacular and want spectator rather than participatory activities.

Maria Winn in her very insightful book, **The Plug-In Drug**, draws the similarities between video use and drug use. In many ways, the effect on the body and mind during viewing strongly resembles the effects of various drugs, and the withdrawal from heavy amounts of viewing to little or none is also a parallel to the withdrawal difficulties of a heavy drug addict.

Only the most radical alarmist would recommend turning off the TV forever. Perhaps more than any other invention, TV has made the world into a global village and has linked persons together who would never have encountered each other's thoughts. But not only is moderation in usage suggested, intense filtering of the message is also desperately needed, particularly by youth who do not have the lengthy background against which to bounce messages that are detrimental to them. Youth groups could be most helpful by critically reviewing the video message. Using the **Growing With Television** curriculum or the **Television Awareness Training** workbook, the group could evaluate how the commercial or entertainment producer stereotypes the audience and what responses these persons are seeking to have happen. Both resources are available through most bookstores or their publisher, Media Action Research Center, Suite 1370, 475 Riverside Dr., New York, NY 10115.

A powerful friend is much less of an enemy if both parties are completely aware of what takes place in the transactions between them. You can believe that the TV broadcasters definitely know their expectations for your time together.

Resources

1. **Keeping Pace with the New Television**, by Mahoney, DeMartino, Stengel, VNU Books, Carnegie Corporation.

2. **Remote Control**, by Frank Mankiewicz, Ballantine Books.

3. **The Plug-In Drug**, by Marie Winn, Viking Press.

See also CABLE, T.A.T., VIDEO CASSETTES

Theology of Youth Ministry

A noted theologian once stated that everyone who deals with life is a theologian. It is just that some people are practicing good theology while others are not. Theology (knowledge of God) sounds so forbidding. It is true that this field of study has been carried on for a long time and has branches which are scientific in form. Yet, your knowledge that Jesus is Lord makes you a theologian. Our struggle as a people of God is always a quest to be faithful to the God who calls us.

Theology is more than a set of princi-

The theology of youth ministry can be simply the sharing of your own spiritual quest.

ples or proofs. Growing closer to the love of God never ends. It is a stretching experience which beckons the young and old throughout life. This means that the wholeness of truth is ours and yet always beyond us.

Some folks are uncomfortable with the concept that God is always calling us further on our journey to understanding. They fear that such a growth stance will make their development appear as if they don't know what they believe. The journey of faithfulness doesn't undercut one's security in Christ. Rather, it permits a deepening of faith. Opening your arms and spirit to Christ means that nothing will ever cut you off from the source of your faith. There will be no moment of life which will catch you with a faith too small.

We also believe that the wholistic theology is found as we acknowledge the communion of saints. This means that we are not lone gunfighters who need no one else for our religion. We are called and formed by the Holy Spirit. This gift is not an individualistic present. The Holy Spirit is the source of the community of faith. Our salvation is given through our fellowship with Christ and his people. What a gift this is for us! You may be a lonely youth advisor facing a tough situation. Yet, when you gather in prayer with no one else in sight, you are really gathering with Bill, Dennis, all the folks mentioned in this book along with John Wesley, Martin Luther, John Calvin, Mary and Martha, Jesus and Moses. You are one of the saints in quest to know him more fully.

It is the context of other brothers and sisters, present and invisible, which helps us pursue a theology that is right and fitting. Faith history has been marked by the misuse of our freedom to be wrong about God. Fortunately, we have been given the witness of other sisters and brothers to guide us as we study scripture and listen to the Spirit.

A person who accepts this view of trekking with God realizes his or her own limitations and sin. Forgiveness is a flowing gift which keeps lapping at our lives and washing us clean. By knowing our highs and lows, we can easily and lovingly accept the journey of young people. To understand young people, we do not have to "lower ourselves to their level." We are called simply to match our humanity with theirs. We are all seeking the fullness of our God as people in the world. The immature or lost teen is embraced, not judged. In that person, there go I.

The person of Christ looms large in our theological probing. God permits us to take side journeys of understanding. It is significant that parts of the fullness of God will jump out at us during certain times of our quest. Just when all of our lives are engulfed with one aspect of theology, a brother or sister will reflect another attribute of the Christian life. We will then see what was previously unclear to us.

Christ is the jewel of God's love. The facets sparkle as we fit our gaze on him. We are often blinded by the majesty and seem only to make out one pool of light at the expense of not seeing others. God understands. He frees us for such a rich shifting vision.

It is easy for you to see from these words that our understanding of theology fits youth ministry. The theology of youth ministry is simply the sharing of your own quest. Permit the teens to participate in your journey. You really have nothing else to offer than your own inner faithful trek. Yet, there is always a danger that we might distract the theological probes of others by our concerns. While the young person needs the witness of others' journeys, she or he does not need to see only the conclusions you have found. It will help to see what is important to you. However, you are really providing a witness that the journey of faith is necessary, possible and rewarding for each person.

One group dealt with theology quite intentionally by having the teens spend a great deal of time interviewing people in the community about their faith journeys. Using cassette tape recorders, they found that folks were very grateful to share their theology. In fact, the young people got so good at asking the questions that adults often said that they understood their faith better after the interview! The teens prepared a media show which featured slides and sections of the interviews. They called the evening meeting for the whole church, "The Witness of the Saints."

Resources

1. **God With Us: A Theology of Transpersonal Life**, by Joseph Haroutunian, Westminster Press.
2. **Shaping Your Faith**, by Wally Christians, Word.

See also HOLY SPIRIT, JESUS

Touch

The teen years bring such a variety of responses concerning the physical act of touching. Two youth will go to the same conference, and one will come home saying, "That was the greatest group I've ever been a part of. They were always patting me on the back and giving each other hugs." And the other will say, "I am never going back. It was one of those emotional touchie-feelie groups, and I don't like all those hand-in-hand activities."

Danielle told everyone that she didn't like people touching her hair or back, and the group seemed to have been challenged to get her to change. She left for good. Tom told everyone as they planned a closing service that he didn't like that sissy stuff of being in a circle with everyone having their arms around each others' shoulders, but later he told

Reaching out to people is an expressive statement of how we feel about them.

the adult leader he was glad they went ahead with the circle because it meant more to him than anything else during that meaningful week.

There are times when a five-hour monologue can be best expressed with a hug.

Reaching out to other persons can be our most expressive statements of how much we feel about them. Physically, we demonstrate that we stand by them.

Some youth have valid reasons for not wanting to be touched. Painful remembrances of child abuse in many different forms cause them to value their distance from other persons. Therefore, it may require a slow, tentative process of being able to let down the barriers and letting oneself be vulnerable to another person's affections.

Resources

1. **Keep in Touch**, by Herman Ahrens, Jr., Pilgrim Press.

See also BODY, EMOTIONS

Training

One of the most beneficial resolves you can make as a youth leader is to regularly seek out training opportunities for yourself and the other leaders in your group. The resolve is quite necessary because time will have to be taken from other inviting functions. You will have to do a bit of searching to locate stimulating training programs that offer new insights, creative methods, periods of sharing with other leaders, and more advanced skill development than what you now have.

Of course, all of that is rarely available in one short course. Often you will have to recover some ground you have trod before to pick up some new hints, but the challenging training opportunities are worth searching for. As in any

sport, it is almost always more beneficial to play with someone slightly more skilled than you are to bring out the impetus to advance.

There are several kinds of training events available:

Leadership school—This is usually offered on a city or area-wide basis for approximately one to five days with a number of classes offered for a wide variety of training needs. Usually, the students commute to the school each day and participate in classes of one to three hours in length. The leader usually imparts most of the information, though the students may be asked to do some preparation prior to the next class. Most of the work takes place in small groups arranged for one age level or interest area. Since the subject matter is normally more general in nature than some of the other training events, this is often

the best first-time starter course for a beginning leader.

Workshop—The scope of training is much more defined here. More emphasis is made on skill development, and usually the participants are expected to do "hand on" involvement during the sessions so they can duplicate the skill later for others. Workshops are offered within larger training events of many days duration as well as a half-day period for those who are interested from a wide geographic area. Fees may be slightly higher to participate in workshops because of the materials that will probably be used learning these specialized skills.

Seminars—These sessions presume some experience in leadership, since a true seminar includes periods in which all participants share from their own background in working with whatever subject or age level ministry is listed in the title of the course. Often the participants are asked to bring samples of work that has been accomplished in their regular duties or a position paper on a particular interest that can be shared with everyone.

Lab school—This training includes input from the leader as well as involvement of all participants in trying out leadership skills with persons of the same age level as the focus of the course. The course usually lasts from three to seven days, utilizing four to ten hours a day, and participants will often come from a widespread area. Usually, the general orientation training will be followed by participants being divided into teams which prepare for leadership assignments with the age level students who will be brought in during the later sessions. Following the experimentation in the lab setting, evaluation will be conducted to further hone the skills being sharpened. Almost always, students who are taking the course toward certification are required to attend every hour of every session.

Manuals, handbooks, workbooks—Almost every denomination has produced leadership training books to aid development of youth ministry leadership. Some materials are designed for self-instruction while others are for use during regular work with the youth group. These are invaluable since they can be referred to often, and parts that didn't make much sense at first may take on greater significance as your situation begins to approximate what is being addressed.

When you need help in locating the kind of resources and training that you need at a particular time, your local church educational leadership should be your first place to inquire. In case the kinds of answers you need are not readily available, check next with your regional church office. If you need to go further, write or call your denominational office. Create a staff title to cover your need (person in charge of senior high leadership schools, for instance) and be as specific in your letter as possible.

Resources
1. **Enlist, Train, Support Leaders**, by Evelyn Huber, Judson Press.

See also CONSULTATION, CREATIVE MODELS, GROUP MAGAZINE, RESOURCES, SEARCH, SERENDIPITY, WORKSHOPS, YOUTH SPECIALITIES

Trips

No doubt about it, your youth group will probably profit greatly from taking a few trips together. There is nothing like enduring a common pilgrimage to unite unrelated individuals into a purposeful unit, particularly if the experience is approached with diligent planning.

Travel offers the youth group a unique opportunity to see God in action.

Probably the greatest cause of problems related to trips is the lack of understanding or agreement with an overall purpose of the trip. The most common misunderstanding occurs when some of the participants have serious goals for study or work and other participants see the trip as an opportunity for escape and party time. This can lead to unbelievable stress on the entire group and make the experience miserable. It could have been avoided if those goals had been openly discussed and negotiated.

Another common misunderstanding relates to the participants' roles. Many persons assume that going on a youth trip means that anything goes and no one will take it seriously: "Working on a vacation, you must be kidding!" "Why can't we stay up all night; we can sleep tomorrow on the bus." Yet, others see the trip as a critical operation with rules, regulations, schedules followed precisely: "We'll have to arrive by 4:30 p.m. in order for everyone to get showers and be dressed up by 6:15 to get to that fancy restaurant." Any trip can include a relaxed schedule along with the times when diligent support will be required. Make sure that everyone recognizes the variety of time demands, the part they will have to play and the roles they can depend upon for everyone else.

Some of the most enjoyable and beneficial trips are the ones that combine purposes. One of the most popular is a travel/study trip. The group plans its itinerary in a way that refreshing travel (sightseeing, touring, relaxation) is possible as well as study (Bible, current topic, a major study that seemed best not to do in church school class). Doubly reinforcing is the combination of a study that relates to the place where the group will be (a study of hunger while visiting places where poverty exists or where food is mass-produced or con-sumed; a study of worship while visiting famous sanctuaries, monasteries, temples; a study of communications while visiting newspaper facilities and broadcast studios; a study of the Sermon on the Mount while visiting insurance companies, stock brokers, mortuaries).

Another possibility is a travel/work trip in which the plans call for some time for fun and some time for work (the fun may permeate the work) at a location where labor is needed.

Some groups have had great response to a surprise trip. The participants register without knowing the destination, only the duration, of the trip. The leader will totally plan a trip that has meaning and variety. This requires not only great faith of the group in the leaders but also sensitive perception of the leaders for the desires and needs of the group in order to plan a trip to meet the interests of the group without any of their input.

Regardless of your mode of travel, a number of games can be found to make the whole time more pleasant, especially if long periods of riding are involved.

Youth groups in other cities have connections. Before arriving in a town, they can set up tours, talks, side trips and can quickly gain access to places not available to the average tourist. And quite often church facilities will become available to you making the night's stay and meals possible at a fraction of the normal cost. Even more promising, many youth groups look forward to being host to a traveling group and can provide fellowship and recreation accommodations for a shared experience.

Trips can offer totally new worlds for the participants, especially the youth. They can experience life in a mind-boggling contrast to that which they know in their home community. And because of the group interaction, they can gain insights with which to evaluate new varieties of lifestyles and outlooks.

A most important part of any trip is

giving part of it to those who did not get to go. For this purpose, it is good to take plenty of pictures that tell of what happened to individuals and the group as the trip progressed. Keep an accurate diary of daily events, and record the sounds as you experienced them so that a sound-and-sight presentation can be created.

How One Group Traveled

One group had four adult leaders available to make the trip. The leaders decided to develop four planning committees with an adult and youth co-chairpersons for each. One committee handled transportation (planned the itinerary, checked on the vehicles and drivers), housekeeping (made schedules and secured supplies so that everyone could help with upkeep of the dwellings occupied by the group), and food preparation when this was undertaken.

Another committee planned the food (menus for those meals prepared by the group, purchased food), lodging (selected housing and made necessary reservations) and served as treasurer (kept budget, maintained adequate balance for needs and emergencies).

A third committee was responsible for recreational activities (secured necessary equipment and planned a variety of activities using facilities en route), worship experiences (made assignments for the participation of everyone in devotional periods, meal graces, and end of the day meditations), and first-aid and insurance (kept adequate supply of first-aid materials, information about medical facilities en route).

The fourth committee was in charge of promotion (contacting potential participants, interpreting the intent of the

trip), registration (getting necessary forms signed, approval of sponsoring body and maintaining contact during trip with sponsoring body), and program (lining up interesting activities, keeping alternative program ideas open, thanking those who helped.)

One interesting note about the above system is that each committee had responsibilities prior to the trip and throughout its duration. The committee chairpersons served as an executive body when instant decisions had to be made (financial crisis, discipline, abrupt program changes).

Of course, there is an unlimited number of ways that a group can structure its planning and responsibilities. Some of the previously listed duties could be combined or separated according to the needs of your group. Your group may have additional concerns, such as special training that's necessary for various activities, extra help for handicapped participants, preparation of materials that would be needed by the group, etc.

Pacing is most important on a trip with a group. Long rides need to be accompanied by a variety of recreation and relaxation. Some program input is helpful all along the trip to combat boredom and too much personal concern. And don't assume that the resting done in a moving vehicle will make up for sound sleep between travels.

Traveling brings out some of the best and worst traits of persons, and this is an especially good time to develop caring skills for the needs of each other.

Resources
1. **Youth Group Travel Directory**, compiled by Thom Schultz, GROUP Books, Box 481, Loveland, CO 80537.

See also BUS, PORTABLE MINISTRY, TRAINING

Vacation Bible School

There are many interesting approaches to summer education projects which offer hope.

Vacation Bible School is an important summer ministry for many churches. Children enroll for five to ten days of refreshing and rewarding study experiences that would have been difficult in any other format. "I think we get more accomplished in VBS than at any other time in the year," said one leader in reference to the variety of study that can be done in this special summer opportunity. It is true that VBS reaches neighborhood children who would not normally attend other programs. It is also an important learning/serving occasion for youth who can be utilized as teachers, aides, projectionists, musicians, etc.

Even though few youth are willing to attend youth VBS classes during the morning sessions, they often are quite willing to participate when the event is planned as a Family VBS. Those evening programs often start with recreational activities and include other activities for the youth after the evening classes. The kind of experimental worship and study that persons had considered for other occasions can be tried out in the carefree summer schedule.

Bud and his folks in Cincinnati created an excellent summer VBS which depended totally on teens. They noted that the energy crisis had made the movement of students a questionable act of stewardship. They also wanted to reach children who would not ordinarily come to the church building. Utilizing the skills of a seminarian, the church found a van for the project. They trained several teams of young people.

Members of the church were urged to host the Backyard Bible Club. Each host advertised that the group would be coming to his or her backyard on a certain day of the week. A colorful sign would appear in the front yard. It was helpful to have a local person invite the neighborhood children.

The Backyard Bible Club van would pull up to the house. Kids would swarm in the yard. Teams of young people would go to different parts of the lawn. Each team carried a decorated case filled with materials for the specialized content it had developed. The children would easily form into small groups for study and discussion.

The youth teams made more than 40 such backyard schools happen over the course of the summer. Of course, such teaching opportunities teach the teachers even more than the students.

See also SUMMER

Values Clarification

We make decisions every hour of our lives. Granted, most of them are seemingly small decisions, but all of them help to shape our destiny. Continually making small decisions in one pattern is actually a major decision. Refraining from making decisions is actually to decide on what seems to be the least painful direction.

The study of values clarification is an active pursuit of the underlying values that shape our decisions: how we got them, why we hold them, and ways we might change them if we choose. This pursuit is enabled by a process of identifying what we hold to have more relative value. For instance, in a group we might be challenged to consider a choice between two possible actions and then to discover what values were alive in those decisions.

Youth is a prime time to begin to assess the values that are behind our actions, opinions and options for the future. The clarification process can be a very liberating one that brings more clarity to decision making and more enthusiasm for living out those directions.

For instance, Malcolm had been a youth advisor for over a year when he realized that the group constantly argued over how programs should be planned. Two members of the planning team always wanted to check out future program ideas with the full group while the rest of the team thought this was unwise as well as a waste of time. It was during a particularly heated debate over the subject that Malcolm suggested they take a few minutes from the regular business to do some on-the-spot values clarification. He assured everyone that the concern was not to look for right and

Exercises and activities that help young people determine their values are an integral part of the youth ministry experience.

wrong judgments in the search but simply to sort out the origin and the basis for the opinions.

Fairly soon the two youth traced their ideas for group input to Sid, a former advisor they had admired. As it turned out only those two remembered and appreciated Sid. One remembered that it was during such a process that he felt a part of the group. In the probe some of the others on the team began to realize for the first time that the process Sid used was much simpler than the way they feared it might work. A streamlined version was constructed, the meeting picked up with the business matters, and the group was far more strengthened through this understanding and renewed trust.

Resources
1. **Values Clarification**, by Simon, Howe, Kirschenbaum, Visual Library.
2. **Integrating Values: Theory and Exercises for Clarifying and Integrating Religious Values**, Pfaum.
3. **Meeting Yourself Halfway**, by Sidney Simon, Argus Communications.
4. **Values and Faith**, by Roland S. Larson and Doris E. Larson, Winston Press.

See also ROLE PLAYING, SIMULATION GAMES

Variety

The church youth group is not a love boat or cruise ship. You are not a smiling skipper or pretty social director trying to please and entertain passengers. However, the youth advisor is responsible to see that young Christians have a life together which sparkles, challenges and changes. In other words, your programming each week should reflect the basic nature of the faith. . . authentic excitement.

Too often youth workers reach for gimmicks to keep things going. Gimmicks are tricks used by the leader to call attention to her or his own superiority, with little, if any, usefulness for the group. Instead, leaders should strive to devise and implement creative methods that encourage group growth by drawing attention to the group members and the God we serve. There is a great need to look constantly for innovative learning methods. Throughout this book you will note that the ideas have grown out of an authentic proof of the goals, persons and opportunities of a particular group in a particular setting.

In addition to methods, sometimes the blahs can be encouraged by working with perimeters that are too restrictive. Meeting times, places and frequency of meetings can be varied with great results—just remember to carefully and repeatedly notify everyone (including potential attenders) of these changes. Ask different persons occasionally to help with the program planning—free-spirited characters often have new perspectives that with a little honing can add needed freshness and vitality. Try to draw people in order that they can contribute by their presence and ideas.

There are a number of creative clues to your programming. The four seasons offer ideas. The church year also provides many program possibilities. What is happening in the world and nation (elections, strikes, natural destruction, world hunger, and so on) which needs to be explored together? Has something important transpired in the sports or entertainment field? Once you and your planning group have isolated a dozen different clues to programming, ask another series of questions. What forms do these items suggest in terms of presentation? Should we change location and visit the disc jockey at the local radio station and talk about values in music? Would the hunger program best be studied by experiencing it with a

The youth group is the most creative place to work on earth! That creativity includes a variety of programs and approaches.

fast? In other words, how does the context of the program suggest that it be experienced? This clue will open your group to an amazing variety of approaches.

It is also important to think of your youth group as being in a larger context. There are other Christian youth who can share their lives with you. Your denomination probably has many programs during the year that are offered for several local churches, perhaps at a camp, college or large church. These can be very rewarding for your group members since they can experience many new program ideas that are either just being introduced or are possible because of the size gathering. New ideas can be taken back home for use there. Usually training opportunities for local leaders are a primary function of these events. If your denomination does not organize regional events, plan your own. Invite a nearby church to join you for an evening. You will be pleased by how these exchanges will open up new opportunities for growth.

Don't forget that there are several national and international youth gatherings each year. These can provide an invaluable unique richness and global perspective. Worshipping and growing with other teens from across the country is important for young people. Groups can develop all kinds of fund raising and group building events in preparation for and surrounding these trips.

The youth group is the most creative place to work on earth! The sky is the limit for variety. You are freer than the public schools, local government or business to explore and risk. Create an environment of possibility to help the young people think in new directions. They are often limited by their previous experiences. The spice of life is yours as youth advisors. You are only limited by your imagination and the company you keep.

See also BIBLE KNOWLEDGE, DIVERSITY, GROUP BUILDING, HUMOR, PROGRAM

Video Cassettes

The capacity to produce your own video pieces is now within reach of everyone. You may be confused by the blinding variety of formats and systems.

Video cassettes of classics such as "The Ten Commandments" can be stopped at any point for discussion and activities.

Video producers have not standardized as audio tape companies did years ago. You will find different video tape widths and incompatibility among video equipment.

The video cassette machines appear in countless homes around the country. Many car dealerships have them for loan. Many libraries now have loan equipment for people in the community.

The video cassette is easy to use. The question is how we can best use this new technology. Most of the material prepared for use on video cassettes comes from film or television. As the late Marshall McLuhan reminded us, we tend to utilize material from a previous medium for a new medium. The real question must be: "What can this medium do that other video media could not do?" A video cassette can be started and stopped. It permits you to select the material you want to see when you want to see it. This means that the video cassette material should be designed in a special way to fit its characteristics.

Most of the video cassette systems can be fitted with a camera. This means that you have an enormous resource for youth ministry. Imagine the kinds of video programs you can develop, say, on local missions!

Warren had a group of young people who were restless with their class. He gathered them one Sunday morning and gave them a biblical passage. The task was to videotape a one- or two-minute program on this passage. After the projects were complete, they moved the monitor to each room and showed the video Bible story to the other students. This system worked beautifully.

You will be amazed to find that many of your folks have video systems in their homes. Ask and you shall receive the use of this equipment. Put it in the hands of your students and they will create beautiful video material.

Resources
1. Television Licensing Center (TLC) Guide (a newsletter), Department G-4, Wilmette Ave., Wilmette, IL 60091.
2.**The Videotape Book, A Basic Guide to Portable TV Production**, by Michael Murray, Taplinger Publishing Company.
3. **Using Nonbroadcast Video in the Church**, by Holland, Nickerson and Vaughn, Judson Press.

See also GROUP MEDIA, MEDIA AWARENESS

Visitation

There is nothing like actually visiting potential members, or once-active members.

Some members of the group who are better at visitation than others may wish to take charge until other persons can be trained. In fact, a total group discussion about conducting effective visits will probably be helpful to everyone.

Persons appreciate being notified prior to the visit so that they will not be embarrased unnecessarily. The advance notice also gives a chance for the person to decline the visit, which should be taken as their right. Refusal for a visit is less likely if the person is told that (the name of one person in the group) simply wanted to drop something by for them, and it would be up to the individual to conduct the visit for the group.

Taking an item to give away is usually very helpful. The one making the visit can comment about it, as can the person receiving it. The object might be a book, newsletter, something brought back from the last retreat, something made by the group especially for this person or a card telling of the group's concern for them (maybe signed by everyone.)

Youth are also extremely helpful in church-wide visitations, particularly

Teach your young people visiting skills. They'll benefit from the experience more than those being visited.

when there are youth in the family being visited. Even families with small children are thinking about the time when their children will be youth. They will exhibit far more interest in the church with youth who are active, concerned and working to bring others into the congregation.

For the adult leader, there is no substitute for visiting youth personally, both those regular and potential attenders. Being with a youth in his or her own home is essential to knowing the person and illustrating concern. Making an appointment illustrates extra responsibility and gives the leader a chance to state the reason for the visit. Some youth may prefer for the visit to take place in a nearby restaurant or location other than their home, if there is something there they do not want you to see just yet.

Keep records of your visit to help you remember special insights and conversations.

See also NEWCOMER

Vocation

"What are you going to do when you grow up?"

One of the biggest anxieties young people face is their future career. They can see the comfortable paths to a job fading away. They don't need to read about "the third wave" (futurist/author Alvin Toffler's prediction of radically changing work patterns) to know that all is not well in the land of work. Brothers and sisters who confidently sailed through school to become teachers or lawyers may still be looking for a job in their fields months after graduation. Fathers and mothers may also be experiencing the fall of long established institutions and companies. The steel mill at the end of the street is no longer

The church can show concern for its youth by offering vocational guidance and training as well as spiritual support.

spouting pollution—or pay checks.

It is interesting that the faith community has been so slow to deal with the vocational aspect of its folk. There have been moments of concern about getting youth into "full-time Christian service." Yet, we are one of the few places endowed with the means to help our youth face the total picture of life planning.

The faith concept of vocation is based on the believer's conviction of being "called" by God to a life of meaningful service. Instead of focusing on whether a career should be in "computers or plastics," we are offered an opportunity to raise the real question: What has God called us to be and do? These theological queries are much more practical than they seem. When we start with theological questions, a whole new view of creation and our role in it emerges. The person of faith discovers a sense of hope and the possibility of faithfulness which is not as apparent by just searching for a job slot.

Thelma helped her young people work through this journey of faith discovery. She then worked with them as a team in a probe of the practical aspects of vocational decision-making. Each group chose a profession or work area. They took audio cassette tape recorders and interviewed people of faith who had made choices about their labor. These interviews were shared and debriefed. The youth group then created a collection of these interviews for the church library for use by people in the church.

The Presbyterian Church in the U.S. has set up guidance centers across the denomination for youth to undergo sophisticated vocational testing. This experience enables youth to identify general fields of interest, to locate appropriate training and school possibilities and to receive counseling into the unique opportunities the youth has in the world of work. The regional centers are available to all youth. Their locations can be obtained by writing to the denominational offices (341 Ponce de Leon Avenue, Atlanta, GA 30308).

Many local churches have set up a program for juniors in high school to meet on several occasions on a one-to-one basis with an adult in the local church about their preparation and anticipation toward work. The vocational concern is matched with a meaningful experience with an adult in the church who cares about the teens' fears. This session also offers the youth a chance to talk out some of his or her confusions and expectations as he nears the end of high school. Various resources and workbooks can be chosen to be used by the youth and adults at this time.

It is possible for youth to feel that the church's concern for them lessens as they turn their attention from local schooling toward work, college, military involvement or other vocational preparation. But the church can make its support for them evident during these critical times of choice and anticipation by helping them to discover their God-given abilities and their calling from God to future endeavors.

Resources
1. **My Life: What Shall I Do With It?**, by Shirley Schwarzrock and Gilbert Wrenn.
2. **Work in America, Report of Special Task Force**, MIT Press.
3. **Where Do I Go From Here?: Work, Worship, Leisure**, by Winn and Cockrum.
4. **If You Don't Know Where You're Going, You'll Probably End Up Somewhere Else**, by David Campbell, Argus Books.
5. **Preparing for W*O*R*K**, by John William Zehring, Victor Books.

See also COUNSELOR

Washington-U.N. Seminar

"A once in a lifetime opportunity!"

"A time when the church can introduce the youth to a staggering amount of power in a context of representative democracy for which the Christian community has urgent concern."

It is one thing for a youth group to visit city hall and talk with the civic leaders of the municipality or to visit the state capitol and talk to the members of the legislature and gubernatorial leaders. But it is something else to enable a group of youth to visit the nation's highest officials and our representatives in the United Nations.

Such a trip is a gigantic contribution that a church can give its youth. It will probably be the first time that the youth in your group will have seriously considered the political implications of power and the way that massive decisions are made by a few people. At once, nebulous words like justice, morality, equality, peace, defense and others take on very concrete significance. Persons and budgets are identified with current priorities.

Of course, it is quite possible to make a tourist romp out of this trip and only touch the spots that should be explored and examined in-depth. Many teens may expect that this will be another high school lark of an outing and that once a few monuments and buildings have been stared at through the bus window, the group is free for the rest of the time to goof off. This may not only be an expectation but the only concept of touring known by many persons in the group. Such would be a pitiful waste of your time, energy and opportunity.

There are several ways to improve upon that anemic concept of travel. One possibility is to contact the offices of your senators and representatives to obtain gallery admission tickets to view Congress in action. Other options are White House special passes, listings of what legislation is currently being considered and other intriguing helps. Personal appointments with your elected officials are always possible. (Try not to invest all that valuable time in getting a group picture.) Instead, find out what issues are current, why this official is voting the way she or he is, how you can influence critical votes, the committee involvements of this official. The office aides could suggest other significant places to go, resources to notice, and constructive methods for information digestion.

As the time for the trip approaches, news notices should be distributed to those going on the trip so that they will be oriented as much as possible to arrive eager to learn.

See also PORTABLE MINISTRY, TRIPS

Weather Balloons

The weather balloon is a prime example of usefulness. These rubber beauties come in several different sizes. The smallest is about six feet across with the biggest being about 16 feet in diameter.

The big balloons are special because they can be used with youth in so many different ways. You will want to employ a vacuum cleaner which blows rather than sucks. Air compressors and other equipment don't work as well as the common tube vacuum cleaner. You will also need some string. Even though the balloon will expand to its majestic size, it has low air pressure.

What happens after inflation depends on your imagination. If you enjoy multi-imaged slide and film shows, the weather balloon makes a fine screen! It is best to tie a hymnal to the mouth of the inflated balloon with a foot of string.

Drop the book into a wastepaper basket. The giant sphere will rest on the basket like a huge scoop of ice cream on a cone. Don't use anything heavier than a hymnal. This permits the balloon to bounce with air currents. Station two slide projectors behind the mounted balloon at right angles to each other. Focus the projected image on the front of the balloon. This will give you a three-dimensional image and provides a fine intermix of images. It will make the slide show like none you have ever presented!

The bubble screen can also be suspended from the ceiling. One group used the weather balloon during a Christmas Eve service. By hanging it from a rafter, it was free to spin slowly, which gave the rear-projected image a "breathing" quality. When the high school students projected a picture of the earth, there were gasps from the congregation. "It looked so real!"

Weather balloons can be inflated to eight feet. They offer numerous creative uses.

The rubber monster has many other uses. We have inflated one for use at the conclusion of a camping experience. By gently bouncing it, we had it soaring up to 30 feet over our heads. We became more and more engrossed in this activity. After 20 minutes, it suddenly broke. We gathered around the limp rubber on the ground. "How do you feel about our broken friend?" We talked seriously about how it had served us and then passed away. "How is this balloon like the weekend we have just spent? Is it finished and gone forever?"

On another occasion a speaker used four weather ballons for his presentation before 1400 high school students. He had suspended them and dropped quarters in them to keep them from moving too much. The teens were very excited by the stage filled with the huge objects. The guest loosened one of them and gently released it over the audience. "Be gentle with it. Care for it." The balloon moved across the sea of hands. As the speaker spoke the balloon got smaller and smaller. It was finally just a heap of rubber. Holding it in his hand, he said, "Perhaps the balloon represents our own lives when we have given everything for others."

Weather balloons can be ordered from Edmund Scientific Co., 101 E. Gloucester Pike, Barrington, NJ 08007.

See also EARTHBALL

Witnessing

Youth are natural evangelists. If they discover a new product that seems to work better for them than some other product, they will try to convince everyone to try it out. That is why so many advertisers aim their media campaigns at youth, not that youth have the money to buy the cars or appliances being hawked. But if an advertiser can convince the youth in the family that his product is the best, most desired item in the world, they will lobby those in the family who control the money.

All of the growing youth movements have observed this same fact and have made it the pivotal point in their efforts. Youth can convince youth to follow a cause better than anyone else. They have got the energy, enthusiasm, persistance, motivation, adaptability and tenacity to tell their story until it gets heard.

Many youth groups view witnessing to other youth as their major outreach opportunities, and they are accomplishing that in impressively innovative ways.

One of the most effective methods is clowning. Youth take on the role of the servant to bring laughter to the sad, relief to the overburdened, hugs for the lonely, optimism to the depressed, and a model of altruistic love to everyone.

Youth are writing scripts, whittling on wood and styrofoam and putting together stages to take puppet troupes on tour to tell the Christian message to persons of all ages in any location.

Youth groups rehearse and perform every conceivable musical style and variety of production for months out of each year. Choirs and creative dance ensembles convey their beliefs through sound and sight.

Drama groups are again converting dingy fellowship halls and shopping center malls into theaters for acting out convincing portrayals of truth that move audiences into productive response.

Many youth groups have formed speaking teams who can deliver provocative programs dealing with crucial Christian life issues. Various persons tell of their insights regarding their faith and this variety relates well to persons in the audience. The teams can travel to locations where such a program can be extremely motivating.

Groups illustrate their beliefs by

Telling others about Christ takes many forms—drama, puppets, work projects, singing and teaching, as well as nurturing a one-to-one relationship.

putting them to work, witnessing by doing. Through an unbelievable array of work and service projects youth show their gratitude for God's love by pouring out their efforts in repairing homes, painting community centers, teaching children, helping in camps for the handicapped, etc.

And youth are preparing themselves to minister one-to-one with those who need their support. Youth learn all they can to help their friends who may have been addicted to drugs or alcohol, discarded by their families, lost in the economic scramble, tormented by a cult or any one of a long list of other problems where assistance is desperately needed.

See also EVANGELISM, OUTREACH, VISITATION

Work Projects

The key ingredient for making many youth groups come alive is showing them how to put their faith to work.

"You should see the difference," one advisor remarked. "Attendance and interest was what you might call less than enthusiastic. In February when we were limping along from week to week, Paul came in talking about a summer work trip that some friends were planning. At first the trip sounded like fun, but no one was thrilled about the work. We checked with a woman who coordinates the youth ministry for our denomination in this state, and she told us of a church-sponsored nursery that had been flooded and needed to be rebuilt as soon as possible. When we began to think of real people who actually needed

Work projects have a way of touching the lives of those doing the work.

our help, we couldn't wait to tell them we would be there during spring break and for two weeks in the summer. That was a year ago, and we have two projects planned again for this year.

"You would not believe what the work projects have done for all of us, and for our whole church. Even people in the community give us supplies to take." Of course, the point the advisor makes is not what it does for the group, but when a group tries to live out its beliefs, those beliefs do become a lot stronger.

Anywhere you turn are endless varieties of work projects crying out for your group's help. They are in your backyard or across the globe—from highly skilled construction to fixing the leaking faucet of the older couple who live next door to the church building.

There is no set pattern for initiating a work project. You may wish to determine what you have to offer in the way of time, skills, interest and access to materials, equipment and vehicles. Or you may wish to first survey potential work projects. Your church will almost always have channels for discovering potential projects. Or you may wish to first determine the general availability and interest of the group, the approximate distance they would be willing to travel, and the variety of skills. Then you could look for needs within that area which call for what you have to offer.

As needs are presented, urge the group to be realistic in what they can accomplish. "No, it might not be possible to rebuild that house in two weeks; maybe by taking another group along. . . If Ron, who is a carpenter and electrician, could oversee the group's work, then it might work." A group that has not done much hard labor will be unable to put in a 10-hour workday, at least not at first. Time for relaxation and fun will have to be planned.

As soon as possible, find out what the work project hosts want done. "We had painted the church till we were bushed out every night. Then we realized that they really were hoping for our kids to do some recreation in the evenings with their kids. The painting was a minor concern to them."

Paternalism must be avoided. Watch for the payoff: A group putting out the effort and time may have secret expectations of those who are being helped. Help your group to learn how to offer its service with no expectations. The group you help may outwardly display resentment in order to convey that they retain pride and do not feel less worthy for accepting your help.

You may want to come up with different ways to keep your home church informed of the group's progress. For instance, a youth group in Ohio phoned the congregation during worship. The pastor had connected the phone to the public address system. The whole congregation could hear the young people's report. The congregation prayed for the youth as they ministered in their place.

Our work is a free gift with no strings attached. We work because we love.

Resources
1. **How to Give Away Your Faith**, by Paul Little, Inter-Varsity Press.

See also OUTREACH, PORTABLE MINISTRY, SERVICE, TRIPS

Workshops

The youth advisor has to keep growing. Every person of faith needs to develop. Even though the youth teach the adults a great deal, youth ministry requires continuous reading and learning. One of the most popular modes of personal and professional growth are the workshops and seminars in youth ministry. They are sponsored both by denominations and cooperative groups.

You should know what you need and want before you attend a workshop. Most workshop leaders will be responsive to particular needs. Do you want information on a particular topic or do you want to pick the brain of a well-known leader whose work you know quite well. If you seek the latter, take along a tape recorder. Don't record the session. Catch her or him and request some time for conversation. Interview the leader with the purpose in mind that you will use this material with youth and other youth advisors. Most leadership folk will be very cooperative.

Be aware of the other folks in the workshop. When someone shares something very helpful, make a note of it. Catch him or her after the session and do an interview. You might also want to get the names and addresses of other kindred spirits you have discovered in the course. This is one of the best ways of finding other people who can help you in your ministry.

There are also compelling reasons to include youth in these workshop opportunities. John never attends a continuing education event without taking at least one youth with him. He sees this as an investment in people. For instance, he took three teens to the Floyd Shaffer clown ministry workshop. It cost a bit and took an entire weekend. Yet, these young people have returned and trained others in the group to do clown ministry! You may also find that your area churches may be willing to subsidize such an investment. If they can see how these trained youth will return to train others in the churches, it makes good sense. This is also a fine affirmation of your youth.

You may have to fight for a workshop budget. Workshop subsidies may be the most important item in your youth ministry budget.

You may want to organize your own workshops. This is much more possible than you may think. Many clusters of churches are now developing their own lay schools of theology. Anybody can be hired to teach in your community. While some of the fees and expenses are high, most workshops can pay for themselves with good planning and publicity. Nothing of value is offered free anymore. You will be surprised how much people are willing to pay for a top-quality learning experience.

It may be better for you to organize a workshop day with local leadership. This may seem like an impossible task at first. However, there are probably many folks who have important insights on youth culture and values who live within a short distance of your church. The hardest part of designing a local workshop is choosing a format. If you invite a panel of six speakers from the community to reflect about youth, you may be faced with a meandering six-hour speech. You owe it to these guests to offer a context in which they can give and be their best.

We have found that when several "experts" are asked to share, it is best to use the interview format. A strong host draws out key information from each. If there are three guests, 20 minutes should take care of this section. Then switch to the audience for dialogue with the guests. This will enable the guest to keep on the mark and contribute only that of which the audience has need. Some folks have found that sessions with fewer participants work well with inexperienced workshop leaders by having an experienced host deal with the group process. The leader has the input while the host provides flow.

See also TRAINING

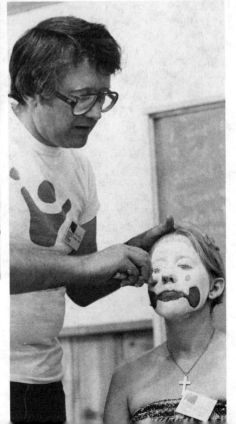

Workshops cover anything from clowning
to youth culture to theology to crazy
games.

Worship

The church has generally geared its worship life to thinking adults. It has said to the young and restless, "Come back and see us when you want to sit and listen."

This process of exclusion starts with children. Most Protestants do not want the littlest among us in worship. This is a strange development. In the frontier days and among farm communities it was natural to have children present for worship. These folks seemed to know that faith is really caught, not taught. The child who becomes a youth needs to learn that he or she belongs to this people. This is only understood by being accepted as someone special among the people of God.

Many churches surprisingly lament that youth do not want to attend Sunday morning service. It is understandable given their previous experiences. There are strong theological reasons for the view that perhaps children are put in our midst in order to minister to us. (See Benson & Stewart, **The Ministry of the Child**, Abingdon Press.) Young people bring something special by their weakness, their acceptance, their physical restlessness, their trust, their forgiveness, etc.

When adults exclude children and youth by being insensitive to their needs and gifts, they are being unfaithful to the gospel. The adults need these new Christians in order to be complete.

Often churches will make a concession to the youth by permitting a "Youth Sunday." This is often a no-win situation. If the young people express the faith which is comfortable to them, some adults will complain. If they try to copy what adults want, the older worshippers will think that the young are cute.

The best way to deal with youth and Sunday morning worship is to treat them regularly as participants. No church can fail to have youth taking offerings, ushering, singing in the choir, providing instrumental support and many other things. A church that accepts youth as full members will see them serve fully as leaders and servers in worship.

Youth advisors usually have no control over Sunday morning worship. But use whatever pressure you can on behalf of the vital contribution youth can make to the people of God.

When you are offered the Youth Sunday opportunity, take it. Help your youth forge a meaningful service which is authentic in light of the historical faith. The easiest way to develop such a celebration is to focus on your basic liturgy. Do not disorient the worshippers. The worship service is not a show. Every liturgy seems to offer the basic ingredients for authentic worship. Encourage the youth to pick out one or two aspects of the service and express these in fresh ways.

One group in suburban Detroit was very concerned about the dryness of the Sunday morning service. The pastor gave them one minute during the service on Sunday. The president of the youth group invited people to leave the sanctuary by a certain door at the end of the worship service each week. She said that the youth were going to greet church members in a special way. One week the youth group gave out flowers. Another week they hugged worshippers. This greeting post added a whole new warmth to the service. The young people had influenced the service without leading it.

Many adults are confused about worship. They assume that their worship style is the historical way to worship. Unfortunately, they have accepted nostalgia in place of historic. Nostalgia always makes the present difficult because it rewrites the past as it should have been. History, on the other hand, is how things really were.

Worship should be a special experience for everyone: God, adults, youth and children.

In a liturgical sense, history consists of 4,000 years of worship practice. There is nothing that you can think of which has not been done in the name of worship somewhere by someone. Youth doing a study of the great hymns are often astonished to discover that some of the melodies were converted from popular drinking tunes. History testifies to the reality that sisters and brothers have praised and glorified God by every possible means and it has been found acceptable.

Being aware of this dynamic, one youth group built in a helpful means of having adults deal with this stress. After the youth service, they invited the whole congregation to a cookie and coffee hour. As folks came into the room, they were given slips of paper. The young person in charge invited people to write comments concerning the service they had designed and led. Peter and Jane, the youth advisors, had worked on how this feedback could best be helped. When criticism about the group's use of music came, the young person in charge read it and then asked if others in the congregation could make a comment about the music. The responses were amazing. Older people in the room defended the young people. It made critics realize that other older people did not agree with the isolated comments. The youth learned that a person does not have to be defensive in the face of negative comments. They also realized that many conservative people liked what they did.

Some clergy are comfortable with youth people in worship. John told his confirmation class that they were important in helping him bring the Word. "I need your response as I preach. It is the Holy Spirit, working through all of us, which make our efforts the Word of God. If I am going too long, give me the across-the-throat signal. I want your comments. I respect what you have to say." You can imagine what this did for the youth in the class.

Two teenage girls were very concerned about the exclusive language their pastor used. They would count the times he used sexist language in his preaching and prayers. Since he was open to teens, they told him about it. He thanked them for their reactions. "I am going to try to be more sensitive. Keep taking the count on me. Let's see if I can do a better job."

Resources

1. **God's Party**, by David Randolph, Abingdon Press.
2. **Preparing the Way of the Lord**, Miriam T. Winter, Abingdon Press.
3. **All Out Days: Laugh and Praise**, by Morris Pike, Friendship Press.
4. **Takestock: Worship**, by Don Wardlaw, John Knox Press.

See also YOUTH SUNDAY

X-Rated

"I felt very uncomfortable at the youth conference held by our denomination. The other kids used such bad language. They swore all the time." This comment by a young woman may seem out of place for a Christian youth gathering. However, times have changed in terms of language and other "street" aspects of life. Teens are familiar with tough language. The songs, talk shows, movies and novels of the youth world are filled with earthy expressions which describe every aspect of life. These patterns are reinforced by high school teachers and coaches who swear profusely and tell off-color jokes. It is natural to find this X-rated material drifting into youth programming.

What do you do when someone swears or tells you a dirty joke? It is easy to fall into a hot or cold pattern of

reaction. A typical adult in this situation might pull the parental role and give a sermon on how un-Christian such talk is. You may be drawing from your beliefs and a sermon will come easy. "Bad words are bad thoughts."

On the other hand, you may be non-chalant about this sudden blast of street talk. Perhaps you just smile and say nothing at all. This method of handling the situation covers the embarassment of being an uptight adult. It may even give you the short-ranged benefit of being one of the "guys" (or girls). Yet, if cheap sex jokes and street language don't seem to be part of your understanding of Christian fellowship with teens, you will be communicating a lie.

There is no simple answer to X-rated moments with youth. If you feel uncomfortable with this kind of expression, you have to be true to yourself. Young people aren't looking for "hipper-than-thou" adults. They need real people.

This means that you don't have to jump into the judgment mode in response to the bawdy story. If you can clear your mind, you might ask yourself some questions: "Why is this person using this expression now? Is he or she testing my reaction?" Perhaps the teen feels comfortable with you and reverts to the kind of communication used with friends.

When you scan such reflections, you can see some new possibilities. One youth group had a reputation for bad language. The new youth advisor helped them work through the problem. He found that they were used to such talk around school and their homes. They were youth barely touched by the church. Ed confronted the situation with the teens. They liked him and they knew that this pattern of communication did not fit his faith and personality. He introduced a nonsense word which his mother had given to the family. He encouraged them to say it when they were angry. It became a substitute for the common words used for swearing. The teens laughed at the meaningless expression. The advisor said it in different ways. The idea quickly caught on with the group. They invented their own expressions. In a few weeks the group's language cleared up. Ed had also unlocked a probe of feelings and values. This was done without a lecture and without accepting a pattern of behavior which was not fitting for the Christian group. Ed also knew that special language patterns are one of the marks of a group's cohesion.

Some groups have found that facing the world of today's films and songs is the best approach. Mature teens from church youth groups have found that today's cinema can be a source of important theological discussions. You may not wish to follow this course. However, why shouldn't we walk with our young companions in the faith as they face the harshness of the world? If they don't have us to talk with, they will certainly have little support for their faith stance in the midst of X-rated overload. At a time when cable television brings soft pornographic films into homes and no street term is excluded from daily conversation, the teen must be encouraged by the youth advisor to think and act differently.

See also COMMUNICATION, CULTURE, LANGUAGE

Youth

Most of the churches in the United States define youth as persons between the ages of 12 and 18 or in grade level 7 through 12, though some churches will include persons one year younger and one year older.

However, international definitions of "youth" will range from 12 or 14 all the way through 25. Some countries extended the age to 35; others say a "youth" is anyone who is unmarried. This is important to remember when your youth attend international youth functions.

Many churches define youth as "the church of tomorrow," meaning that youth will inherit leadership roles from adults. This definition is a mistake that has serious ramifications. Youth are the church today, along with other age groups, and every level of the church can profit from including youth in the decision-making arenas.

Another mistake is to assume that youth are just like everyone else. Every age group is quite different with its own unique gifts and needs. There are times when intergenerational events are rewarding for everyone and other times when youth need to be by themselves. When planning a worship service for the congregation, do not assume that whatever pleases the adults is best for everyone (and "the younger people will grow to like it some day"). The youth may decide to go elsewhere.

Resources
1. **Five Cries of Youth**, by Merton Strommen, Harper and Row.
2. **The Rights of Young People**, by Alan Sussman, Avon Books.
3. **The New Morality: A Profile of American Youth in the '70s**, by Daniel Yankelovich, McGraw Hill.

See also CULTURES

Youth are not the church of tomorrow. They are an essential part of the church today.

Youth Council

If your church has more than one program (fellowship group, church school class, scouting, musical program, drama group, recreation teams or programs, etc.) for the youth, consider forming a youth council. The council need not be a formal committee or have any fancy organizational structure, but it can help the entire church by pulling together occasionally all those youth and adults who have anything to do with the leadership of youth ministry in your church.

Some churches appoint a youth coordinator to help all of these people to do their work and to make sure that the church is offering a program to meet the needs of all the youth in the church. A coordinator can see that the youth council gathers from time to time.

It takes an objective group to look over the entire youth ministry program and see if improvements need to be made. For instance, when a person in the scouting program says that there needs to be more recognition of the youth in the church and the person teaching the senior high church school class says the same thing, the council can evaluate the situation and act to alleviate the problem if necessary.

Often the council posts a large calendar that lists all the events that are being planned. This will help keep scheduling conflicts from arising where youth might feel forced to choose between two programs.

The Youth Council can take inventory of what equipment is available, to see what needs to be repaired or replaced and to explore alternatives to buying equipment. It can see if new facilities are available for various segments of this program. "Some of you were up at the new state campground; would that be good for the retreat we're having next month for the confirmation class?" Mention can be made of new youth ministry resources that have been put in the library or resource center. If the church is planning any new buildings or program directions, this group might have some suggestions to further its cooperative program. If new staff are being hired, this group might want to influence the amount of time to be spent in youth ministry. Budgeting allocation is always a council concern.

This group can look over the lists of individuals who are potentially active in the church and make changes in programs to accommodate these persons. For instance, if the group discovers three handicapped youth in the community who have musical ability, but do not participate in any local church program, it could suggest a schedule and room change that will put the junior high bell choir near a wheel chair ramp.

The Youth Council can bend youth program offerings to fit the youth they are meant to serve.

See also PLANNING COUNCIL, TASK FORCE

Youth Leader

"Now, if you will be as good as Thelma and Tony. I just wish they could have stayed on."

"Marcus was my idea of the ideal youth sponsor."

Such statements might give the idea that there really is a set mold of a youth advisor, and the rest of us should be cloned in that image.

The reality is that there is no ideal youth leader because there are no ideal youth groups, ideal youth situations or ideal youth. Certainly, there are a lot of qualities that might fit an excellent youth leader: sensitivity to needs, strong faith commitment, flexibility, creative, appreciation of youth, caring, curious, thrifty, world citizen.

However, none of us has all those qualities in the quantities that are often needed, though each of us has qualities that enable us to contribute to our particular ministries.

There are times when the youth are super responsible, and the adult leadership is mainly needed for support, advocacy and long-range goal setting. For instance, Noah, the adult leader, usually came into the senior high room and headed for the back row. Much of the time, he did not wish to have a noticeable presence. Everyone knew he was there, because on those occasions when things got rough, he was ready to listen and respond. Some of those times came late at night when the youth needed to ask Noah about a good doctor for a friend or if he would help them work through a financial problem.

Other groups require much more initiative from the adult leadership. The entire planning council always waited for Ruby and Michael, their adult sponsors, to arrive with the program suggestion booklets, mimeographed planning sheets and other materials. Gradually, the other council members took over some of the duties. But for several months it had been necessary for the advisors to take the lead while the new group learned what to do.

In all probability your role as advisor will change as the group changes and as you change. There will be times when the group will look to its adult leadership for initiative and direction. But in time you will discover ways to involve the youth in the ministry with your role becoming one of support and encouragement.

Most of us find that we work better as a member of a leadership team. In fact, several adults working together as advisors can turn out to be a mutually enjoyable and rewarding experience for everyone. Preferably, the leadership arrangement will not be one of rotating the responsibilities, but a true team ministry in which combinations of leadership are pulled together for the best blends of ability.

The question of the age of the youth advisors often arises. Many people think a youth leader has to be 22 years of age or lower, single (or perhaps married to an ultra-attractive spouse), guitar virtuoso and owner of a super modern house at the lake or shore. Obviously, this type person does have a lot to offer youth, understands the same culture, has recently been through similar struggles, possibly can be a positive model influence. If such a person is available, he or she can often be of great help to the group and to various individuals. However, most youth groups need more than youth, wealth and good looks.

On numerous surveys, students in lab schools across the country were asked to name the type teacher or school personnel who they would go to for help (advice, counsel, support, etc.). In most cases the person was over 35 years old. The age group picked last was the early 20's group.

A similar finding has been reported from those working in the area of faith development. It seems that a number of years need to pass between the youth years and those of their leader so that a perspective of faith will develop that can help most youth.

This is not to say that a youth leader needs to be over 35 to be successful. What it does say is that there is no perfect age or type leader needed for youth ministry. Perhaps the best balance is to utilize a variety of ages and types.

Resources
1. **Bridging the Gap: Youth and Adults in the Church**, by Merton Strommen, Augsburg.
2. **Building an Effective Youth Ministry**, by Glenn Ludwig, Abingdon.
3. **Youth, World and Church**, by Sara Little, John Knox Press.
4. **Creative Youth Leadership**, by Jan Corbett, Judson Press.

See also ADULTS, ADVISING, JOB DESCRIPTION, STARTING UP, YOUTH MINISTER

Youth Magazine

One of the longest running resources for youth and their leaders is the quarterly Youth Magazine. This project is sponsored by several denominations as one of their recommended and promoted resources for youth.

Most issues of significance to youth ministry will find their way to these pages in the most readable form for youth. When special concentration is given to an issue, the coverage is inclusive, exhaustive and reliable. The one-to-one conversation tone helps the reader to meet a wide variety of other youth, those interesting to youth, those who are making noteworthy changes in the world, and those who know youth-related issues on a first-hand basis.

The address is 132 W. 31st St., New York, NY 10001.

Youth Minister

A youth minister—professional or volunteer—must include other adults in the ministry.

"If we only had a minister for the young people!" There are churches who raise that possibility when their youth program is lagging. Smaller congregations may consider this concern when they are looking at a new pastor. It is important that clergy take youth seriously. Those churches who have ministers working with the youth program can have very strong programs.

Yet, there are good reasons why a special minister for youth can be restricting. Some clergy in youth situations do not feel that the congregation values their ministry as much as those on the staff who minister to the "real" members. It is also sometimes difficult to get lay persons to accept youth ministry as being their ministry when a minister is supposed to do it. The youth minister must work particularly hard to enable others to do this work along with him or her.

You may be a youth advisor who wishes your church had this kind of professional help. But many clergy folks do not feel comfortable with teens. The emphasis on preaching as an adult intellectual experience forces clergy to think mainly of the adults who will receive this kind of contribution.

If you are a lay person doing youth ministry, you can be a great help to the pastor. You can help him or her get in touch with the contributions offered by youth. The adult needs to see the gospel through the eyes of the young and you may be the only person to make this happen. Arrange times for the pastor to visit the group and create a climate in which he or she will be comfortable. You may be surprised to learn how hard it is for clergy to break into an environment created and controlled by youth.

You might also develop a feedback system by which the pastor receives the youth's perception of your life together as a congregation. One of the easiest and most successful formats is quite simple. Give each person a few pieces of paper at the beginning of the meeting. Have them write questions they would like to ask the pastor. These are to be unsigned. Collect the papers and read the questions to the pastor. After he or she has answered, encourage more discussion. This works very well.

See also AAUGH

Youth News

Many youth groups owe their fantastic participation and excitement to a fantastic and exciting newsletter. Newsletters are built on w-o-r-k, but they can be priceless in keeping the membership informed about upcoming activities or relationships that are developing which will interest non-attenders.

The editor will want to include as many different writers as possible and print as many names as can be mentioned. Pictures add an added dimension to the reporting. Secret columnists making observations about the group can add fun and intrigue.

Naming the newsletter can be a project that includes a lot of persons.

Even with the best newsletter, the group should also regularly submit its news to the church bulletin, local newspaper, regional and national newsletters, as well as local radio and TV stations. In all probability, one of the group members who's taking a course in journalism can suggest the proper way to submit a news item to broadcast or print media.

See also PROMOTION, PUBLICITY

Youth Specialities

Once upon a time a couple of crazy guys by the names of Wayne Rice and Mike Yaconelli published a small book of ideas they'd begged, borrowed and bought from other youth ministry types around the nation. From this humble beginning, these creative and ministry-helping "loonies" have created a wealth of books, weekend seminars and week-long youth workers conventions (The National Youth Workers Convention). Over the years, their focus has remained on the training and equipping of youth workers.

This same group of guys publishes a bi-monthly (or whenever they can get an issue out) magazine called The Wittenburg Door. This provocative publication uses satire and wit to puncture our religiousity. For more information: 1224 Greenfield Drive, El Cajon, CA 92021.

See also CREATIVE MODELS, GROUP MAGAZINE, MATERIALS, WORKSHOPS

Youth Sunday

Many churches designate one day per year as Youth Sunday, where youth assume many responsibilities within the congregational worship service, usually including the sermon.

This is a unique opportunity for all persons in the congregation. For the children it is a chance to see older brothers and sisters and those they admire affirming their faith. For the adults it is a chance to hear a fresh interpretation of the gospel in contemporary terms. For the youth it is a chance to take on the unfamiliar reins of corporate worship leadership and to struggle with what worship really is, how it can be encouraged and how God can speak through the words and actions of persons. For visitors, especially youth, this service says in an emphatic way that the church cares about its youth and youth care about the church.

Youth Sunday offers young people opportunities to work with the pastor, choir director and all those responsible for worship and learn firsthand how they do what they do and why. Young people can also get a unique introduction to worship resources, varieties of expression, historical and traditional backgrounds and practice in creating their own modes of exhortation.

Involve as many youth as possible in this special day. They can serve as ushers, choir members (singing, interpretative dance, choral reading, puppets, clowns, etc.); speakers (prayer, sermon, scripture reading, litany leadership, call to worship, announcements, concerns of congregation, benediction, etc.); bulletin and litany preparation, serving a breakfast or lunch, serving communion, acolyte, musical accompaniment (organist, guitarist, flutist).

Get as many persons involved in the planning of worship as possible. By being personally involved in the preparation, they can better learn the reasoning behind the order of progression of the service.

Youth Sunday can serve many functions, one of them being an awareness that worship every Sunday should serve the particular needs and interests of youth as well as every other specific group of persons in the church. Perhaps with this good experience and the relationships that are established, youth can participate in the leadership much more often than once a year.

See also WORSHIP.

Zits, Frizzies and Mouse Breath

"I can pinch them, medicate them and hide them, but they seem to appear just when I need to be acceptable to my friends, my date or my senior pictures.

Zits are those ugly scourges which pop out at the same time teens pass through the youth ministry period of development. Zits stand as symbols of the discomfort youth feel as they lurch toward maturity. The whole system of organs seems to pump out chemicals which disfigure the face, lubricate the hair with grease and pollute the breath with unkissable odor.

We smile at this flippant recital of puberty's distinctive march toward adulthood. Yet, these physical marks are distressful to teens. The shampoo, mouth wash and patent medicine folk court these anxieties fully. Just scan the ads in teen magazines and listen to media programming.

There are always a few young people in the youth group who are struck particularly hard. The organs rebel against those greasy foods and not only create eruptions, gushers and noxious gases, but they add fat to the body. The physical appearance of the teen person is an incredibly important extension of his or her self-worth.

You are probably not a skin doctor or a beautician, but you are a significant person who has weathered even the zits blitz. You have found a sense of being which enables you to face your own strengths and weaknesses. You can accept a young person who is overweight and pimple laden. This sense of self-worth is grounded upon the acceptance and love of God.

See also CLOTHING, DIETING, ENCOURAGEMENT, IDENTITY, LOVE, SELF-IMAGE

Other youth ministry books from Group Books

Yearbook: Untold Stories—uses the format of a typical high school yearbook to lead young people through a reflective look at the high school years. By Bill Wolfe and Janita Wolfe. $5.95.

Leaders Guide for Yearbook: Untold Stories—a valuable tool that supplies dozens of meeting designs and retreat outlines for use with the **Yearbook**. By Bill and Martha Wolfe. $6.95.

Counseling Teenagers—the most complete and authoritative reference available for understanding and helping adolescents. Written from a balanced Christian perspective. By Dr. G. Keith Olson. $19.95.

The Group Retreat Book—this is the resource for start-to-finish retreat planning, execution and evaluation . . . plus 34 ready-to-use retreat outlines. By Arlo Reichter. $15.95.

Hard Times Catalog for Youth Ministry—how to transform simple, cheap objects into creative valuable tools for youth ministry. By Marilyn and Dennis Benson. $14.95.

The Youth Group How-to Book—66 practical projects and programs to help you build a better group. $14.95.

The Best of Try This One—a big selection of youth group programs, games, stunts, get-acquainted experiences and discussion starters. $5.95.

More . . . Try This One—more youth group games, crowd breakers, fund raisers, discussions and projects. $5.95.

Try This One . . . Too—the third in this popular series of books. $5.95.

Pick up these books at your favorite Christian bookstore, or order direct from the publisher (include $2 shipping cost): Group Books, Box 481, Loveland, CO 80539.